Americans and Asymmetric Conflict

AMERICANS AND ASYMMETRIC CONFLICT

LEBANON, SOMALIA, AND AFGHANISTAN

Adam B. Lowther

Foreword by Donald M. Snow

PSI Reports

PRAEGER SECURITY INTERNATIONAL

Westport, Connecticut • London

Library of Congress Cataloging-in-Publication Data

Americans and asymmetric conflict : Lebanon, Somalia, and Afghanistan / Adam B. Lowther ;
    foreword by Donald M. Snow.
        p. cm.
    Includes bibliographical references and index.
    ISBN-13: 978–0–275–99635–2 (alk. paper)
1. Asymmetric warfare—United States. 2. United States—Military policy. 3. Asymmetric
warfare—Case studies. 4. Counterinsurgency—Case studies. 5. War on Terrorism, 2001–
6. World politics—1989– I. Title.
U163.L69 2007
355.4'2—dc22   2007014362

British Library Cataloguing in Publication Data is available.

Library of Congress Catalog Card Number: 2007014362
ISBN-13: 978–0–275–99635–2

First published in 2007

Praeger Security International, 88 Post Road West, Westport, CT 06881
An imprint of Greenwood Publishing Group, Inc.
www.praeger.com

Printed in the United States of America

The paper used in this book complies with the
Permanent Paper Standard issued by the National
Information Standards Organization (Z39.48–1984).

10 9 8 7 6 5 4 3 2 1

Contents

Foreword *by Donald M. Snow*   vii

Preface   xi

Acknowledgments   xiii

Abbreviations   xv

Introduction   1

1 Military Thought and Asymmetric Conflict   14

2 Understanding Asymmetry in the Twenty-First Century: Strategy,   52
  Tactics, and Weapons

3 Lebanon (1982–1984): The Rise of Terrorism and the Suicide   82
  Bombing

4 Somalia (1992–1994): Into the Post-Cold War Era   102

5 Afghanistan (2001–2004): Winning Wars of Asymmetry   126

Conclusion: The Lessons of War and Implications for Iraq   148

Notes   161

Works Cited   205

Index   231

Foreword

Asymmetrical warfare, the subject of this book, is and probably always has been an enigma, especially to those against whom it is employed, but also to some extent to its practitioners. For those against whom asymmetrical warfare is waged, the enigma involves attempting to counter a style of warfare that is alien and unfamiliar to them conducted by an opponent that would not be able to compete if it fought the way the symmetrical warrior preferred (which of course is the virtual definition of asymmetrical warfare). Not only are asymmetrical means unfamiliar and, generally speaking, inadequately encompassed in doctrine and strategy, they are generally objectionable and, from the view of those subjected to them, confusing, difficult to counter and, especially, difficult to counteract in ways that lead to conventional notions of success.

For the asymmetrical warrior, the problem is different. In a very real sense, asymmetrical warfare is not so much a method as it is a way of thinking about war. Certainly, there are principles of war—the lessons of Suntzu, for instance—that can be and are applied in many asymmetrical circumstances, but there is no set body of rules of engagement, strategy and tactics, and grand designs available to the asymmetrical warrior. Were such a body of instructions available, the enemies of asymmetry would have studied it and figured how to defeat it. If there is an underlying first principle of asymmetrical warfare, it is adaptation—finding and applying methods that will frustrate and foil an enemy that cannot be defeated by standard methods. War fought where one side fights differently than the other (the heart of asymmetrical warfare) is thus a cat-and-mouse game where the asymmetrical warrior seeks to remain one intellectual and physical step ahead of his symmetrical opponent. For the symmetrical opponent, the challenge is getting ahead of the thinking of the asymmetrical warrior, anticipating what that opponent will do before he can do it and acting effectively. Applying

John Boyd's OODA (observe, orient, decide, react) Loop for fighter pilots is also the task of the symmetrical warrior—and not a bad model for the anti-asymmetrical warfare strategist to adopt.

As the Iraq War devolves into the likely recriminations that will be associated with trying to assemble the "lessons learned," the ghost of asymmetrical warfare will once again rear its head. Whatever else the evaluation of the American war effort may produce, it will almost certainly have to make two points. The first is that, over a quarter century after the Vietnam imbroglio, it is not at all clear that the mainstream of the American military has embraced solving the problem of asymmetrical warfare as a problem serious enough to devote its major energies. When it invaded Iraq, the Army and Marines were not prepared for the rear guard tactics they encountered (a form of asymmetrical warfare), and their inability to tame the Iraqi resistance during the occupation was further testimony to the poverty of American understanding. The failure to possess and apply a viable strategy of anti-asymmetrical warfare is not the only reason the United States did not prevail in Iraq, but it is certainly one of them. The second lesson will, or should, be that until the United States figures out how to solve this problem, all the technological superiority in the world that its forces possess will not assure success when it is applied, at least as measured by attaining the political goals for which that force was applied. An American military compared at the turn of the millennium to Rome at the height of its power was, after all, stalemated by a band of insurgents in Iraq.

There undoubtedly will be numerous lessons from the Iraq experience, but one should be especially clear. An asymmetrical approach to warfare worked against the United States in Iraq, and America's future potential opponents are going to study this war, realize that indeed the United States can be opposed successfully if the proper methods are devised and applied, and will make adaptations to the Iraq model to fit their circumstances. If the United States does not recognize that certainty and engage in furtive, systematic study—of a far more serious and heartfelt quality than it did after Vietnam—of how to deal with these realities, it will have no one but itself to blame for the problems, including the failures, it encounters in the future. It is the duty of those who follow and report on military affairs to make sure they make the effort.

Adam Lowther's book is a good first step in this process. He does a very thorough job of laying out the asymmetrical problem and applying it to his three cases, recognizing that they are exemplary of the processes through which asymmetrical warriors go rather than some set of rigid guidelines or linear development in asymmetrical techniques. Asymmetrical warfare by many of the names he discusses has been around for a long time, and although they share commonalities, most of the successful applications share a willingness to adapt to changing circumstances and to present their foes with problems those opponents had not anticipated.

During the Cold War, Soviet military literature was fixated with the problem of technological surprise—the figurative disaster of coming over the top of the hill, looking down and seeing the American military armed with some weapon they neither understood nor could overcome. The task is parallel today. The problem is not technological but intellectual surprise. On the next American battlefield, what tactical and strategic innovations will be waiting over the top of the hill to frustrate us? Will we be able to anticipate those innovations and be waiting for them? What do we need to do not to be surprised next time? Reading the pages that follow is a good start toward approaching and hopefully answering those questions.

Donald M. Snow
Hilton Head Island, South Carolina

Preface

With Operation Enduring Freedom now in its sixth year and Operation Iraqi Freedom well into its fourth year, it is easy for Americans to forget the lessons of past conflicts as the politics of the present dominate the way in which these two operations are understood. The purpose of my analysis of the American experience in Lebanon (1982–1984), Somalia (1992–1994), and Afghanistan (2001–2006) is to highlight some of history's recent lessons so that we may move forward in the current conflicts with an awareness of what past experience offers. While there are a number of other cases that provide useful experience from which we can draw lessons, Lebanon, Somalia, and Afghanistan are the United States's most recent asymmetric conflicts. Since the Iraq War has turned into a prolonged asymmetric conflict and because of the likelihood that future conflict will look much the same, I selected cases with relevant lessons.

As a young sailor in the U.S. Navy and Naval Reserve for most of the Clinton presidency, I participated, in a small way, in a number of American operations around the world. My experiences frequently left me wondering if I and my fellow sailors and marines were ever considered in the calculations that were made prior to choosing American arms. Thus, I am particularly interested in drawing lessons that are relevant to American service personnel currently deployed to Afghanistan and Iraq and engaged against an adversary who refuses to fight by the accepted norms of war. In conflicts of asymmetry it is the average soldier, sailor, airman, and marine who finds himself or herself under constant fire from unseen locations by adversaries without a distinguishable uniform. This has led me to concentrate on drawing lessons at the tactical level and often saying little about higher levels of strategic analysis.

As in any work, there is much that is left unsaid. I do not seek to offer the seminal work on any of the cases I discuss or on the topic of asymmetric warfare. Rather, my goal is to combine a brief description of each case with a discussion of asymmetry in conflict to arrive at a useful set of lessons that can be translated into policy outcomes. Like all authors, I take full responsibility for any mistakes that may appear in the pages that follow. While I have made a significant effort to ensure the accuracy of citations and facts, oversight of factual errors falls squarely on my shoulders.

Acknowledgments

I am pleased to have this opportunity to thank the colleagues and friends who assisted me in my research. Most of my thanks must go to my wife, Jessica, for her tireless assistance in typing notes, editing chapters, and providing any assistance I needed. I also would like to thank Don Snow, John Oneal, David Lanoue, Harvey Kline, and David Beito for their comments. My editor, Elizabeth Demers, and the excellent people at Praeger Security International also played an important role in turning my raw work into a finished product. Thank You.

Abbreviations

4GW	Fourth Generation Warfare
AFO	Advanced Force Operations
AOR	Area of Responsibility
ARVN	Army of the Republic of Vietnam
BIA	Beirut International Airport
BLT	Battalion Landing Team
CENTCOM	Central Command
CIA	Central Intelligence Agency
CINCCENT	Commander in Chief of Central Command
DCI	Director of Central Intelligence
DoD	Department of Defense
DRA	Democratic Republic of Afghanistan
DRV	Democratic Republic of Vietnam
EMP	Electromagnetic Pulse
FARC	Revolutionary Armed Forces of Columbia
FBI	Federal Bureau of Investigation
GWOT	Global War on Terror
IDF	Israeli Defense Force
IED	Improvised Explosive Device
ISI	Interservice Intelligence Agency
JCS	Joint Chiefs of Staff

JSOC	Joint Special Operations Command
KMT	Kuomintang
LAF	Lebanese Armed Forces
MAU	Marine Amphibious Unit
MNF	Multi-National Force
NA	Northern Alliance
NGA	National Geospatial-Intelligence Agency
NGO	Non-governmental Organization
NSA	National Security Agency
NSC	National Security Council
OODA Loop	Observe Orient Decide Act
PAVN or NVA	People's Army of Vietnam
PDPA	People's Democratic Party of Afghanistan
PLO	Palestinian Liberation Organization
PSP	Progressive Socialist Party
QDR	*Quadrennial Defense Review*
QRF	Quick Reaction Force
RMA	Revolution in Military Affairs
ROE	Rules of Engagement
RPG	Rocket Propelled Grenade
SNA	Somali National Alliance
SOAR	Special Operations Aviation Regiment
SOF	Special Operations Forces
SRC	Somali Revolutionary Council
TF	Task Force
UN	United Nations
UNITAF	United Nations Intervention Task Force
UNOSOM	United Nations Operations in Somalia
USC	United Somali Congress
WMD	Weapons of Mass Destruction

Introduction

On the night of September 20, 2001, President George W. Bush stood before a joint session of Congress to address the American people in the wake of the September 11, 2001, terrorist attacks against the United States. Still in disbelief and coping with their grief, Americans watched as the president informed the country that the United States was at war. America now faced a new enemy. According to President Bush:

> The evidence we have gathered all points to a collection of loosely affiliated terrorist organizations known as al-Qaeda. They are some of the murderers indicted for bombing American embassies in Tanzania and Kenya and responsible for bombing the USS *Cole*.
>
> Al-Qaeda is to terror what the Mafia is to crime. But its goal is not making money, its goal is remaking the world and imposing its radical beliefs on people everywhere.
>
> The terrorists practice a fringe form of Islamic extremism that has been rejected by Muslim scholars and the vast majority of Muslim clerics; a fringe movement that perverts the peaceful teachings of Islam.
>
> The terrorists' directive commands them to kill Christians and Jews, to kill all Americans and make no distinctions among military and civilians, including women and children. This group and its leader, a person named Osama bin Laden, are linked to many other organizations in different countries, including the Egyptian Islamic Jihad, the Islamic Movement of Uzbekistan.
>
> There are thousands of these terrorists in more than 60 countries.
>
> They are recruited from their own nations and neighborhoods and brought to camps in places like Afghanistan where they are trained in the tactics of terror. They are sent back to their homes or sent to hide in countries around the world to plot evil and destruction.[1]

President Bush added, "Our war on terror begins with al-Qaeda, but it does not end there. It will not end until every terrorist group of global reach has been found, stopped and defeated."[2] Only later would Americans come to realize that these words were the beginning of what is now the Global War on Terror (GWOT). The scope of the new conflict was further clarified by the president, "We will direct every resource at our command—every means of diplomacy, every tool of intelligence, every instrument of law enforcement, every financial influence, and every necessary weapon of war—to the destruction and to the defeat of the global terror network."[3]

In that same speech President Bush also gave the Taliban an ultimatum: turn over Osama bin Laden and al-Qaeda operatives in Afghanistan or face the consequences. Mullah Muhammad Omar and the Taliban chose to face the consequences. On October 7, 2001, the United States began its invasion of Afghanistan with an air campaign and ground assault by Northern Alliance troops and accompanying American Special Forces. The Global War on Terror was underway.

In the decade since the collapse of the Soviet Union and end of the Cold War, the U.S. military suffered a number of setbacks.[4] These included significant manpower reductions across all services, unsuccessful nation-building efforts in Somalia (1992–1994) and Haiti (1994), protracted peace-enforcement/keeping operations in the former Yugoslavia (1995–present), a successful but unspectacular air-war in Kosovo (1999), bombing of the USS *Cole* (DDG-67) (2000), and the loss of a Navy EP-3 reconnaissance plane to China (2001).

During this same period, the Department of Defense (DoD) struggled to determine its role in an ever-changing world. China, as a rising power, was considered the next likely threat by many analysts and observers within and outside the Pentagon. Little change would be required to the "big box" military the United States possessed. American military experience in the 1990s and the attacks of 9/11 would, however, force the United States to turn from its plans to maintain a military well suited for superpower conflict. Instead, internal conflicts and terrorism soon came to dominate the experience of the U.S. military.

By the end of the Cold War, a small number of Pentagon insiders began suggesting the United States prepare for an enemy of a different kind.[5] Recognizing the unrivaled strength of the American military, it was believed that adversaries of the United States would seek to avoid direct confrontation with the most powerful military in the world and, instead, strike at American weaknesses. Advancing technology and the openness of Western democracies made the United States and its allies susceptible to unconventional attacks. The conceptualization of "Fourth Generation Warfare," as it came to be known, coincided with and influenced the Revolution in Military Affairs (RMA) taking place in the post-Cold War years. Not only was the Pentagon attempting to acquire weapons systems appropriate for the challenges of the future, but a reassessment of fundamental combat doctrine was underway. No single event has done more to shape the current conception of conflict than the attacks of 9/11.

A renewed focus on unconventional conflict or, as it is known in the latest nomenclature, "asymmetric warfare," was the result. No longer would preparation for conventional conflicts dominate intellectual effort within the Pentagon. The fact that conventional military doctrine gained pre-eminence within U.S. military strategic thinking is amazing. Conflicts of asymmetry have long been the "bread and butter" of the United States. The five decades of the Cold War were no exception. This work takes a look at asymmetric conflict and the American experience with it in three recent cases. The ultimate aim is to highlight a number of lessons that should be taken away from the cases examined and to refocus the development of military doctrine on the form of conflict that has long dominated the combat experience of America's fighting men. I do not seek to provide the detailed analysis that an area specialist may provide.

Before turning to the three conflicts examined in the following chapters, I begin with a brief examination of an often forgotten conflict in which the United States confronted tactics similar in their objective to those they are currently facing in Afghanistan and Iraq. In examining the *Werwolf* insurgency that developed as the Reich was collapsing in 1944 and 1945, a theme, which was woven throughout the strategic thought of General George S. Patton, comes to light. As he famously said, "Strategy and tactics do not change. The means only of applying them differ." Patton would also add perhaps his most prophetic words when he said, "We forget the lessons of history." It is with Patton's sage words in mind that the following analysis if offered.

THE AMERICAN EXPERIENCE WITH ASYMMETRIC CONFLICT

October 1944 found the German *Wehrmacht* and *Waffen-SS* reeling from successive defeats as Allied forces rapidly pushed toward the Rhine while establishing air supremacy over continental Europe and *Reichsmarschal* Herman Goring's *Luftwaffe*. With France largely cleared of German forces and occasional thrusts east of the Rhine by General Patton's 3rd Army, Nazi leaders began preparations for the eventuality of an Allied invasion and occupation of Germany.[6] For nearly a decade Nazi Germany dominated Europe, but with American, British, Canadian, and French forces pushing the once mighty *Wehrmacht* east of the Rhine and the Red Army slogging it out with German forces on the banks of the Oder, it became clear to many in the *Wehrmacht* that Germany must soon rely on guerrillas to harass, slow, and stall the Allied advance from both east and west, while also preventing German citizens from collaborating with the Allies.

Tasked to create a force capable of carrying out such guerrilla activities was Inspector General for Special *Abwehr*, SS-General Hans Adolf Prutzmann.[7] As Higher SS and Police Leader (HSSPf) for the Ukraine and Southern Russia during the two and a half years of Nazi occupation, Prutzmann was perhaps Nazi Germany's most experienced anti-partisan commander. Using his experience fighting Russian guerrillas, Prutzmann sought to adapt partisan techniques that worked while avoiding the mistakes of the guerrillas he ruthlessly exterminated.[8]

Established in the fall of 1944, the *Bureau Prutzmann* was designed to create *SS-Werwolf* units with men and boys recruited from the *Waffen-SS*, Hitler Youth, and general population. Taking their name and character from earlier German literature and peasant guerrilla movements, the newly formed *SS-Werwolf* units believed themselves to be protectors of the *Ur-heimat* (German homeland) for which they were willing to kill and die. Although *Werwolf* units generally received between five days and five weeks of additional training in marksmanship, demolitions, and survival techniques, werewolves were frequently unprepared for the difficulties they faced in occupied Germany and its environs.

Organized into 4- to 6-man cells, *Werwolf* units lived in small underground bunkers constructed for storage of supplies and concealment. Although each cell was designed to carry out its mission independent of other cells, it was often necessary for sectors, encompassing 6 to 10 cells, to operate jointly when Allied supply columns or fuel and munitions dumps were targeted. Large unit operations, such as at the section level (six to eight sectors), were relatively rare and when undertaken usually saw lightly equipped and poorly trained werewolves suffer heavy casualties. Werewolves performed best when they functioned as autonomous units cutting Allied communications wire, demolishing bridges, raiding fuel and munitions dumps, poisoning alcohol and food, and assassinating occupation troops and German collaborators.[9]

From the earliest guerrilla attacks launched from the forests of East Prussia to the disintegration of most *Werwolf* units in the 6 to 12 months after the May 8, 1945, surrender, *Werwolf* guerrillas never became more than a minor player in the last gasp of a dying regime. The Nazi effort to develop a guerrilla organization that would live on after the collapse of the regime and serve as a force for a resurgent Nazi power came only after it was too late to develop the necessary base of support for such a difficult undertaking. For many of the 5,000 to 6,000 guerrillas who joined the *SS-Werwolf*, the death of Hitler and the collapse of the regime shortly thereafter offered the necessary incentive to abandon any guerrilla activities and return home.[10] For those "die-hards" whose unflinching faith in the Nazi regime compelled them to fight on, death or imprisonment, usually death, was most frequently the reward for guerrilla activity.

On the western front, American, British, Canadian, and French forces fared relatively better than their Red Army counterparts when encountering guerrillas. American forces suffered 400 casualties from *Werwolf* attacks with 188 deaths from poisoned alcohol and food.[11] British, Canadian, and French forces suffered fewer casualties. The Red Army, however, bore the brunt of *Werwolf* attacks and casualties because it was Soviet Russia that served as Nazi Germany's primary nemesis. While the exact number of Red Army casualties is unknown, evidence suggests that casualties in the East were significantly higher than in the West.[12] German civilians, however, were the group that suffered most from guerrilla activities. Not only were those who collaborated with the Allies targeted for assassination, but the civilian population in the towns and cities in which *Werwolf* attacks occurred suffered severe reprisals at the hands of Allied forces. The Red Army was particularly harsh in its reprisals killing 10 civilians for every Red Army soldier killed in *Werwolf* attacks.[13]

As the Allied occupation of Germany gradually shifted power from the military government to civilian control *Werwolf* attacks subsided, but not without serving as the United States's first experience with guerrilla warfare in the modern era of asymmetry. It is certainly true that American military history offers a great number of examples of American forces engaging guerrillas. The Philippines (1899–1902), China (1901–1941), Mexico (1916–1917), Haiti (1915–1934), the Dominican Republic (1916–1924), and Nicaragua (1926–1933) are but a few examples.[14]

Why then does the example of the *SS-Werwolf* matter? American marines and soldiers were familiar with the strategy and tactics employed by the *SS-Werwolf* long before encountering German guerrillas, as the *Small Wars Manual* (1940) indicates.[15] The American experience with the *SS-Werewolf* marked a transition for the United States from regional power to superpower, with adversaries unwilling to face American forces in a conventional conflict. The United States did go on to fight a largely conventional conflict on the Korean peninsula (1950–1953), but primarily out of accident rather than intent.[16] With few exceptions, American forces have, for the last half-century, faced adversaries unwilling and unable to confront the United States in a conventional conflict.

Since the end of World War II, the United States has deployed American forces 78 times to protect American lives and property. The military might of the United States has been used to retaliate for attacks against American citizens, repel the invasion of allies, contain communism, overthrow unfriendly governments and bring stability to unstable countries.[17] In 7 of 78 instances American military personnel faced a conventional adversary. A pattern of American forces facing an adversary employing an unconventional strategy and tactics dominates the American experience over the past five decades. Unconventional conflicts have, however, rarely received the attention of major conventional conflicts. Few Americans are familiar with the struggle against Filipino guerrillas during the Spanish-American War (1899–1902) or the Marine Corps's seven-year pursuit of Augusto Sandino in Nicaragua (1926–1933).[18] Many are, however, familiar with major events of the Civil War and World Wars I and II.

CONFLICT IN THE TWENTY-FIRST CENTURY

September 11, 2001, dramatically changed the public perception of warfare as the attacks on the World Trade Center and Pentagon made it clear that America's adversaries seek to defeat the United States by utilizing distinctly unconventional means.[19] The military and intelligence services long knew this as their experience in the last half-century suggests. But, with the collapse of the Soviet Union little more than a decade ago, military and political leaders have struggled to remold the American military to fit a world that will not face a Soviet thrust across Western Europe.[20] After the events of September 11, 2001, brought the strategy and tactics of America's adversaries to the forefront of general discourse, unconventional warfare is no longer confined to the bowels of the Pentagon, Fort Leavenworth, and Newport, Rhode Island. Instead, asymmetric warfare is widely assessed in academia, the press, and military circles.

In the five years since the 9/11 attacks much has been written about American efforts in the "Global War on Terror," which includes bringing rogue regimes into the international system and adapting to the changing face of warfare. This work follows along similar lines as it examines three recent cases in which the United States faced adversaries unwilling to "play by the rules" of conventional warfare.

It is often said that the last war defines the manner in which the next war will be fought. This is often true because historians and analysts look to previous experience for "lessons learned." The backward-looking nature of conflict analysis is often criticized for its inability to anticipate changes in an adversary's strategy and tactics. Such criticism belies a lack of understanding of the nature of war, which has changed very little over the past 7,000 years of human history. At the heart of war is the need to overcome an enemy's will to fight. This may be done by destroying an adversary's fighting ability or by overcoming his cost tolerance. If, as General Patton suggests, strategy and tactics have seen little change over time. Rather, technological innovation generates a false sense of evolution in warfare that exaggerates actual change.[21] The difficulty in analyzing past experiences lies not in the inability to anticipate what American forces may face, but in choosing relevant cases from which insights are to be drawn.[22] This study therefore seeks to overcome this difficulty by asking relevant questions, employing an appropriate methodology, careful case selection, and accurate analysis.

APPROACH

To answer these questions I utilize the focused comparison, first elaborated by Alexander L. George in his influential work, *Deterrence in American Foreign Policy: Theory and Practice*.[23] According to George, the focused comparison "resembles the statistical-correlation approach. . .insofar as it examines multiple cases and establishes its results, in the main, by making comparisons among them."[24] Admittedly, the focused comparison uses "thick description" as does the traditional case study method, but it also seeks to rigorously examine the dependent and independent variables, specify hypotheses, address threats to validity and offer parsimonious explanations.

Arendt Lijphart suggests that the comparative method is simply a method of discovering empirical relationships among variables, not a method of measurement, which is my primary focus. The limitation of comparative analysis distinctly limits the relevance of comparative studies and the correlation an author may suggest between variables.

With the collapse of the Soviet Union on Christmas Day 1991, the United States of America became the only state with the economic, military, and political resources necessary to act as global hegemon. In the "unipolar moment" that has lasted more than a decade, the United States has been called upon to act as global policeman in Kuwait (1992), Somalia (1991–1994), Bosnia-Herzegovina (1993), Iraq (1993, 1996, 1998, 2002, 2003), Macedonia (1993), Haiti (1994, 2004), Croatia (1995), Zaire (1996), Liberia (1990, 1997), Sudan (1998), Afghanistan (1998, 2001), and Yugoslavia (1999).[25] In some notable instances the United States declined to intervene including Rwanda (1994) and Sierra Leone (1991). In all instances in which the United States used its military might, it acted to bring stability to the international system by punishing rogue leaders or intervening in the internal crises of failed states. And, in most instances, the international community supported American action, recognizing the benefits a benevolent hegemon provides to the international system.[26] With few notable exceptions, the inability and/or unwillingness of many states to participate in the creation of international stability has left the task to the United States, which is likely to continue well into the twenty-first century. Given the current global environment, the United States is unlikely to face a major power conflict in the foreseeable future. This leaves the American military with the prospects of creating stability in failing or failed states (Rwanda, Liberia, Sierra Leone), confronting rogue regimes (Iran, Syria, North Korea), and prosecuting the Global War on Terror.

In each of these situations, the United States will face adversaries employing decidely unconventional strategy and tactics. To better understand future conflict, this study examines the American experience in three asymmetric conflicts and asks the following five questions: Which aspects of classical military theory provide insight into asymmetric warfare? What is asymmetric warfare and how does it differ from other forms of unconventional warfare? What will warfare look like in the twenty-first century? Has the United States effectively adapted to the asymmetric strategy and tactics of its adversaries? What lessons has the United States learned from its experience with asymmetric conflict?

The first question is addressed in Chapter 1. Questions two and three are the basis of analysis in Chapter 2. The final two questions are the focus of the three case studies which are Chapters 3 through 5.

In answering these questions I seek to shed light on recent American experience with asymmetric conflict and suggest a set of lessons the United States should learn from its experience. Chapter 2 examines the work of major theorists from Sun-tzu to John Boyd. I look at more than 2,500 years of military theory in an effort to determine if a framework for asymmetric conflict existed long before it came to dominate the American experience in the post-Cold War era. During this extensive analysis of military theory two distinct theoretical paths in the development of warfare materialize. Eastern writers, beginning with Sun-tzu, consistently developed strategies and tactics that avert pitched battle. Western writers, however, have long conceived of war as close quarters combat between conventional forces seeking to anhilate the opposing army. This is not to suggest that unconventional conflict is new to the West. Epaminondas, Julius Caesar, and Belisarius, three of the West's great commanders, regularly utilized unconventional means in their conflicts with numerically superior adversaries. Instead, I suggest that elements of Eastern and Western theory are relevant to developing an understanding of military theory and its force in shaping modern conflict. Chapter 2 also underscores Patton's insight highlighted earlier in the chapter by illustrating the similarities in strategic thought of history's great military minds.

Chapter 3 suggests asymmetric warfare is not simply the latest nomenclature, but a distinct form of unconventional warfare utilizing strategy and tactics that differ from guerrilla or internal warfare. In addition, the chapter discusses the changing face of conflict offering an explanation for claims that technology has fundamentally transformed combat for the United States. Again, I return to Patton's insight.

I also suggest that the United States will continue to replace soldiers, sailors, airmen, and marines with technology in a continuing effort to reduce manpower requirements and casualties. The success of these efforts is yet to prove successful in their early stages, particularly as the War in Iraq continues to prove more difficult than expected. Terrorism, as I suggest, will remain the primary tactic of asymmetric actors, which will make it difficult to replace men with high technology.

CASE SELECTION

Lebanon (1982–1984), Somalia, and Afghanistan (2003–) were selected for study because of a number of reasons. The first of four criteria stipulates that the United States must militarily intervene in a foreign state. Where the first criterion includes a majority of American conflicts, the second criterion begins limiting the number of possible cases by including only those conflicts where American intervention lasts a minimum of 12 months. The third criterion requires that American forces possess military capabilities greater than their opponent. Lastly, American forces must face an adversary that refuses to engage in conventional conflict.

Eleven conflicts meet the case selection criteria established in the preceding paragraphs. First among these cases is the guerrilla war that took place in the Philippine Islands during and after the Spanish-American War (1899–1901) followed by the second Mexican-American War (1914–1919), Haiti (1915–1934), the Dominican Republic (1916–1924), Nicaragua (1926–1933), *Werwolf* Germany (1944–1947), Vietnam (1955–1973), Lebanon (1982–1984), Somalia (1992–1994), the War in Afghanistan (2001–present), and the Iraq War (2003–present). Of these 11 cases Lebanon, Somalia, and Afghanistan were selected for analysis.

In addition to meeting the criteria for case selection each of these states is predominantly Muslim, was a failing or failed state at the time of American intervention, hosted known terrorist groups, and is located in one of the regions that is likely to see American intervention in the coming years.

Questions

Five questions are asked in each of the three cases selected:

1. What were the economic, military, and political conditions prior to American intervention?
2. What were American objectives?
3. How did the United States combat the asymmetric strategy and tactics of its adversary?
4. Were American objectives achieved?
5. What lessons did the United States learn from its experience?

Preconditions

In all three cases governments ceased to effectively govern. Lebanon, at the time of American intervention, found itself divided between Muslim factions and the Christian minority. Beirut, once a favorite European and Arab vacation destination, was little more than a war zone by 1982. The Lebanese government, which divided power between Muslims and

Christians, found itself unable to prevent or end the civil war that was tearing the country apart.[27] Syria, Israel, the United States, and the United Nations all entered the fray, but with little success or resolution.

Less than a decade later, Somalia found itself in a similar situation. With the overthrow of Siad Barre on January 27, 1991, Somalia quickly fell into factional fighting as the Hawiye and Ogaden clans sought to assert control over the entire country. No one clan, however, was strong enough to defeat the other. Sub-clan factionalism also proved difficult to control as clan leaders fought to maintain power over geographic territory. By the time President Bush sent marines to Somalia to provide protection for humanitarian relief efforts, Somalis were starving as their country crumbled around them.

Afghanistan also found peace a difficult prospect. After more than a decade of fighting the Soviets during the Soviet-Afghan War (1979–1989), the Mujahideen finally defeated the communist government of President Muhammad Najibullah in 1992. Soon Dr. Burhanuddin Rabbani was elected president, but by 1994, the government found itself fighting the Islamic fundamentalists of the Taliban. For seven years war raged as the Taliban slowly pushed the Northern Alliance into the northeast region of Afghanistan. From 1997 until the American invasion in October 2001, the situation remained stagnant as the Taliban and Northern Alliance fought to a standstill.

Economic decline in all three states was exacerbated by the internal instability brought about by conflict. The economies of Somalia and Afghanistan had, in fact, collapsed leaving many young men without work and little to do but join one of the clan or tribal militias. In Somalia, the sale of weapons and the importation of *miraa* (kat), an addictive narcotic chewed by Somali militiamen, became the leading staples of the Somali economy. Afghanistan, like Somalia, produced no manufactured goods for sale on the international market, save one. Taliban leaders encouraged farmers to grow poppy, which was exported for the production of opiates. Faring slightly better, the Lebanese economy suffered from unemployment and poor economic conditions leading many young Muslims to join terrorist groups such as Amal or Hezbollah. In all three countries economic conditions exacerbated the downward spiral.

With the economic and political deterioration of Lebanon, Somalia, and Afghanistan came the collapse of each state's military. Somalia and Afghanistan lacked a unified military prior to the beginning of conflict. Rather, military units were largely clan or tribal-based. Lebanon, while maintaining a Western-style military, quickly lost control of its units as Christian and Muslim troops formed militias for the preservation of their respective groups. In all three states the national military failed to provide stability in the midst of economic and political turmoil leaving each country to face internal chaos.

Objectives

American objectives in Lebanon and Somalia were much the same. Intervention in Lebanon began as an attempt to stem the bloodshed by providing the stability of an American military presence. Marines on the ground, however, quickly realized they were targets rather than a stabilizing force. In the end, the United States left Lebanon without bringing stability to the small Middle Eastern country. Instead, more than 245 dead marines were payment for the American effort. While the United States fared better in Somalia, attempts to remove warlord Muhammad Farah Aidid from power and end chaos in the East African country led to the deaths of nearly two dozen American soldiers and the continued rule of Aidid.

The invasion of Afghanistan differed greatly in its objectives from the two previous interventions. For some time the United States was aware of the Taliban's support of al-Qaeda and on several occasions President Clinton launched missile strikes against terrorist training camps in Afghanistan.[28] The attacks of September 11, 2001, were the proverbial straw that broke the camel's back. In conjunction with the Northern Alliance, the United States invaded Afghanistan to overthrow the Taliban and eliminate al-Qaeda. The Taliban was quickly destroyed and al-Qaeda terrorists were forced to flee Afghanistan. While al-Qaeda was not destroyed, American objectives in Afghanistan were largely achieved, although the recent resurgence of the Taliban in Pashtun areas of Afghanistan leaves the permanence of American success in grave doubt.

Asymmetry

American efforts to combat the asymmetric strategy and tactics of terrorists in Lebanon, Muhammad Farah Aidid in Somalia, and the combined forces of the Taliban and al-Qaeda in Afghanistan each had differing results. The United States's experience in Lebanon may be a classic case of underestimating one's adversary. American military commanders and civilian leaders expected the presence of marines to serve as a deterrent to further conflict. This mistake led marines to take up exposed positions at Beirut International Airport where a truck bomb driven by members of Hezbollah slammed into the marine barracks on October 23, 1983, killing 241. Naval bombardment and air strikes ensued, but with little success. By February 26, 1984, the last marines left Lebanon.

After two years of clan warfare and several failed international attempts to end the bloodshed in Mogadishu, American marines landed in Somalia December 9, 1992, to launch Operation Restore Hope. With limited success marines were able to provide security for humanitarian relief efforts. Trouble began when the growing U.S. Army and Marine presence expanded along with their mission. Efforts to disarm Somali militiamen, raid arms stores and capture Muhammad Farah Aidid led to repeated conflict between American forces and Aidid's forces. The conflict culminated with the disastrous October 3, 1993, daytime raid designed to capture the uncooperative warlord. Members of the Army's elite Delta Force along with Army Rangers flew into central Mogadishu expecting to find Aidid, but found themselves in an ambush instead. In total, 18 Rangers and Delta operators died while 500 to 1000 Somalis were killed. Aidid remained on the loose until he perished at the hands of Somalis several years after the March 1994 American withdrawal.[29]

When the United States invaded Afghanistan in October 2001 it did so with little more than a few dozen Special Forces operators in combination with the Northern Alliance and the world's most advanced airforce. History may view this war as the first war in which the United States used its technological superiority in combination with asymmetric means to defeat an adversary. In the immediate aftermath of the successful American effort it seems the United States may have turned a strategic corner.

Success

Of the five questions asked in each case, the fourth is perhaps the simplest to answer. Lebanon and Somalia were unequivocal American failures. In both instances the United States failed to meet its objectives. Lebanon was the greater of the two failures. Not only did marines fail to bring stability to Lebanon, they also lost more than 245 of their own. The reasons for this resounding failure are discussed in Chapter 3, which examines the case of Lebanon. Somalia was also a failure, but of less magnitude. When marines first landed on the Somali coast, the mission of Operation Restore Hope was limited to providing security to the columns of relief supplies responsible for feeding the Somali people. This aspect of the mission was a success. It was with the expansion of the mission and the refusal of Secretary of Defense Les Aspin to provide the necessary heavy armaments that the ambush of October 3, 1993, was possible. President Clinton's early withdrawal of American forces was the result. The many intricacies of American involvement in Somalia are discussed in greater detail in Chapter 4.

American objectives in Afghanistan were straightforward: overthrow the Taliban and destroy al-Qaeda. Capturing Osama bin Laden would be an added bonus, but a dead terror chief would suffice. The Taliban was overthrown and al-Qaeda was dealt a severe blow, but Osama bin Laden escaped American efforts to hunt him down. Al-Qaeda also survived but only after several thousand men were killed or captured by American and Afghan forces. Chapter 5 provides detailed analysis of the American invasion of Afghanistan.

Lessons Learned

The fifth question asks what lessons the United States learned from its experience. Often the relationship between current and future events is unclear, making it possible for researchers to equate what "should" have been learned with what was learned. Illustrating causality remains the most difficult task for social scientists and makes the full comprehension of "lessons learned" a difficult task.

Lebanon, if it achieved nothing else, made the United States aware of terrorism as an emerging tactic American forces must learn to combat. No longer would car bombs, kidnappings, and the highjacking of airliners remain a threat to civilian targets alone. After the attack on the marine barracks in Beirut, it was clear that the U.S. military would itself face terrorism and other forms of asymmetric means in the future.

The lessons of Somalia were similar. Much like Lebanon, American and UN commanders viewed Somali militiamen as less than competent. Fighting other rag-tag factions was thought to be one thing, but engaging elite members of the U.S. military was another. On several occasions American and UN raids against arms stores and factional leaders occurred in broad daylight. Expecting further raids, Muhammad Farah Aidid was waiting when the Delta Force and Army Rangers came calling on October 3, 1993. Pictures of Somalis dragging dead Americans through the streets of Mogadishu taught President Clinton to stay out of the internal conflicts of Africa.[30] When the genocide of Rwanda exploded little more than a year later, the United States was nowhere to be found.

With a continuing American presence in Afghanistan, lessons are learned at a rapid rate. The United States has, however, seen that a mix of Special Forces, local allies, and advanced air power are a potent weapon. Although the full ramifications of the War in Afghanistan are not yet fully understood, one thing is certain: the United States will no longer rely on large infantry components to wage war in the third world. Instead, the United States is moving toward lighter and faster forces trained in the tactics of America's asymmetric adversaries.

Chapter 6 examines the evidence of each case in order to draw the broader implications of the American experience with asymmetric conflict over the past two and a half decades. In doing so, the evidence suggests that conflicts of asymmetry are the dominant form of conflict the United States will face in the coming decades, for which the American public and the U.S. military must prepare.

1

Military Thought and Asymmetric Conflict

From the earliest days of human history warfare has played an important role in both the development and destruction of civilizations, and despite our greatest hopes to end it, warfare remains a constant. Military historians and strategists provide us with more than 3,000 years of collective knowledge and thought on the subject for the purpose of educating future generations in the art of combat. In both the East and the West, men have long sought to understand the soul of battle and the art of victory. From the earliest writings of the great Chinese strategist Sun-tzu to Colonel John Boyd's recent development of the OODA Loop, every aspect of warfare has experienced close examination.[1] Rather than adding to the vast body of military theory that exists, this chapter examines the work of a number of respected military historians and strategists in an effort to determine if, in fact, classic military theory holds the key to unlocking a more complete understanding of modern asymmetric conflict.

Contrary to the recent work of some scholars, I suggest that modern asymmetric conflict is a reinvention of concepts developed decades, centuries, and millennia ago. What is often mistaken for innovation is the rediscovery of well-worn ideas modified by the application of technological innovation. In assessing prominent works, the focus is not on the primary theoretical developments in each treatise, but on those contributions that speak to asymmetric conflict. In some instances the concepts I highlight are ancillary to the writer's main focus, but they are illustrative of the author's conceptual understanding of asymmetry in warfare. Here more than in any other chapter Patton's admonition is evident.

EAST AND WEST

The development of asymmetric strategy and tactics took distinctly divergent paths in the East and West. Developing first in China, asymmetric means have long dominated Eastern military theory. The same cannot be said of military theory in the West. In China, strategists developed concepts along a much different line than their European counterparts. Eastern warfare, from its earliest conception in Sun-tzu's *Art of War*, written in the fifth century BC, to the more recent work of Mao Zedong and Vo Nguyen Giap, has long emphasized defeating an adversary without pitched battle.

In distinct contrast, Western theorists have long emphasized the significance of a direct collision between opposing armies. In an environment dramatically different from that of China, European warfare developed with a distinct bias in favor of the decisive battle epitomized in Carl von Clausewitz's *Vom Kriege* (On War). Conflict in the West has, however, seen the development of doctrine similar to that dominating Eastern military thought. The early Roman strategist Vegetius emphasized the use of asymmetry in warfare in the decades before the collapse of the Western Roman Empire.

In light of the distinct differences in the development of Eastern and Western military theory, the two are treated independently in the pages that follow. Because of the East's preference for asymmetric theory, Western states, particularly the United States, should not find it unusual that insurgents in Afghanistan and Iraq are utilizing their current tactics. Abu Musab al-Zarqawi and Osama bin Laden are unlikely to have ever read the works of Sun-tzu, Mao Zedong, or General Giap, yet both men utilize the very tactics they developed and utilized. More than two millennia of conflict between the East and West should have certainly led to a convergence of military theory. This is not, however, the case. Where Sun-tzu played a major role in the development of Mao's "mobile guerrilla warfare," Clausewitz and other Western strategists were unfamiliar with his work. Much the same can be said of Eastern theorists and their unfamiliarity with Western military thought.

Because East and West took divergent paths in the development of military theory, each is examined independently, beginning with early Western military theory. From there I move to the work of Sun-tzu. The chapter then progresses to the current day examining the development of military theory over time. In addition to examining works relevant to modern asymmetric conflict, influential Western works of lesser value to the West's understanding of asymmetry are briefly discussed in order to highlight the evolution of European military theory.

EARLY WESTERN MILITARY THOUGHT (HERODOTUS, THUCYDIDES, AND XENOPHON)

The word strategy comes from the Greek term *strategos*, which is defined as the art of the general. As the developers of strategy, and conversely tactics, it is with the work of the classical Greek historian Herodotus that Western military thought must begin. Strictly speaking, Herodotus was not a military theorist as are many of the men who followed him. He was the "father of history," as the great Roman politician and orator Cicero once called him. It is primarily from Herodotus that the modern world understands the causes, events, and results of the war between Greece and the Persian Empire, which began in the middle of the sixth century BC.[2] Herodotus, in addition to elaborating the reasons for Cyrus's invasion of Greece, provides his readers with an understanding of the strategy and tactics utilized by the Greeks and Persians.

What makes Herodotus significant is his clear description of Greek military tactics. Like his younger contemporary Thucydides, historian of the Peloponnesian War, Herodotus provides detailed accounts of the plans, stratagems, and tactics the Greeks utilized against a superior adversary.[3] According to Herodotus, Greek warfare was based on the hoplite, an infantryman drawn from the yeomanry of the Greek city-states. Heavily armored and carrying a long spear and short sword, the hoplite fought in the phalanx, a tightly packed infantry formation usually eight rows deep. After marching into close proximity with an adversary, the phalanx charged using its crushing weight and protruding spears to break the ranks of the enemy. For nearly a thousand years the hoplite protected Greece from invaders.

Greeks, dependent upon the hoplite, were accustomed to conventional warfare. As Herodotus explains, Athens and its allies never looked to asymmetric means for a defense against a significantly larger Persian invasion force during their protracted conflict. The deciding events in the prolonged war between Greece and the Persian Empire were the battles of Marathon and Salamis. In both battles, outnumbered Greeks using the weight of their heavy infantry (Marathon) and sturdy triremes (Salamis) were able to defeat larger Persian forces in conventional land and naval combat.

Thucydides's *History of the Peloponnesian War* offers an account of the war between Athens and Sparta (431–404 BC) similar in style to Herodotus. And, much like his contemporary, Thucydides details the causes, tactics, and outcome of Greco-Persian conflict. Thucydides's history provides little evidence that the Greeks, the dominant Western society of the time, understood anything other than conventional warfare. Xenophon's *Anabasis*, which offers an account of the expedition, originally led by Cyrus the Younger, to depose Artaxerxes II of Persia and Xenophon's subsequent withdrawal of Greek forces from deep within enemy territory provides an additional account of the strategy and tactics utilized by the Greeks.[4] Again, the development of asymmetric means is not apparent. Greece, as the cradle of Western civilization, rarely faced an adversary employing tactics similar to the modern asymmetric actor. Instead, Greeks usually found themselves fighting one another or their nemesis, Persia. The success of Greece against Persia and the acceptance of set piece battle in internal conflict led to strategic and tactical stagnation within Greek warfare.

It was not until the conquest of Greece by Phillip II of Macedon and his son, Alexander the Great, that Greek warfare experienced significant change. Alexander, culturally Greek, but a native of the Macedonian plains, added cavalry to a modified phalanx and developed tactical formations with greater mobility. As the Greek historian Arrian explains, it was Alexander's modifications to hoplite tactics and his exceptional leadership that led Alexander to conquer much of the known world.[5] The tactical developments of Alexander enabled Greek culture and power to reach its zenith, but stagnation set in once again and Greece lost its preeminent position in the Western world when, at the battle of Pydna (168 BC), Perseus of Macedon was defeated by the Roman consul Lucius Aemilius Paulus. Maneuverability proved the deciding factor as the Roman Legions proved more than a match for the Macedonian phalanx.

ROMAN WARFARE (POLYBIUS, LIVY, CAESAR, JOSEPHUS, AND VEGETIUS)

With the defeat of Macedon and the Greeks at the battle of Pydna (168 BC), Roman power quickly reached its zenith. In addition to waging war against Macedon, Rome continued its conflict with Carthage, which began with the First Punic War (264–241 BC). After defeating Carthage in what was primarily a naval war, Rome gained preeminence in the Mediterranean giving it the economic power needed to continue expanding across Europe, North Africa, and the Near East. In addition to toppling Carthage from its dominant position in the Mediterranean, the First Punic War brought Hamilcar Barca to power setting the stage for the Second and Third Punic Wars (218–201 BC).

Polybius, the Greek historian and scholar, also served as tutor to Scipio Africanus, the Younger, and accompanied him on his campaign in North Africa in which Carthage was razed to the ground. Polybius's account of the Punic Wars offers the first account of Roman military strategy and tactics.[6] Rome, unlike the Greek city-states it conquered, found itself in conflict with adversaries employing a divergent set of strategies and tactics. From the Goths in modern-day France to Carthage in North Africa, Roman Legions succeeded in defeating numerous enemies because they continued to adapt to ever-changing circumstances. According to Polybius and Livy, a later Roman historian of the Punic Wars, the greatest advantage a Roman Legionnaire possessed was his superior training and discipline.[7] Throughout much of Roman military history, the Legions, dispatched to conquer new lands and quell rebellion in unruly provinces, faced enemies that often maintained a significant numerical advantage and, with equal frequency, refused to give battle.[8]

Rome, like the Greek city-states, depended largely on infantry and close-quarters combat to destroy an adversary's fighting force. When Hannibal, commander of Carthaginian forces, crossed the Alps into northern Italy (218 BC), Roman troops were caught off guard by the risk Hannibal had taken in crossing the Alps in the dead of winter. Racing from Sicily to meet Hannibal in northern Italy, the consul Sempronius Longus, after an exhausting march of 40 days, found Hannibal's forces on the west side of the Trebbia River. Initiating the battle, Hannibal sent his light cavalry across the frozen river against the Romans. The Carthaginians feigned a rout in what is one of the East's greatest tactical developments, the Parthian shot, luring pursuing Romans across the Trebbia where they were cut down by heavy cavalry and infantry.[9] Throughout Hannibal's march across the Italian peninsula during the Second Punic War (218–217, 218–204 BC), Hannibal acted unexpectedly, giving battle only when he had carefully planned for victory.

After Rome's defeat at Trebbia, Hannibal marched south where the newly elected consul Gaius Flaminius was set to ambush the Carthaginians at Arretium. Hearing of the ambush, Hannibal marched around the Romans forcing them to pursue his army. At Lake Trasimene, Hannibal ambushed the consular army annihilating the only force standing between Hannibal and the capital.[10] After being badly defeated in two battles in which Hannibal had utilized asymmetric tactics, Rome elected Fabius Maximus dictator. This proved a fortunate turn of events for Rome because Fabius had long advocated refusing battle to Hannibal. Instead, he implemented a strategy, which sought to starve and harass Hannibal until he was forced to withdraw from the Italian peninsula. Fabius's scorched earth tactics quickly proved effective. In concert with this policy, Fabius harassed Hannibal's lines of supply and communication. When Hannibal sought to bring the Romans to battle, they quickly dispersed and retreated to the hills and mountains.

The success of Fabius's strategy and tactics proved little to the people of Rome, who found it contemptuous to refuse battle to an enemy. The effectiveness of Fabius's methods is, however, unquestionable and led to the development of the term "Fabian tactics" as a description for asymmetric tactics. The campaign of 218–217 BC marked the first time Rome developed a strategic plan built on the utilization of asymmetry in warfare. The developments of Fabian were, however, short lived as Rome quickly returned to conventional warfare.

After nearly defeating Hannibal without having fought a single battle, Fabius was replaced by the consuls Lucius Aemilius Paulus and Caius Terentius Varro who, leading the largest Roman army ever assembled

(70,000 men), set out to force Hannibal into a decisive battle. The Roman and Carthaginian armies met near the Apulian village of Cannae where, in one of history's greatest battles, Hannibal drove the Roman cavalry from the field, enabling his cavalry and heavy infantry to surround the Romans. From that point, the Legionnaires were forced in on themselves, creating such a tightly packed mass that they could not draw their weapons. At the hands of a smaller Carthaginian army, 50,000 Romans perished. Cannae was the greatest defeat ever suffered by Rome.[11]

Rather than returning to Fabian tactics Rome raised new Legions and continued the conventional conflict that had proven disastrous. For another 12 years Hannibal waged a bloody war in Italy and Iberia before suffering defeat at the battle of Zama (202 BC), which ended the Second Punic War. With the defeat of Hannibal, Rome rapidly grew in wealth and power. And with increasing power came Rome's expansion into the uncivilized world where the Legions fought adversaries employing tactics dramatically different from their own.

Julius Caesar, perhaps better than any other Roman commander, understood the methods of the uncivilized tribes in Gaul and Britain. After nine years of campaigning in Gaul, Germania, and Britain, Caesar had conquered much of Europe and created an efficient Roman military system, which depended on the superior training and discipline of its Legionnaires to defeat tribal armies fighting on their home soil and at a numerical advantage. Caesar's *The Gallic Wars* provides a detailed account of the people and campaigns faced by Caesar and his Legions.[12]

A prolific chronicler of his experiences, Caesar illustrates to the modern reader why he is often considered one of history's great captains, yet he offers relatively limited insight into his strategic and tactical developments. The same is true of his other great work, *The Civil Wars,* in which he details the collapse of the Triumvirate and his own rise to power.[13] Caesar transformed the Legion into a professional army that, unlike the Legions of the Punic Wars, maintained its Legionnaires for many years, developing the most skilled and disciplined soldiers in the world. However, Caesar wrote as a chronicler of his conquests, leaving those who came after him to their own devices when extracting strategic and tactical insights from his work.

Rome's expansion throughout Europe and the Mediterranean led to frequent and often prolonged conflicts between Roman Legions and native populations. Among the most well-known conflicts is the Great Jewish Revolt (66–73 AD), which was chronicled by the Jewish rebel-turned-Roman citizen and historian, Josephus. Judea, a province of the Empire since 6 AD, chafed under the rule of Roman procurators who forced a devout Jewish people to worship or pay tribute to Roman deities. Led by John of Giscala and Simon ben Giora, Jewish rebels executed a well-crafted asymmetric campaign against the superior forces of Cestius Gallus, whose Legion was nearly obliterated at Beit-Horon. According to Josephus, the Jewish revolt saw early success as its small bands of rebels attacked isolated Roman garrisons utilizing tactics similar to those employed by Fabius Maximus against Hannibal.[14] Nero responded to the defeat of Cestius by sending Vespasian and 60,000 Legionnaires to quell the revolt. By 66 AD Vespasian controlled northern Judea, which suffered near total destruction at his hands.

Caesar, in his Gallic campaigns, developed an effective strategy for combating the asymmetric tactics of the Gauls: depopulation. In many instances, Caesar killed every man, woman, and child in a conquered region or sold the surviving women and children into slavery. He also burned crops, killed livestock, and razed villages to the ground. By razing an area to the ground Caesar denied enemy troops the logistical support necessary to sustaining a viable guerrilla force. These tactics also discouraged potential adversaries from confronting the superior might of Rome.

Utilizing the tactics of his predecessor, Vespasian depopulated much of northern Judea, with Caesar's strategic goals in mind. It was not, however, until 70 AD that Titus Flavius, son of the newly crowned Emperor Vespasian, conquered the Jewish capital of Jerusalem, effectively ending Jewish resistance.[15] Josephus records that Titus's men razed the Temple of Solomon, burning the city and slaughtering its citizens. In total, Judea lost a minimum of 750,000 inhabitants, with estimates ranging as high as 1.5 million. Josephus's account of the Great Jewish Revolt illustrates the manner in which Rome dealt with adversaries who themselves utilized asymmetric tactics. In many instances, those who faced Rome in conventional conflict suffered the destruction of their army and the death of their leadership, but the citizenry went unharmed. The harsher tactics of Caesar, Vespasian, and Titus were reserved for adversaries who refused to stand and fight.

Aeneas the Tactician, writing in the fourth century BC, was the first among Western strategists to systematically examine warfare.[16] It was, however, not until Flavius Renatus Vegetius's *Epitoma Rei Militaris* (A Summary of Military Matters) that a comprehensive strategic and tactical analysis of Roman warfare was written.[17] Writing in the late fourth century AD, Vegetius sought to restore a declining Roman Empire to its former glory by reinvigorating the institution responsible for Rome's dominance of the known world: the Legions.

Epitoma Rei Militaris, considered the greatest work of military theory before *On War*, offers a great deal more than a simple description of Roman warfare at its height. Beginning with the formation of the Legions, book one offers criteria for the selection of Legionnaires and the training needed to restore the physical strength and skill of the once-feared Roman soldier, an area of dramatic decline by the fourth century. According to Vegetius, "Victory in war does not depend entirely upon numbers or mere courage; only skill and discipline will ensure it." He continues, "We find that the Romans owed the conquest of the world to no other cause than continual military training, exact observance of discipline in their camps and unwearied cultivation of the other arts of war."[18] While Vegetius was speaking to the Emperor Valentinian, as commander of the Legions, Vegetius's maxim is applicable to both asymmetric and conventional conflict.

The success of al-Qaeda, for example, is due to the skilled and disciplined operatives that form the organization.[19] This does not suggest that al-Qaeda operatives are as well trained and capable as American or British troops, but it does suggest that the level of skill and discipline achieved by al-Qaeda enables the organization to wage a global terror campaign against the United States and its allies, while continuing to elude the combined efforts of national governments.

Book two examines the organization of the Legions. Here Vegetius elucidates the formation of the Legions and supporting units, distribution of rank, promotion within the Legions, and the role of support personnel. While providing a detailed description of the Roman Legion's composition, book two offers few insights into asymmetric conflict.

Book three, however, proves Vegetius's most prolific contribution. Here he discusses military strategy and tactics, admonishing the Emperor and commanders with maxims similar to those of Sun-tzu. It was because of what Vegetius offered in book three that Henry II of England, Richard the Lion-Hearted, Ludwig the Just, Niccolo Machiavelli, Montecuccoli, and Field Marshal Ligne considered *Epitoma Re Militaris* the single greatest work of military theory ever written. Vegetius begins by warning the Emperor against deploying large armies in the field. He notes that Rome seldom deployed more than two Legions (approximately 20,000 men) to an area of conflict. In a style similar to J. F. C. Fuller, Vegetius warns, "An army too numerous is subject to many dangers and inconveniences. Its bulk makes it slow and unwieldy in its motions; and as it is obliged to march in columns of great length, it is exposed to the risk of being continually harassed and insulted by inconsiderable parties of the enemy."[20] Instead, he favors mobility over mass relying on the superior skill and discipline of the Legions to strike decisive blows at unexpected times and places.[21] During the reign of Valentinian, Rome's position remained precarious as the Legions, long in decline, no longer possessed the ability to defeat an adversary in conventional conflict.

Vegetius, understanding the weakness of the Legions, wisely suggests, "Good officers decline general engagements where the danger is common, and prefer the employment of stratagem and finesse to destroy the enemy as much as possible in detail and intimidate them without exposing our own forces."[22] Reminiscent of Sun-tzu, Vegetius's preference for mobility, speed, and deception illustrates a clear understanding of Rome's adversaries and the asymmetry of conflict.[23] Vegetius does not stop with these suggested reforms. He further emphasizes the need for flexibility in strategic and tactical planning as well as in the mental agility of commanders. Continuing with his emphasis on flexible leadership, Vegetius admonishes commanding generals, in a fashion similar to Sun-tzu's maxim "know thy enemy and know thy self" stating, "It is essential to know the character of the enemy and of their principal officers—whether they be rash or cautious, enterprising or timid, whether they fight on principle or from chance and whether the nations they have been engaged with were brave or cowardly." He adds, "Thus a vigilant and prudent general will carefully weigh in his council the state of his own forces and of those of the enemy, just as a civil magistrate judging between two contending parties."[24]

From this point, Vegetius focuses the remainder of book three on a detailed discussion of Roman order of battle, with one exception. Before offering a detailed description of conventional order of battle, Vegetius speaks to the veteran soldier saying,

> He should form ambuscades with the greatest secrecy to surprise the enemy at the passage of rivers, in the rugged passes of mountains, in defiles in woods and when embarrassed by morasses of difficult roads. He should regulate his march so as to fall upon them while taking their refreshments or sleeping, or at a time when they suspect no danger and are dispersed, unarmed and their horses unsaddled.[25] He should continue these kinds of encounters till his soldiers have imbibed a proper confidence in themselves....If the enemy makes excursions or expeditions; the general should attack him after the fatigue of a long march, fall upon him unexpectedly, or harass his rear. He should detach parties to endeavor to carry off by surprise any quarters established at a distance from the hostile army for the convenience of forage or provision. For such measures should be pursued at first as can produce no very bad effects if they should happen to miscarry but would be of great advantage if attended with success.[26]

Vegetius continues suggesting that a commander should sow dissension within an adversary's ranks in an effort to create discord in the opposing army and society.[27]

Integrating asymmetric and conventional warfare in book three, Vegetius, like Fabius Maximus, illustrates an ongoing need for flexibility, which, in some instances, may call for pitched battle and in others tactical asymmetry. After examining many classical military texts in his effort to develop a comprehensive guide to warfare, Vegetius sees the need to encourage innovation within doctrinal development. By the time Vegetius wrote *Epitoma Re Militaris*, the Roman Empire was split into East and West, with the Goths sacking Rome and the Legions suffering defeat at the hands of the Huns, Goths, Vandals, and other tribes. The declining state of the Roman Army led Vegetius to ask, "Are we afraid of not being able to learn from others what they before have learned from us?"[28]

Valentinian and subsequent emperors of the Western Roman Empire failed to adjust to the increasing pressure of northern tribes. In 410 AD

Rome was sacked and from that point forward, the Western Empire rapidly declined. Had Rome implemented reform and developed an understanding of asymmetry, history may have written a different end for the Roman Empire. The failure to adapt to the changing face of warfare doomed the once dominant empire to a fate from which it never recovered.

THE END OF EARLY WESTERN THEORY (MACHIAVELLI)

The millennia following Vegetius experienced significant evolution in warfare as the era of heavy infantry ended and that of heavy cavalry began. Soon after the final collapse of the Western Roman Empire in the sixth century, the mounted knight came to prominence as the dominant force in European warfare. And with the knight came feudalism, which dominated Europe until the dramatic social changes resulting from the French Revolution (1789–1799) and the Napoleonic Wars (1804–1815). The millennia proceeding Vegetius also marked a decline in the development of Western military theory. It was not until 1520 that a significant treatise on warfare appeared in Europe. At this time the author of the widely read *Il Principe* (The Prince), Niccolo Machiavelli, penned what would be the last military treatise before firearms made their mark on warfare.

Machiavelli's *Dell'arte della guerra* (Art of War) sought to find the laws and principles of warfare by examining the work of Tacitus, Frontinus, Polybius, Xenophon, Livy, and Vegetius.[29] Written in the form of a dialogue between the main character, Fabrizio Colonna, and a group of young men, the *Art of War* was read and admired by military commanders from Frederick the Great to Napoleon. Machiavelli's work, however, made little tactical impact on warfare. Much to Machiavelli's disadvantage, he failed to see the revolution firearms would bring to warfare. Instead, he advocated a form of warfare similar to that of early Rome. Machiavelli's lack of vision left the *Art of War* less than a rival to his greatest work *The Prince*.

New concepts were, however, introduced, or reintroduced in some cases, into Western military thought. Among Machiavelli's greatest contributions is his advocacy of total warfare waged by citizen soldiers and national militias.[30] For the patriotic Florentine, conscription and the establishment of the militia serves to confront the sixteenth century mercenary armies of the European monarchs and instills nationalism within the citizens of a nation.[31] Much as in the *The Prince,* Machiavelli's conception of war as a "no holds barred" contest in which victory is the aim leads him to reject conventional morality as a governing force in conflict. For Machiavelli, war creates its own morality which is based on values such as opportunity and expediency.[32] Machiavelli's explicit rejection of just war proves a precursor to the development of *realpolitik* several centuries later.[33] It also challenges the Western conception of war as an honored activity of the nobility.[34]

Book five of the *Art of War* finds Fabrizio offering strategic and tactical advice to his young listeners, who, familiar with conventional conflict, find Fabrizio's advice exceptional. Here, Machiavelli distinguishes his thought from his contemporaries by advocating the use of deception, ambush, unpredictability and stratagems as fundamental to tactical success.[35] Unlike military commanders of Machiavelli's time, the Florentine sees little purpose in confronting an adversary in open combat, particularly if the adversary possesses superior strength.[36] Instead, Machiavelli focuses on the ends of war (victory) rather than the means by which it is fought. Thus, if asked, "Do ends justify the means?" Machiavelli's response would be a resounding, "Yes!"

In both conventional and asymmetric conflict, combatants frequently take a Machiavellian position concerning the use of tactics, which modern observers find objectionable.[37] The attacks of September 11, 2001, and Osama bin Laden's justification for them is a case in point.[38] Although neither unique to any one form of warfare, the use of tactics, which target noncombatants, is increasingly becoming strategic doctrine for asymmetric actors as they adapt to the superior strength of the U.S. military and are forced to justify the means by which they achieve their ends.

EARLY CHINESE MILITARY THEORY (SUN-TZU)

Older than Western civilization by more than a thousand years, the Sinic world began its examination of warfare at a much earlier time than the West. By the Spring and Autumn Period (722–481 BC), China, the center of Sinic civilization, developed a feudal system similar to that which developed in the West more than a thousand years later. The Spring and Autumn and Warring States Periods were marked by continual warfare as competing kingdoms sought the conquest of their neighbors and the unification of China under one ruler.

It was sometime between the late Spring and Autumn and early Warring States Periods that Sun-tzu penned his famous treatise, *The Art of War*, for the King of Wu.[39] Warfare in China, by the time of Sun-tzu, was developed into a highly ritualized act with combatants expecting an adversary to meet on open ground for set piece battle. In those instances in which a weaker combatant refused to give battle, an attacking force would besiege an adversary retreating behind his city walls. Thus, *The Art of War* was revolutionary in the principles it introduced. Sun-tzu was the first strategist to develop a systematic treatise on warfare, which advocated radically altering warfare, rejecting conventional tactics.

He was not, however, the last. Sun-tzu's *The Art of War*, the writings of Wu-tzu, Ssu-ma Fa's *The Methods of the Ssu-ma*, *Questions and Replies Between T-ang T'ai-tsung and Li Wei-kung*, *Three Strategies of Huang Shih-kung*, and T'ai Kung's *Six Secret Teachings* were compiled by scholars of the Sung Dynasty as the *Seven Military Classics.*[40] Like *The Art of War,* these additional texts emphasize asymmetry and the Tao in warfare. Closely guarded for their military secrets, the *Seven Military Classics* were read by few kings, generals, and emperors.

Rather than discussing each of the *Seven Military Classics,* I focus on *The Art of War,* which receives the greatest attention in the West. It also plays a prominent role in the development of later Eastern and Western theory unmatched by the other six military classics.[41]

Sun-tzu begins *The Art of War* by elaborating his general principles of warfare. Highest among these is the principle of winning without fighting. Here Sun-tzu warns commanders against seeking pitched battles. He counsels, "The highest realization of warfare is to attack the enemy's plans; next is to attack their alliances; next to attack their army; and the lowest is to attack their fortified cities. Thus one who excels at employing the military subjugates other people's armies without engaging in battle, captures other people's fortified cities without prolonged fighting. He must fight under Heaven with the paramount aim of 'preservation.' Thus his weapons will not become dull, and the gains can be preserved."[42] Chinese history is littered with the remains of costly conflicts in which Sun-tzu's highest principle is violated with great and bloody force.[43] Although considered one of China's great works, *The Art of War* and the asymmetry it introduces to Chinese warfare has often fallen on deaf ears. As later sections will illustrate, it was not until the beginning of the twentieth century that Sun-tzu's work played a major role in the conduct of Eastern warfare.

Often credited with providing inspiration to modern asymmetric actors, *The Art of War* actually addresses conflict between states. In many instances, the ascription of concepts and tactics used by guerrillas, terrorists, and other non-state actors to the work of Sun-tzu is erroneous. Asymmetry, for Sun-tzu, enables conventional military forces to overcome their adversaries with the least loss of life and wealth. Sun-tzu's purpose in writing is often overlooked.

To illustrate this point I turn to Sun-tzu's general principles where he says, "Whenever possible 'victory' should be achieved through diplomatic coercion, thwarting the enemy's plans and alliances, and frustrating his strategy." He further adds, "Preserving the enemy's state capital is best, destroying their capital is second best. Preserving their army is best; destroying their army is second best.... For this reason attaining one hundred victories in one hundred battles is not the pinnacle of excellence. Subjugating the enemy's army without fighting is the true pinnacle of excellence."[44] Throughout *The Art of War,* Sun-tzu emphasizes the need for self-control and the obligation of avoiding all engagements without first conducting detailed analysis of the economic, military, and political circumstances in each of the adversarial states. As Sun-tzu says, "Warfare is the greatest affair of state, the basis of life and death, the Way (Tao) to survival or extinction. It must be thoroughly pondered and analyzed."[45]

Setting Sun-tzu apart from many modern asymmetric actors is his emphasis on rational action. Where many twentieth-century guerrilla movements and twenty-first-century terror networks act based on a deep-seated hatred of their perceived enemy, Sun-tzu warns against allowing personal emotions, such as anger and hatred, from influencing military decisions. When emotions direct action a ruler risks losing the mandate of Heaven, which Sun-tzu considers necessary for victory. This emotional and spiritual component of Sun-tzu differs significantly from the *realpolitik* of Machiavelli and the Islamic fundamentalism of Osama bin Laden.

For Sun-tzu, war is the proper use of *ch'i* (unorthodox) and *cheng* (orthodox). In his clear preference for the unorthodox Sun-tzu says, "Warfare is the Way (Tao) of deception. Thus although [you are] capable, display incapability to them. When committed to employing your forces, feign inactivity. When [your objective] is nearby, make it appear as if distant; when far away, create the illusion of being nearby." He continues adding, "If they are substantial, prepare for them; if they are strong, avoid them...If they are angry, perturb them; be deferential to foster their arrogance." Sun-tzu concludes stating, "Go forth where they will not expect it."[46] Colonel Douglas M. McCready juxtaposes warfare, as seen by Sun-tzu, and that of the West saying, "One difference between Sun-tzu's approach and the American way of war can be seen as the difference between the Asian game of Go and the Western game of Chess. In Go, the opponents place their pieces so as to maximize their control and restrict their opponent's options. The enemy loses pieces and the game by being outmaneuvered, not through direct attack. In Chess, the goal is to capture the opponent's key piece, the king. This requires territorial control by capturing enemy pieces so they cannot threaten one's own king and so that they cannot protect their own king."[47]

In making this distinction, McCready addresses one of the central differences between the conventional conflicts of the West and the asymmetry of Sun-tzu: attrition. Interestingly, in *The Art of War,* Sun-tzu never discusses attrition as a fundamental element of warfare. Instead, he focuses on developing strategic and tactical concepts that seek to preserve one's own economic, military, and political assets. It is preservation, as a motivating force, that leads Sun-tzu to move away from the conventional tactics of his time and toward the asymmetry for which he is known. Sun-tzu's most frequently quoted statement on leadership is a warning to aggressive and reckless commanders willing to suffer heavy casualties for the sake of honor and pyrrhic victories. He warns, "Thus it is said that one who knows the enemy and knows himself will not be endangered in a hundred engagements. One who does not know the enemy but knows himself will sometimes be victorious, sometimes meet with defeat. One who knows neither the enemy nor himself will invariably be defeated in every engagement."[48]

Unlike Western theorists who have long seen attrition as a key aspect of warfare, Sun-tzu's emphasis on preservation through asymmetric means requires military commanders to act with a level of skill unnecessary in Western conflict. Where the Western military commander seeks to hone the skills of his men through repetitive drill and simplification of tasks, Sun-tzu seeks to move warfare to as much an intellectual activity as a physical one. This point is illustrated when he says, "[Simulated] chaos is given birth from control; [feigned] weakness is given birth from strength. Order and disorder are a question of numbers; courage and fear are a question of strategic configuration of power (*shih*); strength and weakness are a question of the deployment [of forces] (*hsing*)." Sun-tzu concludes, "Thus one who excels at warfare seeks [victory] through the strategic configuration of power (*shih*), not from reliance on men. Thus he is able to select men and employ strategic power (*shih*)."[49]

Epaminondas, Sherman, Rommel, Patton, and MacArthur grasped the innate truth in Sun-tzu's principles, demonstrating the value of the ancient Chinese strategist's ideas in their respective campaigns.[50] Contrary to the suggestion of recent analysis, the strategic and tactical developments of Mao Zedong and Vo Nguyen Giap are not consistent with Sun-tzu's conception of warfare.

The question then remains, Which aspects of *The Art of War* are most relevant to current developments in warfare and the conflicts in Afghanistan and Iraq? Simply stated, deception, according to Sun-tzu, is the Tao (Way) of war and the objective of conventional (American forces in Afghanistan and Iraq) and unconventional (Taliban and Iraqi insurgents) forces. Sun-tzu was asked by the King of Wu, "The enemy is courageous and unafraid, arrogant and reckless. His soldiers are numerous and strong. What should we do?" He replied, "Speak and act submissively in order to accord with their intentions. Do not cause them to comprehend [the situation], and thereby increase their indolence. In accord with the enemy's shifts and changes, submerge [our forces] in ambush to await [the moment]. Then do not look at their forward motion nor look back to their rearward movement, but strike in the middle. Even though they are numerous, they can be taken. The Tao for attacking the arrogant is to not engage their advance front."[51] American forces in Iraq are experiencing the tactical application of Sun-tzu's reply. They, in turn, have not responded in kind. Instead, American commanders continue to rely on superior firepower, rather than the stealth and deception of Sun-tzu.

LINEAR WARFARE (FREDERICK II, GUIBERT, BULOW, SUVOROV, NAPOLEON, AND JOMINI)

By the end of the Thirty Years War (1618–1648) and the creation of the Peace of Westphalia (1648), the musket and cannon rapidly became the most important weapons in Western warfare. The *tercio*, a Spanish infantry formation of 3,000 men, one-third of whom bore muskets and two-thirds the pike, dominated European warfare in the sixteenth and early seventeenth centuries. Gustavus Adolphus, King of Sweden (1611–1632), recognized the emerging power of firearms and modified the *tercio* by employing two-thirds musketeers and one-third pike-men. He also placed cannons on mobile carriages giving his armies increased firepower and greater maneuverability. Gustavus Adolphus's innovations turned Sweden into a major European power while signaling the beginning of the new era of linear warfare. The strength of the *tercio*, like the phalanx, was in its mass. Firearms, however, required thinner ranks because of the need to increase the volume of fire. Gustavus Adolphus's death during the battle of Lutzen (1632) prematurely ended the career of the seventeenth century's most capable commander, yet the development of linear tactics continued in the century after his death.[52]

From the Peace of Westphalia to the Seven Years' War (1756–1763) Europe remained at relative peace with war kept from turning into pan-European conflict, as was true of the Thirty Years' War (1618–1648).[53] The Seven Years' War once again brought much of the Continent and North America into conflict. Frederick II, the Great, of Prussia proved to be the eighteenth century's most capable commander and a prolific writer of letters, manuals, and military instructions. He did not, however, attempt a comprehensive analysis of war, as would come in the years after the defeat of Napoleon.

Frederick the Great, often considered one of history's great commanders, did not develop the powerful Prussian military system which dominated European warfare for more than two centuries. That credit belongs to his father, Frederick William I. Frederick the Great's contributions turned the Prussian Army into the most disciplined and skilled army on the Continent. He did so by molding Prussian peasants into unwavering soldiers who feared their officers more than the enemy.[54]

Frederick was a commander of his time, maximizing the efficiency of his troops, but also constraining his strategic and tactical developments to the capabilities of eighteenth-century cannon and musket.[55] He did, however, read Vegetius and classical theorists incorporating their thoughts into his own. The maxims of Frederick best illustrate the dichotomy of his time, where linear warfare dominated and the innovation and asymmetry of the classical world played a minor role in warfare:

1. Your strategy must pursue an important objective. Undertaking only what is possible and reject whatever is chimerical.

2. Never deceive yourself, but picture skillfully all the measures that the enemy will take to oppose your plans, in order to never be caught by surprise.

3. Know the mind of the opposing generals in order to better divine their actions, to know how to force your actions upon them, and to know what traps to use against them.

4. The opening of your campaign must be an enigma for the enemy, preventing him from guessing the side on which your forces will move and the strategy you contemplate.

5. Always attempt the unexpected: this is the surest way to achieve success.[56]

Frederick's maxims can be mistaken easily for those of Sun-tzu because of their relevance to asymmetric conflict, yet the great Prussian commander rarely utilized his own strategy in such a manner. Instead, he fought linear battles relying on the superior discipline, skill, speed, maneuverability, and internal lines to defeat his French, Austrian, and Russian adversaries. Frederick did, however, recognize the effect partisans could have on the costs of war, which he gained while fighting Austria. For Austria, Croatian partisans served as skirmishers and harassed Frederick's lines of supply and communication. The disproportionate effect they had during Prussia's two wars against Austria led Frederick to devise his maxims for fighting an adversary more than twice one's own strength:

1. Wage partisan warfare: change the post whenever necessary.

2. Do not detach any unit from your troops because you will be beaten in detail. Act only with your entire army.

3. If you can throw your army against the enemy's communications without risking your own magazines, do so.

4. Activity and vigilance must be on the watch day and night at the door of your tent.

5. Give more thought to your rear than to your front, in order to avoid being enveloped.

6. Reflect incessantly on devising new ways and means of supporting yourself. Change your method to deceive the enemy. You will often be forced to wage a war of appearances.

7. Defeat and destroy the enemy in detail if it is at all possible, but do not commit to pitched battle, because your weakness will make you succumb. With time—that is all that can be expected of the most skillful general.

8. Do not retreat to places where you can be surrounded: remember Poltava without forgetting Stade.

Frederick, often outnumbered two to one, violated his maxims regularly. He lost as many battles as he won, yet he successfully waged war against the three most powerful continental powers (France, Austria, and Russia) and expanded the size of Prussian territory while building an army that became the envy of Europe. Many reasons may explain Frederick's failure to adhere to the maxims he established.[57] What remains clear, however, is that the concept of asymmetry in conflict did not perish during the era of linear warfare.

Jacque Antoine Hippolyte, Comte de Guibert, was a contemporary of Frederick who left a lasting impression on Western warfare. In his *Essai generale de tactique* (1772), Guibert suggests that warfare is an action of the unified forces of the state, rather than the army alone.[58] In order to sustain war waged by the state, Guibert saw conscription as the sole method of gaining the necessary soldiers. The expense of Guibert's reforms called on an already overextended treasury to feed, clothe, and arm an army larger than ever seen in Europe. Thus, he suggests "war should feed war." His final reform called for creating autonomous military units, each with all the necessary men and equipment to wage war—an idea the U.S. Army adopted with the creation of the Brigade Combat Team. Rather than moving as one large mass, as armies of the day were expected to do, each self-sufficient unit was capable of feeding itself and fighting.

Guibert, much like his Prussian contemporary Adam Heinrich Dietrich von Bulow, saw war as an activity of the state. Where monarchs once waged war with private armies funded with the revenue from their estates and the funds granted by the nobility, the taxing authority of the state vastly increased the available funds for warfare. Guibert and Bulow saw the increasing scope of war and the role of state governments in waging it. In *Geist des neuern kriegssystems* (1799), Bulow prophetically declares that states will wage war to expand their perceived territorial boundaries.

Neither Guibert nor Bulow saw war as an activity of disaffected groups within the state as it has become in the era of asymmetry. The concept of a challenger rising to contest the state was inconceivable. Thus, both men expected war to continue moving into the sphere of the state with larger states overwhelming their smaller neighbors.[59]

The Comte de Guibert and Baron von Bulow served their respective nations as military commanders achieving distinguished careers. Neither, however, is considered among history's great captains. Their contemporary, Generalissimo Aleksandr Vasilievich Suvorov, achieved what only Alexander the Great had before him. In a career lasting more than five decades and more than two dozen major battles, Suvorov never suffered defeat.[60] At a time when the Russian military was mired in tactics of an age long sense passed, Suvorov, as a young major, began instituting reforms as commander of the Suzdal regiment, which later ensured victory in all of his many battles against the Poles, Turks, and French.

Eighteenth-century Russian tradition expected the nobility to serve in either the military or bureaucracy. At birth, many Russian noblemen were enrolled in the Russian army, waiting until they were teenagers to begin their service. The advantage of enrollment at birth was rank. Often, boys not old enough to marry entered their regiments as captains and majors having earned rank and seniority while they were children. Suvorov, however, took a different path and was not enrolled in the army until he was a teen, which left him to begin his service as a private. He quickly showed his abilities in battle winning respect and promotion. Suvorov also saw the cronyism of the Russian army and the costs the Russian soldier bore for having an incompetent officer corp.

After many years of service, Suvorov was promoted to major and given command of the Suzdal Regiment, which he soon began to transform into the Russian army's best fighting unit. Where most Russian soldiers were trained in elaborate parade marches, Suvorov spent countless hours leading his men on long and wearying marches. He improved the marksmanship of his men and trained them using simulated combat. Suvorov rationalized the harsh punishment of soldiers and improved their food and clothing. Rather than pocketing the funds the Tsar sent for the support of the regiment, as was the practice, Suvorov spent it on improving the lives and skill of his men.[61] When Suvorov's men finally faced an adversary in Poland, they arrived five weeks early and repeatedly defeated larger Polish forces, fighting on their home soil.

From 1768–1773 Suvorov spent much of his time fighting Polish rebels who struck unexpectedly and then quickly dispersed. Spending his time in Poland hunting the famed Polish nationalist, Francis Pulawski, Suvorov developed tactical insights which he later used to defeat the numerically superior forces of the Turks and French.[62] For Suvorov, skill, discipline, speed, mobility, secrecy of action, surprise, and morale were indispensable components of victory. Often accused of fighting without tactics, Suvorov never failed to adapt to the conditions and adversary he faced. Lacking artillery, siege equipment, cavalry, or men never proved problematic because the great commander never failed to adapt to the current set of circumstances. This willingness to change led Suvorov to defeat Polish, Turkish, and French adversaries who each fought in a very different manner.

Little known in the West, Aleksandr Suvorov's *Science of Victory* served as an operational, strategic, and tactical manual for the Russian army during the life of the Generalissimo.[63] Although it quickly fell out of favor with those who came after him, Suvorov's treatise is among the few works written during the era of linear warfare which proves useful in the current era of asymmetry. His principles of discipline, skill, speed, and mobility are similar to those of Vegetius. Secrecy, surprise, and morale played a major role in victory, which are also of great importance in the writing of Sun-tzu and Vegetius. Among the three theorists, Suvorov alone applied his theory to actual warfare.

With the death of Suvorov on May 18, 1800, there were no great captains left to challenge the growing success of Napoleon Bonaparte. The "Little Corporal" was in France when his subordinates were defeated by Suvorov at Cassano, Trebbia, and Novi. In lamenting the fact that he never faced

Suvorov, Bonaparte marked the passing of the one man capable of defeating him in battle.[64] Much like Suvorov, Bonaparte was a prolific writer of correspondence, law, orders, and other articles. From his writing it is possible to understand Bonaparte's thoughts on asymmetry in warfare.

To understand Napoleon Bonaparte, context is needed. Bonaparte, perhaps more than any commander before or since, with the exception of General George S. Patton, consumed the treatises, histories, and memoirs of great captains such as Alexander, Hannibal, and Caesar. The influence of the past led Bonaparte, early in his career, to place preeminence in warfare on the abilities of a commander. Victory, thought Bonaparte, can be won in any battle with an exceptional captain.[65] Throughout his campaigns, Bonaparte rarely maintained an army equal in size to that of his adversaries. Consistently outnumbered, the French captain relied on the superior fighting quality and *élan* of *La Grande Armee*, which could march faster, fight harder, and strike with greater secrecy than any army of the day. Warfare, for Bonaparte, was as the Comte de Guibert predicted; the full might of the French state waged war against the monarchies of Europe.

Once crowned Napoleon I, the Emperor sought to bend the might of France to his will. According to Napoleon,

> The art of war is a simple art and everything depends upon execution: there is nothing vague, everything is common sense, and nothing about it is ideological. The art of war consists, with an inferior army, of always having more forces than your enemy at the point where you attack, or at the point which is attacked; but this art cannot be learned either from books or from practice. It is [a] feeling of command which properly constitutes the genius of war.[66]

Superior force at the decisive point of battle, a point for which Carl von Clausewitz gained great fame, was, in fact, a fundamental aspect of Napoleonic tactics long before the Prussian strategist first elaborated the point. Traditionally considered a maxim of conventional conflict, it also plays a role in the asymmetric conflicts of the twenty-first century. The ambush is little more than combining surprise with superior force at the decisive point of attack. It is particularly important to follow Napoleon's maxim when in an inferior position since it is possible to overwhelm an adversary bit by bit.

While Napoleon fought what may be considered wars absent asymmetry, he continually relied on tactics relevant to the modern asymmetric actor. He placed great value on discipline, intelligence, secrecy, deception, speed, mobility, and unity of command. When speaking of discipline, he states, "The success of an army and its well-being depend essentially upon order and discipline, which will make us loved by the people who come to greet us and with whom we share enemies."[67] He says of intelligence, "Study the country: local knowledge is precious knowledge that sooner or later you will encounter again."[68]

When speaking on the subject of secrecy and deception Napoleon advises, "In war, intellect and judgment is the better part of reality. The art of the Great Captains has always been to...make their own forces appear to be very large to the enemy and to make the enemy view themselves as being inferior."[69] In correspondence with Marshall Massena, he adds, "You know very well...the importance of the most profound secrecy in such circumstances...You will employ all the demonstrations and appearances of movement that you judge convenient to deceive the enemy about the real strategic objective and persuade him that he will first be attacked by you."[70]

Of speed, Napoleon says, "Great operations require speed in movements and as much quickness in conception as in execution."[71] Mobility was also one of *La Grande Armee's* most important attributes since it was mobility that enabled Napoleon to defeat Allied armies piecemeal on multiple occasions. Finally, unity of command, which Napoleon considered a necessity, enabled the French to defeat the Allies who failed to unite their numerically superior forces under one commander.[72]

In the aftermath of the Napoleonic wars, two of the greatest military theorists penned their influential works. Carl von Clausewitz, who served as chief of staff to General Thielmann during the war, wrote the West's most widely read treatise while serving as director of the Prussian War College in Berlin. *On War,* published in 1832 by his wife after Clausewitz's premature death, has served as a foundational text for young officers from the United States to Russia for more than a century. A contemporary of the Prussian theorist, Baron Antoine Henri de Jomini served as chief of staff to Marshall Ney, and, like Clausewitz, entered the service of the Tsar during Napoleon's invasion of Russia. Jomini went on to organize the Russian staff college and continued in the service of the Tsar until his retirement in 1829. It was during his retirement that Jomini wrote prolifically. He is perhaps best known for *Précis de l'art de la guerre* (The Art of War) (1836), which is, unquestionably, the greatest treatise on linear-geometric warfare ever written.

Although *On War* appeared four years before *The Art of War* it is to the latter that I now turn. Jomini was perhaps the nineteenth century's greatest student and rationalist of linear warfare. Beginning with his early writings, Jomini set out to establish a set of universal principles of war. In his effort to make a "scientific" study of war, Jomini develops concepts such as "theatre of operations" and "zone of operation" as well as others.[73] Jomini's preoccupation with turning warfare into a science led to his development of a set of prescriptive rules for the conduct of war.[74] Ultimately, Jomini concludes that strategy is the key to warfare and is, in fact, governed by universal principles. The key element in war explains Jomini, is to have the greater mass at the decisive point of battle.[75] Jomini is not alone in arriving at this decision. Frederick the Great, Napoleon, and Clausewitz had all seen the utility of such action. Strategy, according to Jomini, embraces the following points:

1. the selection of the theatre of war, and the discussion of the combinations of which it admits;
2. the determination of the decisive points in these combinations, and the most favorable direction of operations;
3. the selection and establishment of the fixed base and of the zones of operation;
4. the selection of the objective points, whether offensive or defensive;
5. the strategic fronts, lines of defense, and fronts of operations;
6. the choice of lines of operations leading to the objective point or strategic front;
7. for a given operation, the best strategic line, and the different maneuvers necessary to embrace all possible cases;
8. the eventual base of operations and the strategic reserves;
9. the marches of armies considered as maneuvers;
10. the relation between the position of depots and the marches of the army;
11. fortresses regarded as strategic means, as a refuge for an army, as an obstacle to its progress: the sieges to be made and to be covered;
12. points for entrenched camps, *tets de pont,* etc.;
13. the diversions to be made and the large detachments necessary.[76]

Attempting to apply the work of Jomini to asymmetric conflict is precarious. Jomini was a patron of linear warfare and concerned with the combat of his day, which consisted of national armies applying linear tactics to create the greatest volley of fire in a given area. Little was he concerned with partisan warfare, despite having served as a senior staff officer under Marshall Ney and Napoleon, who both spent a great deal of energy dealing with the morass that developed in the Peninsular War (1808–1814).[77] In developing a universal set of principles for war, Jomini saw war much like a game of chess with each piece known in advance and placed on the board so that its movements can be predicted well ahead of the next move.

Although it was never the intent of Jomini to develop concepts applicable to asymmetric conflict, *The Art of War* offers some useful advice for the asymmetric actor. Whether a conventional military force or a terrorist network, Article XIII concerning military institutions, offers 12 essential conditions for making a perfect army:

1. to have a good recruiting system;
2. a good organization;
3. a well-organized system of national reserves;
4. good instruction of officers and men in drill and internal duties as well as those of campaign;

5. a strict but not humiliating discipline, and a spirit of subordination and punctuality, based on conviction rather than on the formalities of the service;

6. a well-digested system of rewards, suitable to excite emulation;

7. the special arms of engineering and artillery to be well instructed;

8. an armament superior, if possible, to that of the enemy, both as to the defensive and offensive arms;

9. a general staff capable of applying these elements, and having an organization calculated to advance the theoretical and practical education of its officers;

10. a good system for the commissariat, hospitals, and of general administration;

11. a good system of assignment to command, and of directing the principle operations of war;

12. exciting and keeping alive the military spirit of the people.[78]

Each of these conditions is present to a greater or lesser degree in all combat organizations whether conventional or asymmetric. They are of special importance for asymmetric actors who often exist and operate somewhere between legitimacy and illegitimacy, state sponsored and illegal.

Jomini later enumerates 10 essential bases for military policy of a wise government. Few have direct relevance; numbers seven and nine, however, offer prudent council to asymmetric and conventional actors alike. Number seven urges, "Nothing should be neglected to acquire knowledge of the geography and the military statistics of other states, so as to know their material and moral capacity for attack and defense, as well as the strategic advantages of the two parties."[79] The need for accurate intelligence and an understanding of one's adversary is common sense but has often led to the defeat of a power that underestimates or misjudges its enemy. The need for intelligence is of the greatest importance for the adversary of an asymmetric actor because it is his desire to operate unnoticed.

In essential base number nine, Jomini warns,

> The system of operations ought to be determined by the object of the war, the kind of forces of the enemy, the nature and resources of the country, the character of the nations and their chiefs, whether of the army or of the state. In fine, it should be based upon the moral and material of attack or defense which the enemy may be able to bring into action; and it ought to take into consideration the probable alliances that may obtain in favor of or against either of the parties during the war.[80]

Had Osama bin Laden followed Jomini's advice, he would have understood that President Bush preferred a military response to terrorism where President Clinton preferred legal action. In misjudging the approach of George W. Bush, bin Laden also misjudged the character of the American people and their willingness to shed blood for a moral cause.[81] Similarly, Saddam Hussein incorrectly judged the president's willingness to use force in Iraq, despite the War in Afghanistan (2001–present). Conversely, American leaders underestimated the strength of Sunni-Iraqi irredentism that took the shape of the insurgency in the aftermath of American invasion.

In his discussion of decisive points, Jomini also develops what he calls "political objective points" which are determined by their political, rather than strategic importance, and play an influential role in the considerations of adversaries.[82] Jomini's development of political objective points is, in part, derived from his reading of Clausewitz, who placed great importance on the relationship between political and military factors. Although Jomini's intent was to address the importance of political objectives in conventional conflict, political objective points are the primary target when waging wars of asymmetry. Al-Qaeda, Hamas, Hezbollah, and other organizations waging war against the United States or Israel, for example, concentrate strikes against political targets rather than those of military significance. Rocket propelled grenade (RPG) attacks into Baghdad's green zone, attacks on police stations, and the kidnapping and beheading of civilians in Iraq serve to strike at political objective points.

This look at Jomini gives only limited attention to one of the most influential military theorists in Western history. The continuing, and often unrecognized, impact of Jomini within the American military is slowly beginning to decline as the United States faces a future moving in a distinctly different direction than envisioned by the nineteenth-century Swiss strategist. And, although limited in application, Jomini offers valuable insight into asymmetric warfare. As I now turn to the work of Clausewitz, the West's most influential military theorist, it is worth noting that it was Jomini, not Clausewitz who, for many decades, reigned as the most widely read and admired military theorist in the United States.

Originally read by only a limited number of European officers, *On War* rose to prominence with the rapid defeat of France in the Franco-Prussian War (1870–1871). In the war's aftermath, Helmuth Graf von Moltke, Chief of the Prussian General Staff, remarked of the influence *On War* played in the development of his thinking, setting off a wave of interest in Clausewitz's work.

Unlike his contemporary Jomini, Clausewitz viewed war as an elemental act of violence, which negates social constraints and makes war the arbiter of moral and social norms.[83] Rather than looking for timeless principles of warfare, which Clausewitz believed nonexistent, the Prussian sought to understand the nature of war. Thus, Clausewitz set himself apart from Bulow and Jomini by emphasizing the human elements of war: chance, friction, genius, will, and others.[84] For the Prussian, "War is nothing but a duel on a larger scale. Countless duels go to make up war, but a picture of it as a whole can be formed by imagining a pair of wrestlers. Each tries through physical force to compel the other to do his will; his *immediate* aim is to *throw* his opponent in order to make him incapable of further resistance."[85]

Clausewitz's concentration on the human elements of war makes *On War* timelessly relevant to asymmetric conflict. In addition, Clausewitz understood better than his contemporaries the impact of partisan war on conventional armies.[86] While serving as a deputy to Prince August at the battle of Auerstedt, Clausewitz ordered one-third of his men to fight as skirmishers opposing the flexibility of the French. After Prussia's defeat, Clausewitz, in violation of the armistice agreement between France and Prussia, participated in the raising of the home guards in order that they might fight as partisans against future French invasion. When he later served as the director of General Scharnhorst's office in Berlin, Clausewitz lectured on partisan warfare.[87] In *On War* Clausewitz dedicates a chapter to the subject, making him one of the few theorists of his time to give active attention to asymmetric conflict.

Clausewitz is perhaps most well known for his axiom, "War is merely the continuation of policy by other means." In viewing war as a political act, Clausewitz speaks directly to the many attributes that make asymmetric conflict such a difficult task for states who find themselves embroiled in them. Although often credited with advocating total war, Clausewitz understood well that war is directed by the political objectives for which it is undertaken. Thus, Clausewitz is far more flexible in his conception of war than he is often credited with.[88]

Clausewitz dedicates chapter 26 of book six to "The People in Arms." Here, the Prussian treats insurrection as another means of war, which he considers "an outgrowth of the way in which the conventional barriers have been swept away in our lifetime by the elemental violence of war."[89] Clausewitz begins his discussion by enumerating five conditions under which partisan warfare can be effective:

1. The war must be fought in the interior of the country.
2. It must be decided by a single stroke.[90]
3. The theatre of operations must be fairly large.
4. The national character must be suited to that type of war.
5. The country must be rough and inaccessible, because of mountains, or forests, marshes, or the local methods of cultivation.[91]

In effect, Clausewitz details similar points to those made by later insurgents, recognizing the key attributes that enable insurgencies to develop, sustain themselves, and succeed. Clausewitz explains the significance of geography, noting that the greater the degree of difficulty terrain presents, the greater will be the viability of partisan units.[92] He then moves to the deployment of partisans. Clausewitz, illustrating a well-considered understanding of the asymmetry of partisan warfare, advises, "Militia and bands of armed civilians cannot and should not be employed against the main enemy force—or indeed against any sizeable force. They are not supposed to pulverize the core but to nibble at the shell and around the edges."[93] Clausewitz adds, "A general uprising, as we see it, should be nebulous and elusive; the resistance should never materialize as a concrete body, otherwise the enemy can direct sufficient force at its core, crush it, and take many prisoners. When that happens, the people will lose heart and, believing the issue has been decided and further efforts would be useless, drop their weapons."[94]

Vice Admiral Arthur K. Cebrowski underscores Clausewitz's point by arguing that mass is insurance against the fog of war, which is often an important attribute for the asymmetric actor who depends on the uncertainty created by the tactics he employs for the provision of his safety and the success of his mission.[95] Rear Admiral John G. Morgan further underscores the significance of mass in war. Acknowledging the asymmetry of modern warfare, Morgan suggests that Iraqi soldiers must have an adversary to whom they can surrender.[96] In addition, efforts such as Operation Anaconda (2003) and operations to clear Fallujah (2004) are dependent upon mass to successfully encircle and capture insurgents. Just as conventional forces in an asymmetric conflict seek to create mass at the decisive point, partisans and insurgents must, as Clausewitz advises, remain dispersed.[97]

Clausewitz continues his discussion by further elaborating on the ultimate necessity for partisan forces to employ conventional tactics to defeat an enemy. He adds, "On the other hand, there must be some concentration at certain points: the fog must thicken and form a dark and menacing cloud out of which a bolt of lightening may strike at any time. These points of concentration will, as we have said, lie mainly on the flanks of the enemy's theatre of operations. That is where insurgents should build up larger units, better organized, with parties of regulars that will make them look like a proper army and enable them to tackle larger operations."[98] Clausewitz further discusses the effects of large unit tactics emphasizing the psychological effects of partisan attacks.

Anticipating the Chinese Communist's tactical failure in the Five Encirclements Campaign (1927–1934) and the success of the Long March (1934), the Prussian theorist warns partisans against turning to tactical defense for the preservation of geographic gains. Clausewitz explains the weakness of tactical defense stating, "Moreover, not much is lost if a body of insurgents is defeated and dispersed—that is what it is for. But it should not be allowed to go to pieces through too many men being killed, wounded or taken prisoner: such defeats will soon dampen its ardor."[99] Clausewitz's grasp of the role played by asymmetric actors is clear: they win by not losing. This point later plays a central role in the war waged by Mao and the Chinese Communists against the Kuomintang.

The advice of Clausewitz bears increased relevance in the current global environment where the overwhelming supremacy of American arms leads to a doctrine which seeks conventional battle. As Peter R. Moody and Edward M. Collins point out, modern democracies view war as a distinct moral act which requires direct confrontation with the enemy. This leaves the United States and other Western democracies little room to wage protracted wars against an enemy which refuses to give battle.[100] Clausewitz perhaps falls short because he fails to elaborate the means by which conventional forces can overcome partisans. Conceivably, he saw no solution to partisan warfare if waged in the manner he describes.

Before his death, Clausewitz remarked that *On War* was incomplete and in need of revision because his thoughts on war had evolved since he began writing. The untimely death of Clausewitz prevented him from ever making the revisions he considered essential. Whether revisions would have offered clarification of his views on asymmetric conflict will never be known. His contributions to the Western understanding of partisan warfare are unquestionable. Many later theorists reinvented what Clausewitz, Vegetius, and Sun-tzu before them had long known about conflict.

ALFRED THAYER MAHAN AND JULIAN CORBETT

Rear Admiral Alfred Thayer Mahan, USN, a veteran of the American Civil War (1861–1865) and the first president of the U.S. Naval War College, remains one of history's most influential naval theorists. His first and greatest work, *The Influence of Sea Power upon History, 1660–1783* (1890), is widely regarded as the single most influential treatise on naval strategy and tactics ever written.[101] Mahan, a prolific writer and student of Jomini, applies the linear concepts of the Swiss strategist to naval combat suggesting that naval warfare, like its land-based counterpart, follows a set of timeless principles.[102] Primary among these principles is the need for great powers to maintain supremacy of the seas. In controlling the seas, great powers (Great Britain) are able to ensure the free flow of trade, which enriches a nation. Mahan gained his earliest insight from a reading of the history of the Second Punic War (218–201 BC).[103] During that war, Carthage and Hannibal were restrained in their ability to effectively wage war against Rome because of Rome's dominance of the Mediterranean. Realizing the significant role sea power played in the ultimate defeat of Carthage, Mahan began his study of the influence of British sea power in the seventeenth and eighteenth centuries.

Taking up the central premise of Jomini, Mahan saw the key to winning naval supremacy as the concentration of (naval) force at the decisive point of battle. Thus, Mahan was an advocate of major naval engagements which either led to total defeat or victory. Rather than viewing great power navies as supporting services, Mahan saw in them the key to economic, military, and political dominance.[104] Not only do they fight, but naval assets ensure the free flow of goods or destroy enemy trade and blockade enemy ports.

They transport troops or deny transport to the enemy. Lastly, they keep open the lines of communication between colonial possessions and the metropole.[105]

Throughout his writings, Mahan remains focused on the great power rivalries of his day. The concept of asymmetry in naval combat is one Mahan showed little grasp of.[106] British naval historian Julian Corbett, a contemporary of Mahan, differed greatly in his conception of the role of naval forces in warfare. Corbett's most influential work, *Some Principles of Maritime Strategy* (1911), directly challenges Mahan's conception of the navy's role in warfare.[107] Unlike Mahan, Corbett views the navy as a service with the primary role of supporting land warfare. Where Mahan and the British Admiralty believed that the Royal Navy should seek the decisive battle, Corbett proposes a more limited role for naval elements. Much as Jomini and Clausewitz were advocates of concentrating force at the decisive point in battle, concentration remained a key element of naval combat in the early twentieth century.[108]

Corbett, however, regards concentration as a poor strategy for maintaining command of the sea. Three reasons explain why. First, when naval forces are concentrated an adversary may more easily refuse battle by flight. Second, dispersing one's forces creates an element of shapelessness and surprise, which cannot be achieved by concentration. Third, when concentration is a principle of naval combat, flexibility of action is lost.[109]

Limited conflict, according to Corbett, was and remains the dominant form of warfare. Thus, it is imperative to fight on one's own terms rather than those of the enemy. Additionally, limited conflicts should be fought in such a way that the greatest gains are made at the lowest costs. This translates into support for the strategic offensive, which relies on taking offensive action when risks are low and gains high. The strategic offensive serves as a force multiplier, greatly increasing the effective strength of a state's naval forces.[110]

The strategic and tactical innovations of Mahan and Corbett, while often diametrically opposed, include no conception of naval warfare as an element of asymmetric conflict. Mahan's fixation with total warfare left little room for the small scale asymmetric conflicts of the twenty-first century. Although Corbett's suggestion of surprise, flexibility, and shapelessness are significant, he fails to anticipate the use of naval assets by partisans, guerrillas, and terrorists. Thus, neither man offers insights relevant to the study of asymmetric conflict.

Considering the time in which Mahan and Corbett wrote, it would have been difficult for either to anticipate events such as the hijacking of the *Achille Lauro* in October 1985 or the bombing of the USS *Cole* (DDG-67) in October 2000. For both theorists, naval combat belonged to the state alone. Thus, naval theory has great potential for innovation as asymmetric actors seek new ways to minimize the advantage naval forces provide to the United States and major powers.

THEORY AFTER THE WORLD WAR I (LAWRENCE, LIDDELL-HART, AND FULLER)

Western military theory experienced its next major development in the 1920s as a response to the heavy casualties incurred during the trench warfare of World War I. Across Western Europe a generation of men were lost in the pyrrhic battles of the Western Front where machine gunfire and artillery bloodied the landscape with the corpses of more than five million men. The horrific scenes of the Somme and other major battles where hundreds of thousands of men lost their lives in a single day left an indelible impact on the strategists who spent the postwar decades considering ways to prevent such catastrophic loss in the future.

There was, however, one dramatic exception from the trench warfare of the Western Front. In the sparsely populated desert of Arabia, the Ottoman Empire attempted to maintain control of Medina and smaller towns and villages and the lone rail line linking these remote areas to Palestine, Syria, and the rest of the Empire. As an ally of Germany, the Ottomans found themselves at war with the British, whose possession of Egypt and the Suez Canal were threatened by the proximity of Ottoman and German troops.[111]

As one of the few British officers fluent in Arabic and familiar with the culture and customs of the Arabs, Captain Thomas Edward Lawrence, or Lawrence of Arabia as he is better known, left his post in Egypt to serve as British Royal Army liaison to Sherif Hussein in Mecca. The British sought to encourage the Sherif and his Arab followers to lead a revolt against their Ottoman overlords, which would draw Turks Europe and keep the Ottomans occupied in the vast expanse of the Arabian Peninsula. In return, the British offered technical assistance and material support. Although serving under superior officers, Captain Lawrence quickly became the leader of British cooperation with the Arabs. He soon found himself commanding Arab irregulars and serving with Emir Feisal as one of the "Arab Revolt's" commanders.[112]

As an archaeologist by profession, Lawrence had little military training and even less experience when he began leading what would become one of the most significant asymmetric conflicts in history. Although Lawrence was without the training of a soldier, he was widely read in military theory and understood, conceptually, the strategic and tactical options available to him. The lack of military training proved an asset during the Arab Revolt because Captain Lawrence was unconstrained by the tactics of his day.

Popularized in his account of the Arab Revolt, *The Seven Pillars of Wisdom: A Triumph* (1926), T.E. Lawrence provides the modern asymmetric actor strategic and tactical advice worthy of note.[113] Significant among his many contributions, Lawrence understood the skill, material condition, and mind-set of the Bedouins who comprised the irregular force he led. As important, he also understood the Ottoman soldier, recognizing that they were often poorly trained, unmotivated, and fatalistic.[114] With this in mind, it was then possible for Captain Lawrence to develop a strategy, which utilized the strengths of his allies and attacked the weaknesses of the enemy.[115] The untrained and fiercely independent tribesmen of the desert were undisciplined and accustomed to receiving booty as a spoil of war. This left Lawrence little choice but to wage a guerrilla war, which he did with great success and little loss of life.[116]

Lawrence explains the beginning of the Arab Revolt stating, "So I began with three propositions. Firstly, that irregulars would not attack places, and so remained incapable of forcing a decision. Secondly, that they were unable to defend a line or point as they were to attack it. Thirdly, that their virtue lay in depth not in face."[117] He further explains the strategy of the Arab Revolt saying, "The Arab war was geographical, and the Turkish Army an accident. Our aim was to seek the enemy's weakest material link and bear only on that till time made their whole length fail...Consequently we must extend our front to its maximum, to impose on the Turks the longest possible passive defense, since that was, materially, their most costly form of war."[118]

Lawrence and his Arab allies relied on flexibility, accurate intelligence, geography, mobility, speed, and surprise to strike at Ottoman outposts and rail lines.[119] Fighting on their native soil, a limited number of tribesmen held down large numbers of Ottoman troops, rarely failing to fight on the terms set by Lawrence and Feisel. The hit and run tactics of the Arabs left the Ottomans trapped in their garrisons, too weak and afraid to make a concerted attempt to clear the Arabian Peninsula of irregulars. As the war progressed, Lawrence's strategy made it possible for Arab forces with only limited support to push the Ottomans out of Arabia where they were eventually defeated in Palestine and Syria by a combined Anglo-Arab force.

Written in the decade after the Great War, *The Seven Pillars of Wisdom: A Triumph* has been called the first coherent theory of guerrilla warfare.[120] As much as this may be true, Lawrence's great skill was not in developing new strategic concepts but in applying what he knew from his study of strategy to the situation in which he found himself. Rather than attempting to force the Arab Revolt to fit a European model, Captain Lawrence became the West's most distinguished asymmetric actor by proving to be flexible in thought and action. This flexibility is perhaps T.E. Lawrence's greatest contribution to the study of asymmetric conflict.

For men such as B.H. Liddell-Hart and J.F.C. Fuller, who experienced the carnage of trench warfare, the postwar years were devoted to developing a new way of warfare, absent the frontal charges which left so many men dead on the fields of France. Working in the early 1920s, Liddell-Hart and Fuller developed independent, yet complimentary, approaches to warfare, which played a major role in General Heinz Guderian's development of Blitzkrieg and General Erwin Rommel's mechanized warfare.

Working with his younger contemporary, Major General Fuller moved within the British Royal Army to encourage the development of an all-mechanized army consistent with his *Plan 1919*.[121] Liddell-Hart, 20 years Fuller's junior, gained prominence with his publication of *Decisive Wars of History* (1929), which was later revised to become the twentieth century's most prolific strategic treatise, *Strategy* (1954).[122]

Liddell-Hart develops what he calls the "indirect approach," which is a direct challenge to the warfare of his day and is based on his view that military and political leaders lost sight of the objective of war.[123] Rather than making frontal charges against an entrenched enemy, the indirect approach calls for attacking the enemy's lines of supply, communication, and rear.[124] For Liddell-Hart, attacking an adversary where he least expects it and where loss is minimized is of the greatest importance. This is not simply to suggest that Liddell-Hart advocates attacking the enemy's front when he least expects it, rather he seeks to prevent such attacks by first destroying those assets which make war possible, while also creating turmoil and dissension. In the case studies utilized to illustrate the indirect approach, Liddell-Hart offers a number of examples from the earliest times to the present. Two of note are General William T. Sherman's March to the Sea and T.E. Lawrence's leadership of the Arab Revolt. While Sherman led a conventional army through the heart of the Confederacy, burning crops, destroying homes, and tearing up rail lines, Lawrence led irregular Bedouins on a campaign of hit-and-run attacks against rail lines and isolated garrisons. For Liddell-Hart the indirect approach applies to conventional and unconventional conflict alike.

The former infantry captain develops eight maxims as part of the indirect approach, which he considers the "concentrated essence of strategy and tactics":

Positive

1. Adjust your end to your means.
2. Keep your object always in mind.
3. Choose the line (or course) of least expectation.
4. Exploit the line of least resistance.
5. Take a line of operation which offers alternative objectives.
6. Ensure that both plans and dispositions are flexible—adaptable to circumstances.

Negative

1. Do not throw your weight into a stroke whilst your opponent is on guard—whilst he is well placed to parry or evade it.
2. Do not renew an attack along the same line (or in the same form) after it has once failed.[125]

He adds, "The essential truth underlying these maxims is that, for success, two major problems must be solved—*dislocation* and *exploitation*. One precedes and one follows the actual blow—which in comparison is a simple act. You cannot hit the enemy with effect unless you have first created the opportunity; you cannot make the effect decisive unless you exploit the second opportunity that comes before he can recover."[126]

Dislocation and exploitation are of greater significance to the asymmetric actor because his inferiority *requires* him to rely on the elements of war dislocation and exploitation seeks to utilize. Where a conventional force can take advantage of its superior numbers and technology, the asymmetric actor must rely on alternative means.[127] In Iraq, for example, al-Zarqawi and Saddam loyalists are using car bombs, improvised explosive devices (IED), and other tactical means to first dislocate American forces, Iraqi police, or Interior Ministry troops in an initial explosion, which is then followed by a second attack carried out by insurgents exploiting the confusion and destruction caused by the first attack. On a small scale, these types of attacks are illustrative of Liddell-Hart's indirect approach.

Discussing guerrilla warfare, Liddell-Hart makes two additional points of importance. He suggests that there are three keys to guerrilla warfare: distraction, disturbance, and demoralization.[128] Each affects the physical and psychological elements of conflict, which serves to magnify the effect of the indirect approach. In maximizing the effect of these elements, the probability of defeating an adversary through attacks on lines of communication, supply, and in the rear are increased. Liddell-Hart underscores this point adding, "A guerrilla movement that puts safety first will soon wither. Its strategy must always aim to produce the enemy's increasing overstretch, physical and moral."[129]

TWENTIETH CENTURY EASTERN WARFARE (MAO, GIAP, AND GUEVARA)

Mao Zedong, more than his predecessor Sun-tzu, is the East's most influential military theorist. As a military commander and leader of the Chinese communists from the Chinese Communist Party's earliest days, Mao developed the strategy and tactics responsible for the 1949 victory over the Kuomintang (KMT) in the Chinese Civil War (1925–1949). Developing his first major treatise, *On Guerrilla Warfare* (1934), early in the civil war, Mao went on to lead the Fourth Route Army on the Long March

(1934–1935), which saw Mao and 40,000 of his comrades march more than 6,000 miles while chased and harassed by KMT forces.[130]

Mao suggests guerrilla warfare develops in three phases. In phase I, guerrilla movements organize, consolidate, and concentrate on preserving their existence.[131] This requires that guerrillas win the support of the population, which will play a pivotal role in their success. Without the protection and assistance of the populace insurgents, guerrillas and asymmetric actors will not be victorious. The intelligence, material, food, and recruits provided by the people cannot be replaced.

When Vespasian and Titus instituted a scorched earth policy in Judea during the Jewish Revolt, rebels were forced from northern Judea because the population, which was either killed or forced to flee, could no longer provide assistance.[132] More recent instances offer similar results.[133] When a central government, colonial power, or invading state depopulates the area in which guerrillas operate, the movement collapses. A population unwilling to support a guerrilla movement also causes collapse. The defeat of the *Sendero Luminoso* in Peru was largely due to lack of assistance from local villagers, and sometimes open support of government forces.[134]

In Afghanistan, the Taliban and al-Qaeda were unpopular among a majority of Afghans who disliked the foreign presence of al-Qaeda and the tribal loyalties and fundamentalist views of the Taliban. When the United States proved to be very different from Soviet and British invaders of the past, local tribal leaders quickly shifted support from the Taliban, instead choosing the United States and its local allies. Iraq is proving to be a more difficult situation. While demonstrations against terrorist attacks show a lack of support for Saddam loyalists and al-Qaeda in Iraq, the lengthier the American presence, the greater will be the decline in support for the United States among Iraqis.[135] Thus, popular support is limited for both sides of the current conflict in Iraq, making it difficult for either to win a clear victory.

Phase II calls for the progressive expansion of guerrilla forces. Here guerrillas begin expanding the territory within which they operate, increasing offensive operations and expanding the overall scope of their activity. It is in phase II that guerrillas begin steadily waging a war of attrition against enemy forces and material, attacking in what Mao calls "lightening raids."[136]

It is in moving to phase III that many guerrilla movements make a strategic error by transitioning to conventional operations in order to strike a deciding blow to weakened government forces. As Mao points out, guerrilla movements, in order to ultimately succeed, must topple the national government, which requires conventional operations. Moving to phase III too early can lead to catastrophic defeat such as occurred during the Tet Offensive. American and South Vietnamese forces effectively destroyed the Viet Cong, who mistakenly believed the time was right to launch a final strike against South Vietnam. It took more than four years to recover from the defeat of the Viet Cong and their North Vietnamese allies. Mao, after near defeat in the Five Encirclements Campaign (1928–1934), proved a more adept commander than General Vo Nguyen Giap, military commander of North Vietnam, who repeatedly moved to phase III too early against a superior adversary.[137]

Mao relied on "imaginative leadership, distraction, surprise and mobility to create a victorious situation before battle is joined."[138] He further explains guerrilla warfare as

1. arousing and organizing the people;
2. achieving internal unification politically;
3. establishing bases;
4. equipping forces;
5. recovering national strength;
6. destroying the enemy's national strength;
7. regaining lost territories.[139]

Mao then asks the question, "What is guerrilla strategy? Guerrilla strategy must be based primarily on alertness, mobility and attack."[140] This does not suggest Mao favors decisive battle. He does not. Much as Liddell-Hart, Lawrence, and Clausewitz before him, Mao warns guerrillas against seeking the decisive battle adding, "There is in guerrilla warfare no such thing as a decisive battle; there is nothing to the fixed, passive defense that characterizes orthodox war."[141]

The "death by a thousand cuts" strategy supported by Mao is similar to that utilized by asymmetric actors today. Where the communists understood that the ultimate goal of the war against the nationalists was the destruction of Chiang's government and its replacement by communism, the same is not true for many twenty-first-century asymmetric actors. Instead, they seek to force the withdrawal of a foreign power's occupying forces. For the asymmetric actor this means phase III is never entered, which sets conflicts of asymmetry apart from the mobile guerrilla warfare of the Chinese Civil War.

Where Mao makes his greatest contribution to military theory is in his discussion of the political elements of guerrilla warfare. Understanding the dominant role politics plays in war, Mao established a code of conduct for the Fourth Route Army, which required soldiers to treat peasants, with whom they interacted, with dignity and respect. In doing so, Mao sought to generate the support of the populace necessary for communist success. Areas controlled by communist forces also saw landlords punished for "exploitative" behavior, land rents reduced, public health improved, the introduction of local democracy, and major reeducation campaigns designed to introduce the peasantry to communist ideology.[142]

After the Japanese invasion of Manchuria and their expansion south, Generalissimo Chiang moved his KMT forces into central China, ceding the most productive areas of the country to the Japanese. Mao, however, suspended operations against the Nationalists and moved against the Japanese. This endeared the communists with large segments of the Chinese population because they alone challenged the Japanese invasion and occupation. For Mao, waging a guerrilla war against the Japanese was a calculated risk undertaken because of the political gains it might bring. Chiang's unwillingness to confront the Japanese was a terrible miscalculation because it demoralized his troops and led to the evaporation of support for the KMT.[143]

Asymmetric conflicts are similar in their political aims. While seeking to attrite the enemy and force his withdrawal, asymmetric actors wage a public relations campaign to win the support of the populace while turning them against the external power. Asymmetric actors do, however, violate one of Mao's fundamental rules: they target civilians with acts of terrorism. Recent public protests in Iraq underscore the negative political effect of such acts, which continue to target civilians.[144] Chinese military theory takes an exceptionally negative view of terrorism because it, in fact, turns the mass against the military force utilizing it.[145] In those instances in the West where communist guerrilla movements were defeated, in Bolivia (1967), Chile (1981), Peru (1992), and elsewhere, the use of terrorism against civilians led to the withdrawal of support among the populace. Understanding that guerrilla warfare *is* at its foundation political, Mao prohibited the use of terrorism.[146]

Mao's contemporary, Vo Nguyen Giap, military commander of the Viet Minh during the War of Liberation against the French (1945–1954) and commander of the People's Army of Vietnam (PAVN or NVA), wrote two significant treatises on guerrilla warfare that must not be overlooked. General Giap developed his strategic and tactical innovations under circumstances which more closely mirror those of twenty-first-century asymmetric conflict than Mao. It was Mao, however, whose writings served to stimulate the former high school teacher as he sought to defeat an experienced French commander in General Navarre.

The strategy employed by General Giap ultimately forced American withdrawal from Vietnam.[147] For Giap, guerrilla warfare develops in three phases (consolidation, expansion, and destruction). Differing from Moa, however, Giap places a greater emphasis on the political elements of guerrilla conflict. According to Giap, "The war of liberation of the Vietnamese people proves that, in the face of an enemy as powerful as he is cruel, victory is possible only by uniting the whole people within the bosom of a firm and wide national united front based on the worker-peasant alliance."[148] Where Mao limited the indoctrination of the Chinese peasant, Giap seeks to thoroughly unify the political will of the Vietnamese people.

Placing added importance on the intellectual unification of the Vietnamese, Giap views "people's war" as developing in six initial stages:

1. Develop and consolidate the organizations for national salvation.
2. Expand the organizations to the cities, enterprises, mines, and plantations.
3. Expand the organizations to the provinces where the revolutionary movement is still weak and to the minority areas.
4. Steel the Party members' spirit of determination and sacrifice.
5. Steel the Party members so that they may have capacity and experience to enable them to lead and cope with the situation.
6. Form small guerrilla groups and soldiers' organizations.[149]

The jargon of communism often clouds the meaning of its authors, but it is clear that Giap places great importance on political elements early in the development of a guerrilla movement. In addition to placing great emphasis on the political aspects of war, General Giap emphasizes the dominance of propaganda over combat saying, "political activities were more important than military activities, and fighting less important than propaganda."[150]

Giap follows his discussion of politics and guerrilla warfare with a description of the war waged by the Viet Minh and the Democratic Republic of Vietnam. Of greatest relevance is his discussion of the mobilization of the economy, military, and people for war. In essence, the People's War waged by the Vietnamese communists was a total war, waged for total ends (the overthrow of the Republic of Vietnam), by total means.[151] France and the United States, however, fought a limited war. For the French, the objective was the destruction of the Viet Minh, which they almost achieved, but for the limited means employed. The United States fought for the preservation of a noncommunist South with limited resources.

As is often the case, the side waging total war, in this case the Vietnamese communists, maintained a psychological advantage gained by viewing conflict as a life or death struggle. Asymmetric actors are similar in their perception of the conflict in which they are engaged, which provides a psychological advantage to the asymmetric actor as well.

In the years following the withdrawal of American forces and the defeat of the Republic of Vietnam by the North, General Giap wrote an explanation of his success entitled *How We Won the War*, which offers some additional insight into the successful guerrilla campaign.[152] Giap suggests that the Viet Cong and NVA were successful against American and Army of the Republic of Vietnam (ARVN) forces because they regularly seized opportunities to take the offensive, giving communist forces the momentum at the point of attack.[153] Speed also played a key role in the success of the North, which was combined with superior mass at the decisive point of attack to ultimately demoralize and annihilate ARVN forces.[154]

Throughout the three phases of the war in Vietnam, leading to the ultimate defeat of ARVN forces in the Ho Chi Minh Campaign of 1975, General Giap utilized the combined strength of what he called, "Revolutionary War."[155] This includes the regular army (NVA), regional forces (Viet Cong), the militia, and guerrillas. Prior to the 1975 offensive and with the exception of the Tet Offensive (1968) and a second offensive in 1972, General Giap relied on the guerrilla capabilities of the Viet Cong and NVA. During the final offensive in 1975, the North was able to over-whelm the South from within (guerrillas) and without (conventional forces). And, while one of the largest and best equipped militaries in the world, ARVN quickly succumbed to the pressure of the unrelenting Northern onslaught.

Although an Argentine by birth, Che Guevara, the doctor-turned-Marxist guerrilla, viewed guerrilla warfare in a similar manner to his Asian counter-parts. In his treatise on the subject, *Guerrilla Warfare,* Guevara emphasizes the importance of safe base areas, mobility, speed, and the strategic attack.[156] He does, however, differ from Mao and Giap in one significant area, which he elaborated in three "fundamental lessons":

1. Popular force can win a war against the army.
2. It is not necessary to wait until all conditions for making revolution exist; the insurrection can create them.
3. In underdeveloped America the countryside is the basic area for armed fighting.[157]

Guevara differs with Mao and Giap in numbers one and two. It is there that the Latin American revolutionary minimizes the political and psychological attributes of warfare, which were so important to both Mao and Giap. Failing to cultivate the assistance and sympathy of the local population cost Guevara his life when a deserter from his guerrilla band informed the Bolivian army of his position. He was quickly captured after a short battle and executed in October 1967.

Guevara's failure to properly judge the political environment in Bolivia was a major miscalculation. His mistaken view that a small band of revolu-tionaries can spark a general revolution is one asymmetric actors are tempted to make. Osama bin Laden's attempt to overthrow the Saudi royal family is one example. The current insurgency in Iraq is another. In both instances asymmetric actors initiated combat before first gaining the support of the populace and, in both cases, insurgents failed or are failing to achieve their objectives.

Of greatest relevance to twenty-first-century asymmetric conflict is Guevara's discussion of guerrilla tactics. Two points are prophetic and speak directly to the current insurgency in Iraq. First, Guevara warns, "There is one point very much in controversy in opinions about terrorism.

Many consider that its use, by provoking police oppression, hinders all more or less legal or semi-clandestine contact with the masses and makes impossible unification for actions that will be necessary at a critical moment. This is correct, but it also happens that in a civil war the repression by the government power in certain towns is already so great that, in fact, every type of legal action is suppressed already, and any type of action of the masses that is not supported by arms is impossible."[158] He goes on to further warn guerrillas against the use of terrorism saying, "We sincerely believe that terrorism is of negative value, that it by no means produces the desired effects, that it can turn a people against a revolutionary movement, and that it can bring a loss of lives to its agents out of proportion to what it produces."[159] Insurgents in Iraq would be wise to heed Guevara's warning, given the increasing unpopularity of terrorist attacks.

Guevara's second point is one insurgents in Iraq are currently exploiting effectively. According to Guevara, "One of the weakest points of the enemy is transportation by road and railroad. It is virtually impossible to maintain yard by yard over a transport line, a road, or a rail yard. At any point a considerable amount of explosive charge can be planted that will make the road impassable; or by exploding it at the moment that a vehicle passes, a considerable loss of lives and material to the enemy is caused at the same time that the road is cut."[160] The current use of IEDs by insurgents in Iraq is an illustration of the effectiveness of roadside bombs. Had Guevara followed his own tactical advice more closely, rather than his ill-conceived strategic plan, he may have succeeded rather than lost his life.

CONCLUSION

Throughout human history man has devoted great effort to the understanding of one of humanity's more endearing institutions: war. These pages have examined a number of the most influential treatises on warfare and the thoughts and actions of some of history's great captains in an effort to determine if influential works of the past offer insight into twenty-first-century asymmetric conflict. The emphasis has been on the strategic and tactical contributions of those authors and the application of specific innovations to the current conflicts in Afghanistan and Iraq.

In addition to the principle aims of this chapter, an underlying theme emerged. For many of the theorists examined, a common set of strategic and tactical elements plays an important role in the thought of each writer. Elements such as mobility, speed, surprise, and others frequently appear in the work of men that span more than two millennia of military thought. As the United States moves forward into the twenty-first century, American leaders, civilian and military, would be wise to look to the past when determining the face of the future. For as much as technology and time have changed the face of warfare, history shows that the elemental characteristics of conflict span the centuries and are as relevant today as they were more than two millennia ago.

2

Understanding Asymmetry in the Twenty-First Century: Strategy, Tactics, and Weapons

In the wake of the September 11, 2001, terrorist attacks on New York City and Washington, DC, Americans were forced to face what the military and intelligence services knew for the better part of a decade. The United States was the victim of its own success. Rapidly defeating Saddam Hussein in 1991 proved to prospective adversaries that the Americans are not easily defeated in a conventional conflict. Despite the lessons of Vietnam and casualty aversion of the United States, the superiority of American forces turned the "generation of American casualties" promised by Saddam Hussein into a difficult task. In total, just over 200 Americans died in the Persian Gulf War (1991) with the majority of those casualties resulting from friendly fire.

The lessons of the Gulf War (1991) were simple. Any attempt to challenge the United States must utilize asymmetric means. Not only did our allies and adversaries learn this lesson, American war planners did as well. Although the Department of Defense and its slow-moving bureaucracy took some time to shift from a threat-based to a capabilities-based force structure, significant retooling of the military has occurred over the past decade as the United States prepared to fight the wars of the twenty-first century.

The twentieth century has often been called the century of total warfare, with World War I and World War II serving as the principle examples. The twenty-first century, however, is on track to be the century of asymmetric warfare. Understanding this dramatic shift in conflict and the role the United States is to play in twenty-first-century conflict requires that we answer five questions:

1. What is asymmetric warfare?
2. How does asymmetric warfare differ from other forms of unconventional conflict?
3. What is the American experience with asymmetric warfare?
4. What asymmetric threats does the United States face?
5. What is the future of warfare?

This chapter seeks to answer these questions as it pays particular attention to the role asymmetric conflict has and will play in shaping the U.S. military and its strategy and tactics. Contrary to the perceptions of many observers, the United States has a long and successful history of fighting adversaries who seek to minimize the conventional superiority of American forces. In some instances, it was the United States that sought to apply asymmetry in conflicts.

The reality of asymmetric conflict is that it is a form of warfare as old as war itself. Weak actors have long sought to minimize the strengths of their adversaries just as the strong have sought to bring the weak to battle. As the United States and its military forces move forward into the twenty-first century, they will face an old adversary that is ever adapting to meet the superior fighting ability of the American military.

WHAT IS ASYMMETRIC WARFARE?

Over the past 3,000 years, asymmetric warfare was given many names. For Sun-tzu, asymmetry was the pinnacle of the art of war.[1] Tacitus called asymmetric warfare the barbarian's way of rebellion.[2] T.E. Lawrence called it desert warfare.[3] Mao Zedong used the term mobile guerilla warfare.[4] For Vo Nguyen Giap it was people's war and for Che Guevara it was simply guerrilla warfare.[5]

The term asymmetric warfare did not enter the American lexicon until it first appeared in the 1997 *Quadrennial Defense Review* (QDR).[6] After its initial use, the term began making frequent appearances in government and civilian publications, often replacing other terms (insurgency, guerilla warfare, low intensity conflict, etc.) that were previously the staple of terminology. Secretary of Defense William Cohen defined asymmetric warfare when explaining that future adversaries will likely try to "circumvent or undermine U.S. strengths while exploiting its weaknesses, using methods that differ significantly from the usual mode of operations."[7] The Joint Chiefs of Staff have defined asymmetric warfare as "unanticipated or nontraditional approaches to circumvent or undermine an adversary's strengths while exploiting his vulnerabilities through unexpected technologies or innovative means."[8] President Clinton, in *A National Security Strategy for a New Century*, describes it as "unconventional approaches that avoid or undermine our strengths while exploiting our vulnerabilities." The report goes on to add, "Because of our conventional military dominance, adversaries are likely to use asymmetric means, such as WMD, information operations or terrorism."[9] Lieutenant Colonel Kenneth McKenzie Jr. adds that asymmetric warfare is best described as "leveraging inferior tactical or operational strength against American vulnerabilities to achieve disproportionate effect with the aim of undermining American will in order to achieve the asymmetric actor's strategic objectives."[10]

In assessing these definitions of asymmetric warfare it is important to point out that adversaries employing asymmetric approaches against the United States do so on foreign soil.[11] As McKenzie explains, actors employing asymmetric approaches have three strategic goals. First, and preferably, they seek to prevent the United States from committing to a policy of intervention or invasion. By threatening to deploy chemical and biological weapons against coalition forces in the weeks leading up to the Persian Gulf War ground invasion (February 24–28, 1991), Saddam Hussein sought to use asymmetric warfare (the use of WMD) to deter a coalition invasion. Second, if the United States has committed to intervention or invasion, asymmetric approaches may create a situation where the strategic interest in the use of force is far outweighed by the costs incurred. Thus, American forces halt entry or accelerate a withdrawal. For Somali warlord Muhammad Farah Aidid, his strategy was simple: compel American forces to leave Somalia (1992–1994). Third, regional actors hostile to the United States may employ asymmetric approaches, such as terrorist attacks, while attempting to maintain their relationship with the United States.[12] One example of such an approach is that of Iran. While Iran seeks to expand its trade relationship with the United States, it plays a major role in supporting Sunni insurgents in Iraq.[13]

Grand Strategy

B. H. Liddell-Hart in his classic work, *Strategy*, explains grand strategy in the following manner.

> Grand strategy should both calculate and develop the economic resources and man-power of nations in order to sustain the fighting services. Also the moral resources—for to foster the people's willing spirit is often as important as to possess the more concrete forms of power. Grand strategy, too, should regulate the distribution of power between the several services, and between the services and industry. Moreover, fighting power is but one of the instruments of grand strategy—which should take account of and apply the power of financial

pressure, of diplomatic pressure, of commercial pressure, and, not least of ethical pressure, to weaken the opponent's will.[14]

The nature of asymmetric conflict and the relative weakness of the asymmetric actor in relation to his adversary place asymmetric means outside the norms of the "American way of war" and, often, the Geneva Conventions on the Laws of War (1949). In the veiled fashion in which he frequently issues public statements, Osama bin Laden explained the grand strategy of al-Qaeda saying, "As for the United States, I tell it and its people these few words: I swear by Almighty God who raised the heavens without pillars that neither the United States nor he who lives in the United States will enjoy security before we can see it as reality in Palestine and before all the infidel armies leave the land of Mohammed."[15] In a statement released October 10, 2001, bin Laden said, "Let the United States know that with God's permission, the battle will continue to be waged on its territory until it leaves our lands, stops its support for the Jews, and lifts the unjust embargo on the Iraqi people who have lost more than one million children."[16]

As a non-state actor, al-Qaeda approaches grand strategy in a very different way than do states seeking to employ asymmetric means against the United States.[17] Al-Qaeda relies on laundering the legitimate proceeds of commerce and the contributions of Muslims to finance its war against the United States. A fundamentalist interpretation of Islam and the unhappiness of millions in the Arab world are used to recruit and sustain the "willing spirit" of al-Qaeda. Since the al-Qaeda network functions like a hub and spoke, cells (the "several services") function autonomously, waiting to be activated.[18] Osama bin Laden and al-Qaeda rely upon the popular support they receive in the Arab world to pressure Arab governments into working toward constraining the foreign policy of the United States and, most importantly, bin Laden and al-Qaeda rely on acts of terror to shorten the reach of the United States. While Liddell-Hart spoke of the manner in which grand strategy is developed by states, non-state actors employing asymmetric approaches develop their own grand strategy, which can best be described as an effort to influence the foreign policy of an opposing state.

Strategy

According to Liddell-Hart, strategy is "an application on a lower plane of 'grand strategy.'"[19] The great Prussian strategist Carl von Clausewitz in *On War* defines strategy stating, "Strategy is the use of the engagement for the purpose of war."[20] For Liddell-Hart, strategy is "the art of distributing and applying military means to fulfill the ends of policy."[21] It is at the strategic level that asymmetric wars are won or lost for either side. For adversaries of the United States, the key to success is dependent upon determining America's strategic interests and attacking them. Throughout the 1990s al-Qaeda successfully determined that attacks on the United States and its interests abroad would not lead to significant retaliation.[22] It was only with the September 11, 2001, attacks that al-Qaeda misjudged America's strategic interests and has paid a heavy toll since.

For asymmetric warfare to achieve its strategic purpose, asymmetric means must establish their effectiveness. In order to demonstrate success, three conditions must be met. Asymmetric approaches should prove unexpected, as were the September 11, 2001, attacks. They must shock the defender making completion of the mission impossible. It is this second aspect of the asymmetric approach that generates the all-important psychological effect. It is here that al-Qaeda's war against the United States was ineffective. While Americans were shocked by the September 11, 2001, attacks, the United States did not abandon Saudi Arabia nor did it end its support of Israel. Spain, however, after the March 12, 2004, Madrid bombings, rapidly pulled its forces out of Iraq. Al-Qaeda achieved the psychological shock it sought, which subsequently led to the defeat of an incumbent prime minister, Jose Maria Aznar, who, prior to the bombing, held a significant lead over his opponent.[23] One final aspect of effectiveness is important. Asymmetric approaches must cause damage to the target in excess of the costs to carry out the operation. This final aspect is perhaps most important for the actor employing asymmetric means. As the weaker party in a conflict, the side utilizing asymmetry cannot attrite at an equivalent rate to his opponent.[24]

In strategic planning there are two options available to the planner: annihilation and attrition. A strategy of annihilation requires the victor to destroy his adversary's ability to fight while a strategy of attrition requires the victor to inflict casualties at such a level that his adversary's cost tolerance is overcome.[25] For both strategies, defeating the will of the enemy is central to victory. Liddell-Hart called Clausewitz's understanding of this point his greatest contribution to strategy. Annihilation is not an option for the asymmetric actor. He knows he cannot destroy his adversary but must rely on defeating his will to fight. Ho Chi Minh and General Giap understood this well and placed the defeat of the American "will" at the center of North Vietnam's strategy of attrition.

Tactics

Clausewitz said, "Tactics teaches the use of armed forces in engagement."[26] Liddell-Hart further elaborated on Clausewitz's description saying, "When the application of the military instrument merges into actual fighting, the dispositions for and control of such direct action are termed 'tactics.'"[27] Strategy and tactics have often been confused for one another and, as some might say, the distinction is a semantic one.[28] Clausewitz understood this point saying, "The distinction between tactics and strategy is now almost universal, and everyone knows fairly well where each particular factor belongs without clearly understanding why."[29] Asymmetric warfare blurs the distinction to a significantly greater degree than does conventional warfare. Terrorism, for example, is a strategic component of asymmetric warfare, yet each terrorist act is a tactical action.

Adversaries of the United States have and will utilize very different tactics when attacking at home and abroad. In both instances they will seek to target American weaknesses.[30] Domestically, infrastructure, large population centers, and information systems offer enticing targets.[31] The current insurgency in Iraq offers an excellent example of what American forces can expect in future conflicts. By employing the IED, small arms ambush, rocket attack, and car bomb the asymmetric actor strikes at the vulnerable points of Coalition forces. Not only is the recognition of the United States's weaknesses important in determining the tactics that will be utilized against the United States, the capabilities of an adversary are a primary factor. The Taliban, al-Qaeda, China, and Iran can only attack DoD computers from a safe location if they have the technology and personnel to carry out such an attack. Thus, knowing the capabilities of one's adversary is invaluable in defeating the asymmetric tactics they utilize.

HOW DOES ASYMMETRIC WARFARE DIFFER FROM OTHER FORMS OF UNCONVENTIONAL CONFLICT?

The first accounts of unconventional warfare, terms used interchangeably, are 2,000 years old.[32] The Bible, according to David Rooney, offers the first written description of asymmetric warfare in its chronicle of Judah's effort to overthrow the Seleucid Persians governing Judea in 160 BC.[33] Asymmetric conflict stands as the oldest form of unconventional warfare. It was very soon after men first clashed in close quarters combat that the weaker adversary learned that it was not to his advantage to face his enemy on the even plain of battle. Like his modern counterpart, the ancient warrior knew his success lay in striking at his adversary's weakness.

Asymmetric and guerrilla warfare are similar in many respects but differ at the broadest of levels: grand strategy. The grand strategy of the guerrilla seeks the overthrow of the current government and/or political system. The asymmetric fighter, however, generally seeks to force a change in his adversary's foreign policy. In the case of al-Qaeda, this includes compelling the United States to cease its support for Israel and remove American forces from Arab lands.

The guerrilla's strategy is much the same as that of the asymmetric fighter. Both wage a war of attrition in which the objective is to overcome the will of the adversary. Mao Zedong's mobile guerrilla warfare moves through a series of stages, with the last a conventional stage.[34] If, and when, the conventional stage is entered, the strategy of the guerrilla moves to one of annihilation where guerrillas seek to destroy the government's ability to resist.

Tactically, guerrillas and asymmetric actors rely on "irregular, part-time, often non-uniformed forces that employ such tactics as ambush, hit-and-run, and avoidance of contact where superiority at the point of engagement does not guarantee victory."[35] Guerrilla warfare does not, however, utilize many of the tactics that are the hallmark of modern asymmetric conflict. With few exceptions, guerrillas target government forces and their supporters for attack. Guerrillas do not, however, indiscriminately target the civilian population as asymmetric actors frequently do. The guerrilla seeks to gain the support of a population, rather than alienate it. Thus, terrorism has rarely been a tactic of guerrilla warfare.

Guerrilla movements differ from asymmetric conflicts in other important ways. Asymmetric warfare, as I have thus described, is a conflict in which adversaries are not of equal strength leading one side to develop a strategy and tactics, which are, in many instances, outside the accepted rules of Western warfare. Asymmetric conflicts also tend to be external conflicts in which a powerful state intervenes in the internal affairs of a weak or failed state. The United States intervened in Lebanon (1982–1984) in order to stabilize a collapsing regime. Intervention in Somalia (1992–1994) sought to alleviate starvation and restore stability in a failed state. The United States invaded Afghanistan (2001–present) because the Taliban refused to turn over Osama bin Laden and al-Qaeda operatives.[36] In each of these three countries internal conflicts raged as warring factions sought to dominate one another in the absence of a stable regime. The internal conflicts that often serve as a precursor for American intervention are marked by insurgencies against an existing government or where government has collapsed.

The Making of an Insurgency

In his classic work on the subject, *Why Men Rebel*, Robert Ted Gurr describes the circumstances necessary for guerrilla movements to take root, grow, and succeed.[37] The following discussion serves to further distinguish between guerrilla and asymmetric warfare. Such a distinction is relevant because the preconditions, goals, and approach of guerrillas and asymmetric actors vary significantly.

The fomentation of a guerrilla movement begins when a segment of the population feels it is not getting what it deserves and the government is to blame. This feeling of "relative deprivation" develops in a four-step process. First, the disaffected population must realize that they are deprived of something. Second, they realize their condition is not universal and others possess what they lack. Third, the group questions not only the equity of their circumstance but also its fairness. Fourth, the affected segment comes to the conclusion that they can alter their condition through political action.[38]

Relative deprivation takes one of three forms. Decremental deprivation develops when expectations remain the same but the ability to meet those expectations declines. Aspirational deprivation exists when expectations rise dramatically while society is incapable of meeting those expectations. Progressive deprivation is a condition in which expectations rise while society's ability to meet those expectations declines.

In addition to the psychological conditions mentioned, guerrilla movements develop in states where terrain (mountains, forests, jungles, vast steppe) encumbers government forces as they attempt to destroy nascent insurgencies. These geographic conditions enable guerrillas to survive, expand, and eventually succeed. Early in an insurgency, the emphasis is on redressing the grievances of inhabitants in the area in which guerrillas operate. And, as insurgents build support within the local population, they are then able to take the offensive against government forces.

Asymmetric conflicts, however, are not waged to improve the living conditions of the lower classes and overthrow a corrupt regime as this description suggests of a guerrilla movement. Not only do guerrillas and asymmetric actors desire different outcomes, they differ in the conditions that lead to their creation, and the strategy and tactics they implement. Some may consider it semantics to suggest that guerrilla and asymmetric warfare are not the same. If asymmetric warfare is defined as conflict between two unequal sides, then it is, in fact, a semantic distinction. But, as I suggest, guerrilla warfare has distinguishing characteristics that set it apart from asymmetric conflict, making each a distinct form of unconventional warfare.

New Internal Wars

Guerrilla warfare made its presence known on the global stage in the twentieth century with an unprecedented number of efforts to install communist regimes around the world. The global state of affairs dramatically changed, however, with the close of the Cold War. As client states of both superpowers experienced a precipitous decline in financial and military support and the East-West overlay of the Cold War was lifted, old grievances came to the forefront. Disaffected groups were finally free to compete for the limited resources once firmly held by regimes backed by the Soviet Union or the United States.

The 1990s were the decade of the new internal war, a decade which saw the explosion of internal conflict within unstable, failing, and failed states in Africa, Central and Southeast Asia, and the Balkans.[39] Where superpower support had once mitigated centuries old ethnic and religious conflicts, the absence of a legitimate post-Cold War regime led disaffected groups to take up arms.[40] It was not the ethnic and religious grievances alone that caused states to experience internal conflict. In all of the conflict-plagued states poor economic performance, high levels of poverty, underdeveloped infrastructure, and a poorly skilled and educated citizenry were hallmark characteristics.[41] Many of the former socialist states lacked a fundamental understanding of entrepreneurship and capitalism, which is vital to a developing economy. Such conditions left young men from Somalia, Rwanda, and Afghanistan unemployed and with little to do but butcher those they blamed for their poverty.

No longer able to maintain stability, weak states were plunged into rebellion and civil war as violence became the method through which disaffected groups sought to change the status quo. Unlike the insurgencies of the past, the new internal wars lacked the strategic purpose fundamental to the communist revolutions of the twentieth century.[42] Instead, poorly trained and led bands spent much of their time plundering and killing civilian populations rather than following any recognized grand strategy for defeating government forces and replacing the regime in power. Rebel leaders often concentrated on enriching themselves at the expense of impoverished civilians.[43]

Internal wars often utilize conventional and asymmetric tactics, but this does not necessarily dictate into which form of conflict internal wars fall. Asymmetric warfare is characterized by a grand strategy which seeks to deter or end the intervention or invasion of a foreign power. This is not the case in internal wars. Like traditional insurgencies, they arise because of unstable conditions within a state that may include poverty, religious conflict, and a failed regime. Whereas the majority of twentieth-century guerilla movements sought the violent overthrow of corrupt regimes and the imposition of a communism, internal wars are largely struggles over ethnic and religious grievances.

After five decades of the Cold War, the West was loath to provide military assistance and financial aid to war-torn states that were not of strategic interest. Should Somalis, Rwandans, or Liberians exterminate one another neither Europe nor the United States would feel little impact. The cost of the Cold War gave the West ample reason to stay out of the internal war of the third world. For the United States in particular, there were neither communist guerrillas nor direct threats to American interest. Thus, intervention in the wars of the world's backwaters was unpopular with the American people.

For developed states there were three options: benign neglect, selective intervention, or large-scale development.[44] Benign neglect, simply ignoring the crisis, was often a preferred option, but one that became increasingly difficult as the international news media illuminated the death and destruction of internal wars.[45] Large-scale development of more than a dozen states in Africa and Central and Southeast Asia was untenable and unpopular in the West. This left the lone superpower the option of selectively intervening in internal wars where deprivation was most horrific. After the debacle in Somalia (1993), President Clinton was slow to act in Rwanda and selective in his use of military force elsewhere.

Although the United States sent forces to Somalia, Rwanda, Haiti (twice), Bosnia, and Kosovo in the 1990s, American intervention was minimal. In limited instances, France and Great Britain intervened in the internal wars of their former possessions but, as was often the case, it was too little too late.[46] For Great Britain, efforts to bring stability to Zimbabwe and other Commonwealth countries proved equally difficult.[47]

In the post 9/11 era, greater attention is being given to the world's trouble spots. As the United States and its allies continue the GWOT, American decision makers are well aware of the fact that unstable states are a breeding ground for terrorists. The neglect of the West that marked the 1990s has been replaced by watchful vigilance and a global agenda on the part of the Bush administration to bring democracy and open markets to the developing world. In an era dominated by the events of September 11, 2001, it is important to understand that the United States is not facing an asymmetric adversary for the first time in American history. Rather, the United States has a long history of facing asymmetric actors and overcoming the varying tactics they utilize. The following section offers a brief history of the American experience with asymmetric conflict, offering some context in which to place the current Global War on Terror and the Iraqi insurgency.

WHAT IS THE AMERICAN EXPERIENCE WITH ASYMMETRIC WARFARE?

June 25, 1798, is a forgotten day in American history for all but the devoted military historian. It was the day the U.S. Congress authorized President John Adams to take action against French privateers, responsible for ravaging American merchant vessels in the Atlantic and Caribbean.[48] The congressional statute served to spark the Quasi-War, in which American sailors and marines landed in the Dominican Republic, where they captured a French vessel, and defeated French privateers throughout the Caribbean. Most importantly, it marked the first time the United States deployed forces abroad.

Captain Thomas Truxton and the sailors and marines of the frigate Constellation achieved astounding victories over French privateers who sought to prey on poorly defended merchant vessels while using the geography of the West Indies to hide from the searching eye of Truxton. At the same time, Truxton used deception and surprise to capture an unaware French privateer from underneath the guns of Puerto Plata. For the United States, the Quasi-War was a victory which led to the end of French attacks on American merchants while offering the young nation its first overseas victory and its first experience with asymmetric conflict.[49] Victory in the Quasi-War did not allow the traditionally isolationist Americans to liquidate their Navy, as they had done soon after peace with Britain was achieved in 1783. Instead, the experience foreshadowed the "military operations other than war" that have come to dominate the use of force by the United States.

As the United States rapidly expanded in the nineteenth and early twentieth centuries, the nation's men and goods spread across the globe as the nation grew in power and wealth. And, as all great powers before her came to learn, the need to protect one's citizens and their property requires the use of military force. In the 207 years since the cessation of hostilities between the United States and France (1800), American forces have deployed 244 times to end piracy, protect or evacuate Americans, exact reprisals for destruction of American property, protect the United States's strategic interests, fight conventional wars, and provide humanitarian assistance.[50]

The United States has declared war five times in its history and fought four undeclared conventional wars.[51] In the overwhelming majority of instances in which America's military might was utilized, the conflict was asymmetric. Early in American history stronger European powers preyed on the United States and kept an undersized Navy and Marine Corps in near constant action. The spread of American products and citizens abroad led to the need for protection of persons and property. When the domestic situation deteriorated in Latin America, China, or the Pacific Islands, as it frequently did, small numbers of sailors and marines were sent into combat. As the United States grew to rival the great powers of Europe in economic and military might late in the nineteenth century, it sought to aggressively assert American interest abroad by promoting the Open Door Policy (1899) in China, enforcing the Monroe Doctrine (1823) in Latin America, and acquiring overseas territories.

Max Boot, author of *The Savage Wars of Peace: Small Wars and the Rise of American Power*, groups America's experience with "small wars" into three eras: commercial power, great power, and superpower.[52] The commercial era (1798–1899) was a period in which the Navy and Marine Corps intervened in countries around the globe to protect Americans and their property.[53] Whether it was the Barbary Wars (1801–1805, 1815), the Marquesas (1813), China (1859), Korea (1871), Samoa (1899), or any of a number of smaller conflicts, American sailors and marines were on constant guard and in near constant conflict with an adversary that greatly outnumbered the better trained and equipped American contingents sent to assert the rights of the United States.[54]

The great power era (1899–1941) saw the United States expand its ever-growing power as it increasingly intervened in the domestic affairs of other nations. In the century leading up to America's first large-scale unconventional conflict, sailors and marines alone served to combat the tactics of pirates, Boxers, and Pacific Islanders. This changed, however, when the United States annexed the Philippines.[55] Emilio Aguinaldo, leader of Philippine insurgents, led more than 200,000 Filipinos in operations against an American force that never exceeded more than 20,000 men.[56]

Using effective counterinsurgency strategies,[57] the United States successfully convinced Filipino insurgents, after capturing Aguinaldo, to end their three-year struggle and accept American rule.[58]

In addition to large-scale efforts in the Philippines, the United States intervened in an unprecedented number of internal conflicts in Latin America. Whether it was marines fighting guerrillas in Haiti (1915–1934) or soldiers chasing Poncho Villa (1916–1917) through northern Mexico, there was always ample opportunity to engage in asymmetric conflicts.[59] Firmly established as the master of the Western hemisphere and with a Navy second only to that of Great Britain, the United States began an active and aggressive effort to protect its interests around the globe, which often left the United States at odds with European states who employed local peoples to confront American troops. In many instances, locals did not need provocation from Europeans to take exception to American expansion.

World War II interrupted the era of small wars forcing the United States to mobilize its population and resources in an unprecedented fashion. With the end of the war and the onset of the Cold War, the spread of communism, often by guerrilla movements, became a constant for the American military.[60] The bipolar period was a series of brush fire wars, with Vietnam serving as the preeminent conflict of the Cold War. The United States ultimately proved victorious and emerged the lone superpower and, therefore, the state expected to secure the international order. The post-Cold War superpower era has seen a constant state of intervention for the United States as it seeks to prevent the spread of chaos throughout Africa, the Balkans, and elsewhere. Most recently, intervention has turned to invasion as American troops are currently engaged in the greatest asymmetric conflict to date.

What marks the American experience with asymmetric conflict is its dominance in the American military experience. Few and infrequent are conventional conflicts. Past conflicts, by in large, fit the criteria established for asymmetric conflicts, albeit imperfectly. As President George W. Bush, Secretary Donald H. Rumsfeld, and America's military commanders continue to wage protracted wars in Afghanistan and Iraq, it should never be forgotten that the United States has a long and successful history in conflicts similar to those faced in the current day. In centuries past, Rome and Britain maintained vast empires where asymmetric conflict was almost constant.[61] The United States should expect much the same as weaker adversaries challenge the order imposed by the global hegemon.

WHAT ASYMMETRIC THREATS DOES THE UNITED STATES FACE?

Throughout the Cold War the U.S. military was structured to fight a large-scale conventional war with the Soviet Union. While the "mother of all battles" never came, U.S. strategic policy remained focused on the Soviet threat. The numerous unconventional conflicts of the Cold War received limited attention until well after the collapse of the Soviet Union. Beginning with the 1997 QDR, the Department of Defense acknowledged serious flaws in the two major regional wars strategy that replaced the Soviet threat in the immediate post-Cold War period.[62]

Joint Vision 2010 was the first Pentagon effort to take a comprehensive look past the Cold War and examine new the threats facing the United States in the future.[63] By the time *Joint Vision 2020* was published four years later, the Pentagon was well aware of the changing nature of conflict.[64] Where past presidents relied on Mutually Assured Destruction to deter a global nuclear war between the United States and the Soviet Union, presidents Bill Clinton and George W. Bush could no longer depend on such a deterrent. The twenty-first-century nuclear threat is a very different one in which states are no longer the most troubling. Non-state actors, such as al-Qaeda, may prove more dangerous.

Terrorist organizations are also finding new ways to utilize biological and chemical weapons, which pose a greater threat than ever before. During the Cold War they were not a major concern for the United States. International treaties and a gentleman's agreement between the United States and the Soviet Union precluded their use by either side well before ratification of the Chemical Weapons Convention (1972) and President Nixon's ending of all offensive development of biological and chemical weapons (1972). Terrorism was also minimized by the superpowers during the Cold War. For Soviet and American leaders, terrorism was a threat to both. The Soviet Union sought to prevent communist groups from utilizing terrorism, even as the USSR attempted to install communist regimes around the world.[65]

Two additional asymmetric threats have made their presence known in the post-Cold War era as technology has shaped conflict. First, terrorism currently poses the greatest risk to the United States and its citizens. America's forward-deployed forces are particularly at risk. During the 1990s, attacks on the Khobar Towers (housing for Air Force personnel in Saudi Arabia) and the USS *Cole* (DDG-67) illustrate the relative ease of carrying out a terrorist act. Terrorism, however, has proven less effective in shaping American foreign policy than its had hoped. Thus, state and non-state actors around the globe began to develop methods of attacking the information infrastructure of American industry and government. China, for example, has developed military units dedicated to developing the country's cyberwar capabilities. In the combat scenarios run by the People's Liberation Army (PLA), the United States is the primary adversary and target of cyber attacks.[66]

In the years following the collapse of the Soviet Union, the world changed dramatically, as did the threats facing the United States. During the five decades of the Cold War, conflict was marked by a rule-set understood by both of the superpowers. Major conflict was averted and the Cold War ended with a thud.

In the wake of 9/11, weapons of mass destruction rose to new prominence. Recent works by Graham Allison and other prominent scholars suggest that there is a credible threat to the United States and its forces from these weapons, particularly when they are utilized by asymmetric actors such as Osama bin Laden and al-Qaeda.[67] Because of the strong concentration on WMD in recent literature, the discussion now turns prospective ways in which chemical, biological, and nuclear weapons *may* be used against the United States and its forward-deployed forces. In addition to these threats, terrorism and cyber war are discussed because of their rise to prominence in recent years.

Terrorism

Terrorism is a form of political violence currently utilized by adversaries of the United States to strike at the soft underbelly of American society. In Iraq and Afghanistan the desire is to destabilize fledgling governments and overcome American cost tolerance. It has been used to successfully force the withdrawal of Spanish troops from Iraq and is a primary reason for Italy's early withdrawal from Iraq.[68] As the primary tactic of the Iraqi insurgency and reconstituted elements of the Taliban, a discussion of terrorism provides a firm understanding of a powerful weapon in the asymmetric actor's arsenal. Terrorism's major characteristics are as follows:

1. Terrorism is premeditated and aims to generate a climate of fear.
2. Terrorism is directed at a wider audience than the immediate victims.
3. Terrorism involves attacks on random and symbolic targets, such as civilians.
4. Terrorism's violence is outside the social norm of the society, in which they occur, thus causing outrage.
5. Terrorism is generally used to influence political behavior.[69]

Terrorism, a tactic with a long and bloody history, rapidly replaced the Soviet Union as the primary threat to the United States.[70] In the decade since the collapse of the Soviet Union, terrorism has seen significant change. Unlike hierarchical terror organizations of the twentieth century, which were structured similar to militaries, the Islamic fundamentalist terror networks of the twenty-first century have a highly decentralized structure in which semi-autonomous cells[71] carry out attacks ordered by a central leadership.[72] The result of this restructuring is an unprecedented level of independence from state support and control. Al-Qaeda, through its system of businesses and money laundering operations, is capable of self-sufficiency, to a degree impossible two decades ago.

Cooperation between terror networks also has seen dramatic change reaching unprecedented levels. In the wake of September 11, 2001, al-Qaeda members have been linked to the Revolutionary Armed Forces of Columbia, Chechen rebels, and numerous other terrorist groups.[73] The size of Islamic fundamentalist terror networks is also much greater than that of previous terror organizations. During the height of terrorist activity in the 1970s and early 1980s, terror organizations such as the Japanese Red Army and Red Army Faction sustained no more than 20–30 hard-core members.[74] Al-Qaeda, however, is estimated to have trained more than 10,000 men, of which at least 4,000 are believed to be members of terror cells. One final marked trend in modern terrorism is its purpose. The *RAND-St. Andrews Chronology of International Terrorism,* a comprehensive database on worldwide terrorist incidents since 1968, points out that none of the original 11 terror groups included in the database were religious. All were either ideological (communist) or ethno-nationalist. Today, Islamic fundamentalists dominate the terror world, with few exceptions.

Recent terrorist acts suggest several developing trends. First, there is a trend toward the use of high explosives in urban centers.[75] Second, there is a general trend toward attacks of greater lethality. Third, a trend exists toward attacks designed to inflict damage to a state's economy. Fourth, hostage taking has increased significantly.

In addition to these trends are threats most pressing for the United States. Al-Qaeda and related groups are better educated, trained, funded, and have greater access to technology than previous terrorists. Not only did the training camps of Afghanistan provide recruits with small arms training and demolitions expertise, but the universities of the West provide the chemistry, computer science, and engineering degrees needed to improve the lethality of terrorist attacks. No longer must al-Qaeda or other terror networks purchase fully developed biological, chemical, or nuclear weapons. Instead, al-Qaeda scientists acquire equipment, material, and laboratory space for its member-scientists. Fortunately for the United States and its allies, it is proving difficult for al-Qaeda to bring all of these components together. Fissile nuclear material is particularly difficult to acquire, despite Hollywood's suggestions to the contrary.[76] According to the terrorism data collected by the Center for Nonproliferation Studies (CNS), the use of weapons of mass destruction for terrorism is rare.[77] In 1999 there were 175 reported terrorist acts, including threats never acted upon. In the overwhelming majority of instances where a non-state actor possessed or used a chemical agent, it proved to be tear gas.[78]

In order to find a large-scale biological or chemical terrorist attack, it is necessary to look back to March 20, 1995, when Aum Shinrikyo released a sarin gas attack on the Tokyo subway, killing 12 and sending 6,000 scared Japanese to the hospital.[79] Most recently, the anthrax attacks in the United States killed five and sickened a dozen.[80] Instructive in these attacks is the ability of a terrorist to hide his identity.[81] While even large-scale biological and chemical attacks have proven difficult to carry out with few casualties, the threat of a biological or chemical attack causes significant psychological distress.

As the Bush administration assesses the threat environment created by terrorism, the economic costs have proven to be most significant. With an immediate loss of $1 trillion in hard assets and stock values after the September 11, 2001, terrorist attacks, the United States continues to pay an additional $50–$100 billion annually in increased security costs.[82] Should a successful WMD attack occur in the United States, the economic and psychological costs could well exceed those of 9/11.[83]

The United States has two options when attempting to prevent terrorism. First, there are anti-terror policies, which are defensive and seek to deter terrorism. Airport screeners, customs agents, and the border patrol are all vital parts of the American anti-terrorism effort. In an open society, anti-terror efforts are difficult.[84] For these policies to prove effective, Americans can expect restrictions on the liberties they enjoy. This has begun already in office buildings, airports, and public buildings. In contrast, counter-terror policy is proactively seeking out terrorists and neutralizing them.[85] U.S. Special Forces, CIA Operations Bureau, FBI Counter Terrorism Unit, and American military are the core of the United States' counter-terrorism effort. President Bush has frequently explained that part of the Global War on Terror is engaging al-Qaeda and other terrorists on their own soil, before they reach the United States.[86] General Montgomery C. Meigs underscores the significance of this policy, suggesting that France could have crushed Hitler before he engulfed Europe in war had the political will existed prior to 1938.[87]

Hoover Institute scholar Bruce Berkowitz offers three options for American decision makers.[88] The first option is diplomacy and legal prosecution, which dominated American anti-terror policy during the 1990s and the four-decade-long French anti-terror effort. This option has not yet proven effective in combating terrorism. In the statements of Osama bin Laden cited earlier, the terror chief stated that American efforts to prosecute al-Qaeda members in American courts illustrate the weakness of the United States.[89] For the French, special magistrates have long played the leading role in the fight against terror with mixed results.[90]

Preemption is Berkowitz's second option. Afghanistan and Iraq are examples of such a policy. Given the limited use of preemption as a counter-terrorism strategy, it is difficult to gauge its effectiveness. Proponents suggest it is a highly effective way of destroying terror networks on their home soil while opponents counter that it is costly in American blood and gold and inflames anti-American sentiment around the globe.[91]

The final counter-terrorism option is covert action. Since the September 11, 2001, attacks, significant resources have been allocated to these operations as U.S. Special Forces and CIA operations officers have worked with their counterparts in the Philippines, Columbia, and elsewhere. Given the secret nature of covert and direct action, it is difficult to determine how effective these operations are. For example, vague and often less than accurate news accounts suggest the direct action taken in the Philippines and Singapore is proving effective. But, there is little definitive proof.

As General Meigs points out, the adaptive nature of al-Qaeda and other terror networks makes it difficult for the United States to anticipate and prevent terrorist attacks. The basic overview of terrorism offered above is just that. Detailed analysis of terrorism is beyond the scope of this discussion, in which I suggest that terrorism is the single greatest threat facing the United States in the Global War on Terror.

Nuclear

Graham Allison's recent work, *Nuclear Terrorism: The Ultimate Preventable Catastrophe,* paints an alarming picture of the threat nuclear terrorism poses to the homeland. State and non-state actors who find themselves in an adversarial relationship with the United States have a heightened interest in acquiring nuclear weapons because of the perceived protection they provide against American intervention or invasion. Iran, North Korea, al-Qaeda, and Hamas are but a few examples of both state and non-state actors actively pursuing offensive nuclear weapons. For all but Hamas, the United States is the primary adversary and the reason for the pursuit of nuclear weapons. Recently, Iran and North Korea violated international agreements restricting their nuclear programs because of increased fears that without nuclear weapons they will find themselves in a serious conflict with the United States. Al-Qaeda and other terror networks are known to be actively seeking one or more functioning nuclear devises and the material to construct a dirty bomb.[92] All of these activities are of serious concern to the Bush administration.

One important point should be made before discussing the nuclear threat further. In the discussions of terrorism, weapons of mass destruction serve as tactical assets. Weapons of mass destruction and cyber warfare do not constitute a strategy, but weapons used to achieve an objective that may be part of an asymmetric strategy. This is to say that a discussion of asymmetric threats need not consider each threat as mutually exclusive. The detonation of a nuclear device or dirty bomb in New York, Los Angeles, or Washington, DC, is one of many ways a terror network may strike the United States.

A number of scenarios in which a nuclear weapon is used against the United States exist, but three are viewed as viable risks.[93] In the first scenario a nuclear device is smuggled into the United States by a member of al-Qaeda. The one-megaton bomb is detonated as it sits inside a van on a busy Manhattan street. Everything within a one-quarter-mile radius is instantly destroyed. All buildings within 4.5 miles are destroyed or heavily damaged. Moderate damage exists to buildings and homes up to 7.4 miles from the center of the blast.[94] Depending on wind conditions, fallout would cause serious internal injuries to humans and animals up to 160 miles from the site of the blast with the severity of injuries increasing as the epicenter of the blast is approached. As many as one million New Yorkers would perish as the city becomes uninhabitable for a decade or more. An airburst or larger bomb will cause greater destruction and loss of life. The previous scenario is one the Departments of Energy, Homeland Security and Defense ran before and after 9/11 as they sought to determine the destructive power of a nuclear strike.[95] As Graham Allison has noted, "In my own considered judgment, on the current path, a nuclear terrorist attack on America in the decade ahead is more likely than not."[96]

American nuclear policy has long been that a nuclear attack against the United States would result in a counter-strike.[97] The difficulty in this scenario is determining responsibility. In the aftermath of an attack, an effort must be made to determine how the bomb entered the country, the bomb's point of origination, the source of the fissile material, and who created the bomb. This is no easy task, particularly when terror networks are adept at operating covertly.[98]

In a second scenario, American troops are in the first phase of a Middle East invasion when a short-range ballistic missile carrying a low-yield nuclear weapon strikes the center of advancing troops. There are 5,000–10,000 immediate casualties, which causes the president to withdraw. Military intelligence was taken by complete surprise with the first attack making it difficult for the president to determine whether a nuclear threat persists. The first strike was on foreign soil complicating any response. Additionally, it is not known whether there is a long-range strike capability on the part of the adversary. Continuing the invasion could place regional allies in danger of a nuclear strike.[99]

The final scenario envisions Space Command detecting an object launched from the Middle East, North Korea, or China heading for the United States. As the object reaches the upper atmosphere somewhere over Kansas it explodes. Commercial airliners crash after their electronics fail, the North American electricity grid is severely damaged, and computer circuitry is destroyed by the electromagnetic pulse (EMP) generated in the blast. If detonation occurs in the Van Allen belt, the belt is charged with electrons knocking commercial and military satellites out of service.[100] There are few casualties from the explosion and no city is laid waste, but billions of dollars in damage and a degraded military capability are the result. Once again American leaders must decide how to respond. Without Boston, Los Angeles, New York or Washington, DC, in ruins, can the United States rationally retaliate with a nuclear strike?

Few states currently posses the necessary intercontinental ballistic missile technology to manage such an attack.[101] North Korea's continuing improvements to their Tae Po Dong class ballistic missile and their willingness to sell advanced weapons systems to adversaries of the United States increases the threat EMP weapons pose to this country. But, there are few states who possess the technology to carry out such an attack.

Exactly why the Cold War ended without a nuclear holocaust is left for historians to determine. The fact remains that despite rivalries between the United States and the Soviet Union, India and Pakistan, Israel and its Arab neighbors, the nuclear option has never been taken. Adversaries of the United States actively developing nuclear weapons consider their nuclear programs defensive and a deterrent to "American aggression." The same is true of al-Qaeda. And while its members are willing to die for their cause, they may not be willing to risk the lives of their parents, siblings, wives, and children, which would be the result of detonating a nuclear device in the United States.

Former Senator Sam Nunn and the Bush administration are particularly concerned about the threat of nuclear terrorism which is viewed by government and scholarly sources as a credible threat.[102] As al-Qaeda and other terror networks increase their independence from state sponsorship, the ease with which a nuclear strike could be carried out in anonymity increases. This can only decrease the deterrent effect of an American response.

Biological

Biological weapons are proving to be a significant concern for the United States.[103] For many regimes and terror networks the lure of biological weapons is too strong to resist. They are inexpensive to produce and require a lower level of technical expertise and advanced equipment to create than do nuclear weapons, yet they serve much the same deterrent effect. In spite of the Biological Weapons Convention (1972), the number of states pursuing a biological weapons program has increased. During the Cold War the Soviet Union maintained the most advanced biological weapons program in the world. Since then, many Middle Eastern states have turned to the biological option as unemployed Soviet scientists seek to ply their trade for the right price.[104] Terror networks are also proving to be interested in the purchase and development of biological weapons. Many of the same scientists willing to work for Iran, Iraq, and North Korea after the Soviet Union's collapse are willing to sell biological agents to al-Qaeda and other terror networks.[105]

Biological agents are divided into five categories: viral, rickettsial, bacterial, fungal, and toxins. Each is a highly toxic biological organism, toxins are the exception. According to Anthony H. Cordesman, biological weapons are used to target "infantry concentrations, air bases, ships, ports, staging areas, command centers, munitions depots, cities, key oil and electrical facilities, and desalinization plants." Cordesman also states that biological weapons are "potentially far more effective against military and civil area targets than chemical weapons."[106]

When used against military units, biological weapons rarely cause large numbers of casualties. They do, however, force military units to don protective gear, which degrades offensive combat capabilities and slows an advance. A biological attack against American forces could, at best, hope to achieve this very objective.[107] An attack against a civilian target, however, would result in many more casualties because of the public's lack of preparation. A biological attack's purpose is not a high casualty count. It is economic disruption and psychological trauma that are the goal of such an attack. During the anthrax attacks in the United States (2001), the Capitol Building was vacated for more than a week and the House and Senate office buildings for even longer after a single anthrax-laden letter was sent to Senator Tom Daschle (D-SD).[108] In addition to the cleanup effort, members of Congress were given a 60-day treatment of cyprofloxicin. The total number of casualties from all of the anthrax attacks reached five, but most important was the psychological effect.

Biological weapons have not, as yet, proven to be an effective weapon against military or civilian targets. Tactically, biological agents are difficult to weaponize because they are highly volatile, degrade quickly, and are susceptible to heat. This makes it very difficult to use biological agents in missiles and projectiles where heat and lengthy storage periods work against the effectiveness of a biological agent. The same difficulties arise when considering their use against civilian targets. Biological agents are difficult to widely disperse and when dispersed, rapidly succumb to biodegradation and corruption.

For al-Qaeda and other terror networks, biological weapons are viewed as the best option among weapons of mass destruction. Since they are relatively simple and inexpensive to produce and, once dispersed, can be spread from person to person, biological weapons are preferred. The fact that many biological agents are highly contagious also increases the "fear factor," which is highly valued by those who would resort to their use.[109]

Chemical

Chemical weapons are the third component of the WMD triad and are least effective. Similar to their biological counterpart, chemical weapons vary significantly in the characteristics that make them more or less effective. Chemical and biological weapons serve much the same strategic purpose: to deter the United States, delay an invasion force, and strike terror into a civilian population. They are not, however, equal to biological or nuclear weapons in the threat they pose.

World War I (1914–1918) was the first instance in the history of warfare where chemical weapons played a major tactical role.[110] Their success was, however, limited. For the British and Americans, the probability of surviving a gas attack was much greater than that of a frontal assault on German trenches. Chemical agents, while less volatile and susceptible to degradation than biological agents, are also less effective, requiring more to achieve less effect.[111] For example, it would take 1,728 kilograms of sarin agent to produce a 50 percent casualty rate among an unprotected infantry in a typical formation spread over 1.3 kilometers.[112]

The United States learned from its experience with chemical weapons in World War I, training American troops to the highest level of preparedness. In the event of an attack, air, ground, and naval forces possess the training and equipment necessary to quickly and safely decontaminate equipment and personnel without significant delay of action. Emergency management officials in large metropolitan areas are also trained and prepared for the release of chemical agents. In the wake of the September 11, 2001, attacks, funding under the Nunn-Luger-Domenici Domestic Preparedness Program has increased dramatically, enabling state and local emergency responders to improve the equipment and training necessary in the event of a chemical attack.[113]

While it may be possible, as it was in the Iran-Iraq War, to attack an adversary with chemical artillery and cause significant casualties among unprotected troops, this is not a viable prospect when considering chemical weapons for a terrorist attack against a civilian population.[114] In order to cause serious casualties in a large metropolitan area, the aerial delivery of a chemical agent, whether aerosol or powder, would require numerous low-level flights over the target area.[115] When Aum Shinrikyo dispersed sarin in a crowded Tokyo subway during rush hour on March 20, 1995, 12 people died and 6,000 suffered minor injuries, with few suffering long-term complications.[116] Sarin, one of the deadliest nerve agents in the world, was dispersed in an enclosed space where commuters were tightly packed, yet there were only 12 casualties. Had a single gunman entered the same subway station and begun firing wildly into the crowd, a much higher casualty count would have resulted.

While the thought of a chemical attack causes considerable anxiety among political and military leaders, the threat remains primarily psychological. When prospective developers of chemical weapons compare the costs of to the advanced detection and denial systems the American military brings to combat, chemical weapons are diminished as a viable option. When effectiveness is also included and compared to conventional weapons, chemical weapons are an expensive and ineffective counter to the United States. They are also proving less than ideal as a weapon for use by terror groups but remain a threat against which civil and military leaders must prepare.[117]

Cyber

The collapse of the Soviet Union at the end of the twentieth century was a momentous event and success for the United States. More ubiquitous, however, was the rise of the internet. What had once been a project of the Defense Advanced Research Projects Agency revolutionized communications and the transfer of information during the 1990s. The internet, and the interconnectivity that it brings, also opens government and business to attacks against their networked systems. What were once attacks by young computer "geeks" sitting in their bedrooms hacking into business or government networks "just to see if we could do it" has now become a tactic both governments and terror networks are preparing to utilize in an attack against the United States.

The FBI defines cyber terrorism as "the premeditated, politically motivated attack against information, computer systems, computer programs, and data which result in violence against noncombatant targets by subnational groups or clandestine agents."[118] A definition of cyber war differs little from that of cyber terrorism with two exceptions. In cyber war, attacks are carried out against noncombatants *and* military targets, and they are state-sponsored attacks rather than non-state actors. Ample evidence suggests both are a growing threat. Al-Qaeda and other terror networks currently possess the knowledge and ability to attack commercial and government web sites, a tactic Palestinian terror groups have been actively utilizing against Israeli information networks for years.[119]

In testimony before the Special Oversight Panel on Terrorism, Dr. Dorothy E. Denning explained that it would take a group two to four years to move from simple-unstructured attacks to advanced-structured attacks and six to ten years to utilize complex-coordinated attacks capable of causing mass disruption.[120] Simple-unstructured attacks may be something as simple as web vandalism, where an attacker hacks into a commercial or government web site and alters the home page. In an advanced-structured attack, the aggressor is capable of infiltrating multiple systems with, for example, a denial of service attack which can shut down a network by overloading it. Complex-coordinated attacks are of the greatest concern to civilian and military leaders because it is this form of attack that is capable of disrupting, damaging, or destroying critical infrastructure such as the North American power grid, emergency response systems, and the computer networks linking military units around the globe.

In addition to al-Qaeda, China, France, Israel, and Russia have advanced cyber warfare programs.[121] China and Russia, in particular, have programs designed to target the information infrastructure of the United States.[122]

The characteristics that draw terror networks to cyber terrorism are the same that draw states to cyber war. First, cyber warfare requires lower levels of investment in equipment than other forms of asymmetric warfare. There is neither the need for laboratories to produce biological, chemical, or nuclear weapons, nor the often difficult need to acquire components used in them. A skilled programmer, a laptop, and an internet connection are all that is necessary to engage in cyber warfare. Second, cyber warfare gives an attacker a level of anonymity not possible in other forms of warfare. Sophisticated cyber warriors are capable of masking their identity and location by utilizing "slave" computers, which create a false identity for an attacker. Third, the number of cyber targets is exponentially greater than the number of conventional targets. Commercial targets are numerous, offering an attacker the ability to select an optimum target. Fourth, cyber warfare is waged in safety. Attacks against the United States have come from China, Serbia, the Philippines, and many other countries.[123] Finally, the effects of cyber warfare are increasingly widespread. From the ILOVEYOU virus to denial of service attacks, an increasing number of people are affected by cyber attacks. As they increase in sophistication, attacks may prove capable of doing more than deleting files on unprotected hard drives.

The cyber threat has not gone unnoticed in the halls of Congress, the Pentagon, and the White House. As early as 1997 the Pentagon acknowledged the threat to its information infrastructure in the QDR.[124] President Clinton also understood the threat and issued Presidential Decision Directive 63 (PDD-63), which created the National Infrastructure Protection Center at the FBI.[125] Congress has responded with efforts of its own, but has yet to pass effective legislation to protect America's information infrastructure.

Information security experts Bruce Schneier and Art Coviello do not share the same concern. They believe the cyber threat has been overstated. According to Schneier and Coviello, denial of service attacks temporarily prevent the use of email but do not constitute an act of cyber warfare.[126] This attitude is more prevalent among business leaders while federal and state officials are working to secure information networks and encouraging private firms to take similar precautions.[127]

Forward-Deployed Forces

In the decade prior to 9/11, al-Qaeda and its allies waged an asymmetric war against the United States' forward-deployed forces attacking American troops and personnel in Somalia (1993), Saudi Arabia (Khobar Tower bombing, 1995), Nairobi (American embassy, 1998), Dar es Salaam (American embassy, 1998), and Yemen [USS *Cole*, (DDG-67) 2000]. In the wake of the Afghanistan and Iraq invasions, American troops continue to fight a war in which a majority of American casualties come from the use of tactical asymmetry.

An adversary employing an asymmetric strategy against American forces has one of two strategic objectives. First, he may seek to deny the U.S. military access to the area of operation. This is as an anti-access strategy. Second, he may seek to force the early withdrawal of American troops. This is as an anti-deployment strategy. An adversary may resort to terrorism in combination with WMD to achieve their objective or low intensity insurgency.[128]

By deploying the world's most advanced military, the United States makes itself highly susceptible to anti-access strategies. In the opening phase of the Iraq War, American hardware was prominently on display. This high dollar hardware is designed to protect American lives but comes at a very steep price. The Navy is typically first to arrive in the area of operation. A battle group is often composed of a single aircraft carrier, several guided missile cruisers, several guided missile destroyers, one or more nuclear submarines, marine transports, support ships, and more than 100 aircraft. The combined value of this hardware exceeds $13 billion, providing an adversary an elusive but high value target.[129] Likewise, the Air Force and Army deploy aircraft, tanks, and other hardware that are expensive and difficult to replace.

Denying the United States access to an area of operation need not come at a high price. Bottom-rising and free-floating mines are inexpensive weapons capable of sinking or seriously damaging American warships. Low cost cruise, ballistic, and surface-to-air missiles are available from states and black market arms dealers.[130] Aircraft must also consider shoulder-fired missiles and rocket propelled grenades, which are among the least expensive and widely available weapons. Costs range from $600 to $40,000. Losing a $6 million helicopter and its crew to a $600 RPG is unacceptable and a cost that may exceed the United States' cost tolerance. This problem is exacerbated by the urban environment in which aircraft must now operate. Hidden fire from the urban jungle is difficult to locate and requires a precision response.

Anti-access measures are similar, with two primary exceptions. When the United States resorts to intervention, legitimate government has or is near collapse. In Lebanon (1981–1983) and Somalia (1991–1993), government had become ineffective as warring factions exerted territorial control. This meant American troops faced an adversary that is difficult to separate from the citizenry, using low technology weaponry in an unconventional manner.

During a full-scale invasion, such as Iraq, the United States may face a military or paramilitary force fighting to preserve the regime. Once the state's conventional forces are defeated, asymmetric tactics may be utilized if the regime refuses to capitulate. Even after capitulation, former regime elements may continue fighting, waging an asymmetric war. Such is the case in Iraq where Sunni-Baathists continue to wage a prolonged insurgency against Coalition forces. In Afghanistan, elements of the Taliban are reconstituting and beginning to make gains in the southern provinces.

If an invasion's opening phase is successful and the United States gains a firm foothold, an adversary shifts from an anti-access to anti-deployment strategy. Forcing the early withdrawal of American forces is a difficult task and requires the United States' cost tolerance be overcome through heavy casualties and the destruction of hardware. Urban combat eases the difficulty of this task. Regardless of the reason for American action, urban combat greatly restricts the advantage of advanced technology and makes it imperative that collateral damage is limited. The urban environment also makes it easier for combatants to move in and out of the civilian population unnoticed. Iraqi insurgents are utilizing this to the detriment of Coalition troops. The increase in Taliban attacks suggests that a similar strategy is being pursued almost five years after the initiation of Operation Enduring Freedom.

The dominant role urban combat now plays in anti-deployment strategies also shapes the tactics used against American forces.[131] Iraq is an excellent example of the tactical difficulties the United States can expect in the future. As of early 2004, car and roadside bombs were responsible for the deaths of 266 Americans. Small arms fire took 256 lives, which, between the two, represent more than 50 percent of casualties in Afghanistan and Iraq (2001–2004).[132] Low technology tactics such as these are inexpensive, require limited training, and will remain the greatest threat in the future.

As the United States continues in its role as global hegemon and leader in the Global War on Terror, American troops can expect to face strategic asymmetry designed specifically to deny and deter the application of American foreign policy. In its continued role as provider of international security, the United States will undoubtedly be called upon to provide stability to unstable nations. Those with much to gain from instability will resort to the tactics discussed above. This will require that the United States address the threat American servicemen and women face in the fulfillment of their mission.

WHAT IS THE FUTURE OF WARFARE?

Into the Fourth Generation

Months after Poland elected the first noncommunist president in the East Bloc and just weeks before the fall of the Berlin Wall, William S. Lind and a group of officers from the Army and Marine Corps wrote a seminal article in the *Marine Corps Gazette* suggesting that warfare was entering a fourth generation.[133] In the first generation, smoothbore muskets and linear warfare were the norm. World War I marked the second generation, where the machine gun and trench warfare ruled the day. Third generation warfare revolutionized grand strategy by again introducing total war into the equation. Here mechanized armies marched across Europe and Asia to defeat fascism and save communism. With the mechanization of the armed forces, tactical superiority became synonymous with mobility.

Fourth generation warfare, as envisioned by Lind, is different. Just as in World War II, society can expect to be the center of the battlefront. Warfare will not see a return to a time when society's elites sat upon the hilltops surrounding Manassas, Virginia, to watch the first battle of Bull Run in the fields below. Instead, war will take place in towns and cities where elites and average citizens reside. Maneuver will remain, as it was in third generation warfare, a necessary component of victory. Where mass was the key to victory for von Clausewitz, it has given way to the superiority of maneuver, just as it had in the third generation. Finally, wars of the future will require overcoming an adversary's will to resist rather than the destruction of his military capability.[134]

Technology, long a major force in the evolution of warfare, will undoubtedly play a primary role in the future. For Lind, the continuing advance of technology is blurring the lines between strategy and tactics as asymmetric approaches, such as terrorism, allow a small number of combatants to inflict disproportionate damage on society.[135] Technology, however, is not the sole force driving warfare in the fourth generation. Ideology plays a major role in the shape of the future. Unlike warfare during the struggle between communism and capitalism, non-Western cultures and movements, such as Islamic fundamentalism, must reject the Western way of war, turning to asymmetry to compensate for military and technological backwardness.

Looking forward to a future of asymmetric conflicts, Lind and other advocates of military transformation initiated the slow processes that came to be known as the Revolution in Military Affairs in the 1990s. The RMA is most pronounced in the technological superiority of the American military. A revolution in strategy and tactics has not, however, developed at such a rapid pace.[136] Among the services, the Cold War mind-set still persists despite more than a decade of fourth generation conflict illustrating the need for new approaches to conflict.

Defining Danger

As the global hegemon, the United States can expect to play a central role in the international security matrix. Although American leaders were slow to establish new rule-sets for a post-Cold War world, the wars in Afghanistan and Iraq forced the Bush administration and the Pentagon to reconcile current force structure, weapons programs, and doctrine to the danger the United States faces and is likely to face in the years to come. America's future conflicts are likely to share 12 key attributes:[137]

1. The United States will continue to intervene in the domestic conflicts of non-democracies and preemptively act against authoritarian regimes.

2. Not only is the United States likely to take military action in states that are non-democracies, but action is likely to be taken against states without a tradition of democracy or liberal government.[138]

3. Economic and political stability will have a tendency to be tenuous in the states where American forces find themselves.

4. An element of the instability generating American intervention is the continuation of long-running conflicts between ethnic or religious adversaries.[139]

5. These states will have significant levels of poverty and inequality generated by government policy and practices that provide substantial benefits to one segment of society and are unavailable to another.[140]

6. In cases in which the United States intervenes in the midst of long-running conflict, it is unlikely that there will be a clear distinction between the good and bad guys as America's adversaries are likely to change.[141]

7. Conflict will continue to persist in non-Western states, often in states that have made a particular effort to reject Western influence.[142]

8. Globalization of economics, politics, and culture threatens to eliminate the control illiberal regimes exercise within their borders. Thus, the United States can expect to find itself engaged in conflict in the places where globalization has had the least effect: fighting the forces opposed to globalization.[143]

9. States with high levels of military-to-military interaction with the United States have westernized militaries that are often moderate, forward looking, and desirous of stability rather than conflict with the United States. Those states with no or low military-to-military interaction with the United States are likely to come into conflict with the West.[144]

10. Future conflict is likely to take place in densely populated urban environments where America's adversaries will utilize the cover civilian populations provide.[145]

11. Future alliances will remain fluid as allies come and go depending upon economic and national interests and domestic politics.[146]

12. The Persian Gulf War and the wars in Afghanistan and Iraq taught America's future adversaries an important lesson. If you seek to confront the United States it must be done utilizing asymmetric means.[147]

Combat in the coming decades will undoubtedly require the United States to carefully choose the time and place of battle. American leaders can no longer wait for combat to come to them, as was the case at Pearl Harbor. Future warfare will resemble a chess game on a scale larger than ever before. When considering whether to intervene in the internal turmoil of a failed state or taking preemptive action against a state known to support al-Qaeda or a related terror network, American leaders must think several moves ahead.

Grid Centric Warfare

The strategic environment in which the United States will operate in the coming decades is one the Pentagon seeks to control by maintaining total information dominance. Analysts and senior officers have given great consideration to achieving this ambitious goal and consider it a key element of successfully waging future conflicts. Publications such as *Global Trends 2015, Joint Vision 2020,* and *The Four Thrusts* address the American military's need for a comprehensive integration of C[4]ISR data.[148]

Since the beginning of the RMA in the 1970s, technological advances have focused on improving and developing capabilities in eight major areas.[149] First, the United States has made dramatic strides in the development of precision-guided munitions. Second, "dominant maneuver," the ability to move ground forces anywhere at anytime, gives the United States improved capabilities. The addition of the M1-Al Abrams Main Battle Tank, Bradley Fighting Vehicle, and Striker vehicle are important components of dominant maneuver.[150] Third, and most important to air and naval forces, is the ability to minimize an adversary's capacity to determine the type and number of aircraft and combat vessels in a combat zone. To solve this problem the United States has developed stealth technologies. Fourth, advances in sensor technology (passive, space-based, airborne, ground, and naval) enable the United States to collect vast amounts of intelligence radio signals, sonar readings, video images, and telephone conversations. Fifth, space systems are among the greatest advances of the RMA, with improvements in data collection, satellite imagery, global positioning, and communication.[151] Sixth, the United States, led by the Air Force, has developed the world's most advanced unmanned aerial vehicles and is continuing to develop low-cost, pilotless technologies that are capable of flying into combat zones and hovering over targets for long periods of time.[152] Seventh, the military is actively working to improve and integrate new information technologies at all operational levels, improving the speed at which units can act and the reliability of information.[153] Finally, to protect the United States' information dominance, the Pentagon has developed substantial information-warfare capabilities suitable for both offense and defense.[154]

The drive for battlefield dominance through information superiority suggests the United States will not only continue to field combat systems that far surpass the capabilities of even its closest allies, but also offer units in the field a level of knowledge that is unsurpassed. For those on the cutting edge of information integration, the globe is quickly becoming a grid, much like a topographical map, in which analysts and operators can specify a grid coordinate and pull up all available data on that location and people in the area. Satellite imagery collected by the National Geospatial-Intelligence Agency, phone conversations of terrorists recorded by the National Security

Agency (NSA), terrorist profiles compiled by the Central Intelligence Agency (CIA), and recent intelligence collected from FBI informants would all be available to authorized users. Such an integrated network of information would provide Central Command the information necessary to make key strategic and tactical decisions with greater speed and accuracy. Precision-guided munitions could be directed with greater certainty of hitting the desired target. Human targets and their capabilities could be determined moments before a Special Forces unit moves to eliminate a target.

In the field, a company commander responsible for securing a Baghdad or Kabul neighborhood will have the ability to access real-time satellite imagery of the streets he and his men must clear. A soldier in the same company will be capable of conducting thermal imaging scans, sending the results back to Central Command for analysis. The ability to send and receive multiple source data will provide soldiers in the field and commanders an unprecedented capability.

The global grid envisioned here exists, in part, already. Real-time information moves to and from the battlefield almost instantaneously and soldiers and commanders have access to intelligence that far exceeds that available in the past. Two problems, however, prevent the development of a network with total information awareness. Data collection is spread among multiple departments and agencies within the federal government, each protecting the information they possess.[155] Until a unified information management system is created in which access, rather than information ownership, is the key, American troops will enter combat with incomplete knowledge of the battlefield. The second problem stems from the volume of data collected and the inability of current analysts and information management systems to separate relevant from irrelevant information. This is a difficult task that is proving to be overwhelming for agencies such as the NSA, which is tasked with interpreting the often encrypted messages of terrorists and other adversaries.

As the United States moves forward into the twenty-first century, warfare will continue to evolve as America's adversaries adapt at an ever-increasing pace to the technological superiority of the U.S. military. Adversaries, whether state or non-state actors, are developing strategies and tactics that rely on asymmetric approaches to strike the United States. American success will be determined by the Pentagon's ability to adapt. Grid centric warfare is one way the Pentagon is seeking to do just that while acting with greater speed and information.

CONCLUSION

The previous pages made an attempt to define, clarify, and explain a number of points. This was done by attempting to answer the following five important questions:

1. What is asymmetric warfare?
2. How does asymmetric warfare differ from other forms of unconventional conflict?
3. What is the American experience with asymmetric warfare?
4. What asymmetric threats does the United States face?
5. What is the future of warfare?

No longer is it possible for America's adversaries to stand and face the overwhelming might of the world's most powerful military. Defeating the United States is dependent on the successful utilization of asymmetry in warfare. Victories over Barbary pirates, Filipino *Insurectos*, Nicaraguan *Sandinos*, and Haitian *Cacos* taught Americans how to fight and win asymmetric conflicts. Post-Cold War conflicts have also provided the United States with additional experience. Somalia serves as an example of American failure while Bosnia-Herzegovina and Kosovo are yet to prove a success or failure.

As the United States continues to provide security and stability in its role as hegemon, threats from those who oppose the order imposed by American military might will continue to look to asymmetric conflict as a solution. Terrorism, WMD, and cyber war are proving difficult to manage. Increasingly, the United States is turning to technology as a solution, widening the tech gap between the United States and all others. For the Pentagon, the future is net centric. Information will flow at an increasing rate to and from the battlefield as integrated networks are developed. This will enable American troops to "get inside" the decision cycle of their adversaries and dominate the battlefield.

Throughout human history warfare has been ever present. Few points in recorded history are marked by prolonged periods of peace. And, while man has long been able to depend on conflict, the outcome is never guaranteed. Thus, the United States can never depend upon its technological superiority to defeat adversaries who are continuously adapting.

The chapters that follow examine three cases in which the United States found itself engaged in conflicts of asymmetry. Lebanon and Somalia were failures for the Reagan and Clinton administrations. Political and military leaders failed to adapt to the changing face of conflict. The third conflict, Afghanistan, has avoided many of the same pitfalls of the past, yet success remains uncertain. Each of the cases is examined with the goal of each chapter to provide a set of lessons learned which are then aggregated in the final analysis. The current chapter offers a broad understanding of asymmetry in its many forms. Now I turn to the details of the individual cases and a deeper analysis of the American experience with asymmetric conflict.

3

Lebanon (1982–1984): The Rise of Terrorism and the Suicide Bombing

Lebanon is the first of three cases in which I examine the American experience with asymmetric conflict. In each case five questions are asked:

1. What were the economic, military, and political conditions in Lebanon prior to American intervention?
2. What were American objectives?
3. How did the United States combat the asymmetric strategy and tactics of its adversary?
4. Were American objectives achieved?
5. What lessons did the United States learn from its experience?

These questions provide the structure and focus of the analysis. The emphasis of analysis remains on the tactical application of military force. A brief history of each country is also provided, as is the political context for American intervention, but the bulk of each case is dedicated to the analysis of the application of asymmetric means against the United States and the American response.

Lebanon is the first of three cases to meet the criteria established above and, interestingly, the first major American military action after withdrawal from Vietnam. Interestingly, Vietnam proved a greater tactical success than would the second American intervention in Lebanon (1982–1984). Like Vietnam, Lebanon was a political failure on a much smaller scale. It was in Lebanon that the United States had its first glimpse into many of the tactics that have come to be the bane of American forces in Iraq. For the United States, roadside bombs and suicide attacks came to prominence as terrorist tactics in Lebanon. While the United States learned from its experience in Lebanon, it made many of the same mistakes in the decade that followed when American troops sought to stabilize Somalia.

WHAT WERE THE ECONOMIC, MILITARY, AND POLITICAL CONDITIONS IN LEBANON PRIOR TO AMERICAN INTERVENTION?

After erupting in 1975, the Lebanese Civil War lasted nearly two decades, finally coming to an end in 1991. The conflict between Muslims and Christians, which served as an underlying cause of civil war, began almost 13 centuries earlier when the Christian region, now known as Lebanon, saw its first influx of Muslims. Lebanon, home of Christianity since the first century and the Maronite sect since the fifth century reacted violently to the eastward push of Islam. While violence was never constant, Maronites felt ill at ease in a world that came to be dominated by Islam.[1]

Understandably, Maronites welcomed Crusaders who made their way to the Holy Land from the tenth through the thirteenth centuries. Remaining one of the lone strongholds of Christianity in a region dominated by Islam, Lebanon developed strong ties to the West that endure to this day. The story of modern Lebanon, however, begins in the nineteenth century at the height of European colonialism. Maronites, sharing a common religion, language, and customs with the West (France), became wealthy merchants and traders, particularly in the nineteenth and early twentieth centuries.[2]

With Lebanon set to gain its independence from France in 1943, the endemic conflict between Maronites and their Druze, Shia, and Sunni neighbors required a solution. Based on the national census of 1932, a document known as the National Pact (1943) was developed to govern a newly independent Lebanon and distribute power among the major ethnic and religious groups.[3] The Druze and Shia, however, were largely left out of this power-sharing arrangement. Initially, the president was to be a Maronite and the prime minister a Sunni. Shiites were later guaranteed the Speaker's post in the National Assembly.[4]

Left out of the National Pact altogether were the Druze, a Muslim religious faction considered heretical by Sunni and Shia Muslims and longtime residents of the Chouf Mountains to the south and east of Beirut and the coastal plain. By 1949 Kamal Jumblatt, de facto leader of the Druze, established the Progressive Socialist Party (PSP) with Syrian support. This support enabled the PSP to continue its efforts to alter the established order, often through violent means.

Gamal Abdul Nasser, President of Egypt (1954–1970) and father of Arab nationalism, quickly established a close relationship with the Soviet Union in the 1950s. Nasser's efforts to eliminate Western power and influence in the Middle East and establish Egypt as the leader of the Arab world came to a head with Israel's invasion of the Suez and the occupation of the canal by British and French forces in 1956. Intervening on behalf of its client, the Soviet Union threatened to destroy the occupying forces, which subsequently withdrew after American pressure was applied to avoid a showdown.

America's interests in growing Soviet influence reached a critical point in 1958 when the pro-western King of Iraq, Faisal II, and his prime minister were assassinated in a military coup.[5] Simultaneously, efforts to overthrow King Hussein of Jordan were thwarted. With the outbreak of violence in Lebanon during the month of May and concerned that he and his government would face a fate similar to Iraq, Lebanon's President Camille Chamoun requested the support of American forces on July 14, 1958.[6]

President Eisenhower assented to Chamoun's request citing the destabilizing effects of Arab nationalism, the overthrow of Faisal II, the plot to overthrow King Hussein, and the peaceful nature of the Lebanese people as reasons for sending marines to Lebanon.[7] According to President Eisenhower, the mission of American forces was to "protect American lives—there are about 2,500 Americans in Lebanon—and by their presence to assist the Government of Lebanon to preserve its territorial integrity and political independence."[8]

On July 15, 1958, marines from the Sixth Fleet landed on the beaches of Beirut.[9] Quickly securing Beirut International Airport (BIA) and the city's port, the marines were soon reinforced by soldiers from the Army's European Command. At their peak, American forces in Lebanon exceeded 10,000 men. With a formidable American presence patrolling the streets of Beirut and neighboring towns and villages, the rioting that began in May after the assassination of anti-Chamoun newspaper editor Nassit el Metui quickly ended and Lebanon returned to a state of peace.[10] With little fanfare, the American mission ended in success.

Today, Operation BLUEBAT is considered one of America's most successful military operations. Civil war was averted, Soviet effort (real or perceived) to further alter the strategic balance in the Middle East was prevented, and the United States flexed its muscle in a region with substantial economic and political interests. In an operation that saw the last American forces depart Lebanon before October 15, 1958, the Eisenhower Doctrine was validated by the force of American arms.[11]

When the United States returned to Lebanon 25 years later, conditions in the country were dramatically different. Civil war (1975–1976) and factional violence (1976–1991) had ravaged the country by 1982. Many

Lebanese were impoverished by the violence and a large segment of Lebanon's infrastructure lay in ruins. Although civil strife is endemic in Lebanese history, the tipping point in Lebanon's 16-year conflict can be traced to a more recent event: the immigration of tens of thousands of Palestinian refugees in the late 1960s.

Overwhelmed by the number of Palestinian refugees living in Jordan and threatened by militant Palestinians, King Hussein evicted many of the 400,000 refugees from Jordan. Leaving Jordan, many Palestinians settled in Southern Lebanon where they continued waging a low intensity war against Israel.[12] The destabilizing effects of a foreign military on Lebanese soil, in the form of the Palestinian Liberation Army (PLA), soon caused the Lebanese government to attempt a similar eviction of Palestinian militants.[13] Lacking the military strength to expel a force of over 6,000 Palestinian fighters, the Lebanese Armed Forces (LAF) and President Suleiman Frangieh requested the assistance of Syria, which deployed 40,000 troops in Lebanon to fight Palestinian militants.[14]

Syria had long sought to incorporate Lebanon into a greater Syria, which the Lebanese government soon came to suspect was the case as Syrian force occupied greater and greater portions of Lebanon in the months following their initial intervention. Continued Palestinian attacks on Israel and a growing menace posed by Syria led Israel to invade Southern Lebanon in March 1978. As the expanding violence continued, Israel aligned itself with the Christian militias waging war against the Syrian-backed Druze and Sunni militias. By 1982, the Shiites in Southern Lebanon were receiving support from their co-religionists in Iran as they also waged war against the Phalange and other Christian militias, as well as Israel and the LAF, which sought to establish government control over the entire country.

The Israeli Defense Force (IDF) dramatically altered the balance of power in Lebanon in June of 1982 when it launched a major invasion from positions south of the Litani River in Southern Lebanon. Israeli forces launched air strikes, heavy artillery, and mechanized infantry against Palestinian positions south of Beirut and Druze/Syrian positions in the Chouf and Beqaa Valley. As Israeli forces rapidly pushed the PLA north and destroyed Syrian aircraft, artillery, and tanks, President Reagan's envoy to the Middle East, Ambassador Philip Habib, persuaded Israel to halt its advance as the IDF reached the outskirts of Beirut and began pounding Palestinian positions in the city.[15]

In accordance with the terms agreed upon by the PLA, IDF, Government of Lebanon, and the United States, American marines would oversee the withdrawal of Palestinian fighters who would depart Beirut from the city's port and be removed to host countries.[16] It was into this highly volatile situation that marines of the 32nd Marine Amphibious Unit (MAU) entered Beirut on August 25, 1982.[17]

WHAT WERE AMERICAN OBJECTIVES?

When the marines of the 32nd MAU (BLT 2/8) landed on the beaches of Beirut, their objective was simple. They were to secure the port of Beirut, disarm and embark Palestinian fighters onto the Greek ship *Sol Georgious,* docked at the port, and complete the mission by returning to American war ships waiting off shore. In two messages received by Colonel James M. Mead, commanding officer of the 32nd MAU, before going ashore, General Robert H. Barrow, commandant of the Marine Corps, explained the marines' mission saying, "You will soon be engaged in carrying out an extremely important mission in Beirut. Clearly, it is also a most difficult and delicate one. Your soldierly virtues, especially discipline, will in all likelihood be severely tested. At this critical hour you will serve as the primary instrument of our national will to further the course of peace in that region." General Barrow went on to add, "As Marines you will meet the challenge and acquit yourselves, not only honorably, but with distinction. The eyes of your countrymen will be on you as surely as their hearts are with you."[18]

A second message from President Reagan elaborated on the marines' objective stating, "You are about to embark on a mission of great importance to our nation and the free world. The conditions under which you carry out your vital assignment are, I know, demanding and potentially dangerous. You are tasked to be once again what Marines have been for more than 200 years—peacemakers. Your role in the Multinational Force—along with that of your French and Italian counterparts—is crucial to achieving the peace that is so desperately needed in this long-tortured city. I expect that you will perform with the traditional esprit and discipline for which the Marine Corps is renowned. Godspeed. Ronald Reagan."[19]

Simultaneously, Secretary of State George Schultz continued diplomatic efforts to reach a permanent solution in Lebanon.[20] President Reagan and his counterparts in the region understood that a multinational peacekeeping force served only temporary needs. A long-term solution would either be won on the battlefield or through diplomatic negotiations. The marine presence in Lebanon was designed to give the latter time to develop.

Successfully completing their mission by the second week of September, Secretary of Defense Caspar Weinberger offered accolades to Colonel Mead and the marines of the 32nd MAU on a flawless mission.[21] Israel's Minister of Defense, Ariel Sharon, also offered his compliments to the marines for their efficient removal of thousands of Palestinian fighters.[22] The success of the marines was viewed as a positive step toward long-term peace efforts. With Palestinian fighters no longer trapped in Beirut and the city no longer under siege, stability was given a legitimate chance.

Only weeks after the marines withdrew to ships of the Sixth Fleet, events in Lebanon took a turn for the worse as Israeli war planes began pounding

Palestinian, Druze, and Syrian positions along the Beirut-Damascus Highway and in the Beqaa Valley.[23] Two events played a crucial role in President Reagan's decision to send the marines back to Lebanon. First, President-elect Bashir Gemayel, leader of the Maronite Phalange, was assassinated on September 14, 1982, by a bomb placed in a room adjacent to the room in which he was speaking before a Lebanese women's group. Second, in retaliation for Gemayel's death, Phalange militiamen entered the Sabra and Shantilla refugee camps on September 16, two days after Gemayel's death, killing 800 Palestinians while searching for those responsible for the assassination.[24]

Realizing that violence would escalate out of control, Amin Gemayel, elected by the National Assembly to replace his brother, requested that the Multi-National Force (MNF) return to Lebanon. Returning on September 29, 1982, Colonel Mead and Lieutenant Colonel Robert B. Johnston led their men back into Beirut where they were tasked with holding Beirut International Airport after Israeli forces withdrew to the south, while the French and Italian elements of the MNF held adjacent sectors north of the airport.[25]

In a letter to the Speaker of the House and president pro tempore of the Senate, President Reagan described the objective of the marines saying, "Their mission is to provide an interposition force at agreed locations and thereby provide the multinational presence requested by the Lebanese Government to assist it and the Lebanese Armed Forces (LAF)."[26] He added, "I believe that this step will support the objective of helping to restore the territorial integrity, and political independence of Lebanon. It is the continuing effort of the United States to bring lasting peace to that troubled country, which has too long endured the trials of civil strife and armed conflict."[27]

For the marines, deploying to Beirut was viewed as a peacekeeping operation in which the rules of engagement (ROE) strictly limited the ability of the marines to take offensive action to provide security in their sector. The highly circumscribed ROE may have been adequate for an operation absent hostility, but as the marines would soon find out, this did not describe Lebanon.[28]

The rules of engagement were simple:

1. When on post, mobile, or foot patrol, keep loaded magazine in weapon, bolt closed, weapon on safe, no round in the chamber.
2. Do not chamber a round unless told to do so by a commissioned officer or unless you must act in immediate self-defense where deadly force is authorized.
3. Keep ammo for crew served weapons readily available, but not loaded. Weapon is on safe.
4. Call local forces (LAF) to assist in self-defense effort. Notify headquarters.
5. Use only minimum degree of force to accomplish any mission.

6. Stop the use of force when it is no longer needed to accomplish the mission.
7. If you must receive effective hostile fire, direct your fire at the source. If possible, use friendly snipers.
8. Respect civilian property; do not attack it unless absolutely necessary to protect friendly forces.
9. Protect innocent civilians from harm.
10. Respect and protect recognized medical agencies such as the Red Cross, Red Crescent, etc.[29]

For the marines of BLT 22/8 these rules of engagement were burned into their minds as they served as the basis for determining which course of action each marine would take when a situation arose.

As Colonel Thomas M. Stokes and the 24th MAU (BLT 23/8) arrived on October 29, 1982, to relieve the 32nd MAU, Beirut remained quiet with the only signs of conflict coming when Israeli positions, south of BIA, came under fire from Druze and Palestinian positions in the Chouf. When Colonel Stokes took control of the American sector, the marines were experiencing the calm before the storm. BIA was opened to commercial traffic. Shiites in the neighborhoods adjacent to the airport, which the marines called "Hooterville," welcomed marine patrols. All was proceeding according to the plan.[30]

Challenges to American objectives first arose in January 1983 when armored Israeli patrols entered the American sector at BIA. For the Israelis, it was an opportunity to test the marine response.[31] Throughout January, Israeli vehicles were stopped and sent back to their positions. In the most serious incident, a marine officer climbed atop an Israeli tank where he drew his pistol and ordered the Israelis to exit the airport.[32] Such testing of the marines soon ended as Colonel Stokes met with his IDF counterpart to put an end to Israeli incursions.

The 24th MAU was relieved by the 22nd MAU (BLT 22/6) during the third week of February. Returning for the second time as commander of the marine contingent in Beirut, Colonel Mead continued to maintain a force posture which sought to preserve the neutrality of the United States among the warring factions.[33] Given the lack of artillery, tanks, limited rules of engagement, and the tactical weakness of the marines' position at BIA, there was little choice for the MAU but neutrality.

The first signs of trouble came in March 1983 when marines were ambushed by small arms fire, taking five casualties.[34] Four men were arrested, but ties to one or more of the Islamic factions could not be established. This incident failed to raise alarm bells. Instead, on April 16, in an attack mirroring the bombing of the marine barracks six months later, a van loaded with 2,000 pounds of explosives drove into the lobby of the American embassy in Beirut, detonating after the driver fled. The embassy was destroyed and 63 civilian and military personnel were killed.[35]

For the marines in Lebanon, the destruction of the embassy fundamentally altered the objective of their mission. Officially, however, the mission's objective remained the same. No punitive efforts were taken against the Iranian-backed group which claimed responsibility for the attack. Instead, diplomatic efforts to reach a solution to the Arab-Israeli conflict were renewed and restrictions on the rules of engagement were relaxed slightly to give the marines greater freedom of action.[36]

Beginning May 5, 1983, fighting intensified between Christian militias and Druze forces occupying the Chouf and Kalde. This left BLT 22/6 in an exposed position between two opposing forces. They neither had the mandate nor the firepower to force either side to cease operations. In addition to the difficult tactical position in which the marines found themselves, they were also required to rely on the LAF for protection should an element of the multinational force come under heavy fire.

The weakness of the LAF left the marines' position exceptionally difficult. As a national military, the LAF was poorly equipped, led, and trained. Morale was low and the division between Christian and Muslim soldiers within the LAF greatly weakened its combat effectiveness. Thus, when the marines came under heavy fire beginning in late August, the LAF was unable to provide the protection needed to eliminate Amaal and Druze positions firing on BIA.[37]

When Colonel Timothy J. Geraghty, commander of the 24th MAU, and Lieutenant Colonel Howard L. Gerlach, BLT 21/8 commander, relieved the 22nd MAU and BLT 22/6 in late May 1983, neither man could have predicted the dramatic escalation they would soon face. In the immediate aftermath of their arrival, the new BLT and supporting elements spent the first days of June substantially improving the defensive positions they held around the airport. In a city that was deteriorating into chaos, the American objective remained the same.[38] This left the force of 1,500 men in a precarious position.

The MAU/BLT position and the commander's effort to maintain neutrality was further weakened by the overt assistance the United States provided the Government of Lebanon. Advanced training provided to LAF air assault units by senior marine noncommissioned officers linked the United States to a government the Druze, Palestinians, and Shiites viewed as Christian and pro-Israeli. President Reagan maintained overt support for the Government of Lebanon while also seeking to create a stable environment in which Lebanon could solve its problems. Yet few in Washington realized that the marines in Beirut were becoming increasingly viewed as part of the problem, rather than the solution.

On August 10, marines returned fire for the first time against Amaal militiamen harassing combat posts at BIA and patrols in neighborhoods near the airport.[39] It was not, however, until August 28 that heavy combat spilled into the airport as LAF strong points in the area came under sustained fire from Druze positions to the east.[40] On August 29, Alpha Company and adjacent LAF forces found themselves coming under small arms fire as well as steady grenade and mortar attacks from Amaal positions in the burnt out buildings 100 to 200 yards from the airport. Returning fire, the marines and LAF poured lead into Hooterville. When the fighting subsided, two marines were dead and seven wounded.[41]

Staff Sergeant Alexander Ortega was killed by a single bullet wound to the head. Lieutenant George Losey, an Alpha Company platoon leader, suffered massive trauma and died after an 82 mm mortar round struck his command tent.[42] Almost immediately, the White House expressed its sadness after the casualties were confirmed and reiterated, "Our forces are there at the request of the Government of Lebanon in helping to provide security for the Lebanese people."[43]

As the IDF pulled back to the Litani River during the first week of September, LAF and Druze forces fought for control of evacuated towns and villages in the Chouf.[44] Poor performance by the LAF brought BIA under continued fire and the guns of the Sixth Fleet into action. After two marines were killed in fighting on September 6, the United States escalated its role in assisting the LAF by providing naval gunfire support from the USS *Bowen*, which fired into Druze batteries in the Chouf.[45]

While the objective of the multinational force never officially changed, it is apparent that Washington viewed the role of the marines in a different light in the first days of September 1983. As attacks from Amaal and Druze positions intensified throughout the month, the marines no longer saw themselves as a force of interposition, but in a fight for their lives. Fighting continued on a daily basis throughout September and October with the combat posts furthest from the airport's main complex receiving the heaviest fire.

Combat in September and October gave Colonel Geraghty reason to bring mortars, artillery, naval gunfire, and Cobra attack helicopters into the fight.[46] For President Reagan, the escalation in attacks against the marines at BIA was viewed, at least in part, as a Soviet effort to force the United States' withdrawal from the Middle East.[47] In the president's struggle against the Soviet Union, the United States would not back down.

Events culminated on the morning of October 23, 1983, when a van loaded with 12,000 pounds of explosives ran several marine checkpoints crashing through barricades and into the lobby of the BLT Headquarters where hundreds of marines were spending their Sunday morning catching up on sleep.[48] Within days of the bombing, Vice President George H.W. Bush, Commandant of the Marine Corps General Paul X. Kelley, and other high-ranking civilian and military personnel visited Beirut to view the devastation and determine the course of action the United States should take.

President Reagan delivered an address to the nation four days after the tragedy where he again reiterated American objectives and the need for intervention in Lebanon. The president cited four reasons for American involvement:

1. The Middle East is a powder keg.
2. The region is important to the economic and political life of the West.
3. Since 1948 the United States has accepted the moral obligation to ensure the survival of Israel.
4. Syria must not be allowed to incorporate Lebanon into a greater Syria, which is host to more than 7,000 Soviet advisors.

President Reagan added, "As to the narrower question—what exactly is the operational mission of the marines—the answer is, to secure a piece of Beirut, to keep order in their sector, and to prevent the area from becoming a battlefield."[49] He went on to say that the peace process would be accelerated; the United States and its allies would continue to support the Government of Lebanon, and the Multinational Force would receive the protection needed. Support for maintaining the American presence in Beirut remained high following President Reagan's October 27 speech with polls showing 67 percent of Americans favored keeping marines in Beirut.[50]

In his public statements in the months that followed, President Reagan continued to hold firm on the objectives first stated in the weeks before marines first landed in Beirut (1982).[51] By February 1984 the Long Commission's work was complete and it was clear to the president and the Joint Chiefs that there was little the United States could achieve by remaining in Lebanon.[52] More Americans had fallen in the months since the attack on the BLT Headquarters and the prospects for a diplomatic solution were grim. By late February, the marines were gone.[53]

The USS *New Jersey* began pounding Druze positions in the Chouf within minutes of the departure of the last marines. Its 16-inch guns laid waste to fighting positions used to attack the airport in the previous months. Strike aircraft also hit positions east of Beirut. The loss of two American fighters soon ended punitive strikes against Syrian and Iranian allied groups.

The final end of the American presence in Beirut came on July 31, 1984, when marines guarding the makeshift American embassy returned to ships of PHIBRON 6, waiting in the Mediterranean. For two years the United States attempted to resolve the lingering conflict in Lebanon but, ultimately, went home empty handed. Bringing peace to a war-ravaged country proved a more difficult task than 1,500 marines and a politically sensitive administration could handle.

HOW DID THE UNITED STATES COMBAT THE ASYMMETRIC STRATEGY AND TACTICS OF ITS ADVERSARY?

When the MNF entered Lebanon in 1982, guerrilla warfare dominated the tactical milieu in the war-ravaged country. Acting as a force of interposition, American, French, Italian, and later, British forces sought to deter continued conflict through intimidation. It was not aggressive action on the part of the MNF that the United States and its allies relied on to pressure the warring factions into peace, but the available military strength and determination of the intervening countries. The lightly armed MNF was outmanned and outgunned by all sides in the Lebanese conflict. It was their role as impartial arbiter and the threat of large-scale intervention that gave the MNF any hope of success. When Syria and Iran realized by mid-1983 that MNF states were unwilling to escalate their role in the conflict, intimidation failed and Amaal and Druze forces sought to dislodge the MNF.[54]

Upon taking control of the airport in late September 1982, the first task the BLT faced was clearing the thousands of mines littering the perimeter of BIA.[55] This initial effort generated the first marine casualties as one de-mining team struck an unexploded mine costing one marine his life. Outside of this single incident, the second half of 1982 offered the marines little to concern themselves with.[56] Fighting was largely between Druze and Israeli units in the Chouf and, on occasion, Druze and Phalange forces further north. When marine patrols began making their way through the streets of Shiite neighborhoods in November 1982, the inhabitants offered refreshing drinks and snacks to marine patrols. According to Colonel Mead, "The Muslims waved to, slapped hands with every Marine with whom they came into contact. They returned the smiles of our proud young peacekeepers. They cried."[57]

In addition to offering a friendly face and candy to children, the marines sought to gain the trust and support of local residents by assisting them in small-scale projects. In February 1983, heavy winter snows in the mountains southeast of Beirut left many villagers trapped and in need of food and medical attention. Neither the LAF nor American aviators were able to reach the isolated villagers by air, which left the MAU to rescue those in need. The mission was difficult but successful as the marines traversed the icy passes in their amphibious assault vehicles, bringing sick villagers back to Beirut.[58] Despite efforts to provide relief and security to Lebanese civilians, MNF forces began to find Lebanese Muslims increasingly hostile. A March 16, 1983, ambush of American and Italian patrols was among the earliest signs that the MNF would soon find itself engaged in an asymmetric conflict with Amaal, Druze, and Palestinian fighters.[59] While four men were arrested for the ambush, there was no broader response to the attack. This signaled those opposed to the MNF that their attacks would go unpunished.

Perhaps the single event which signaled the onset of asymmetric conflict was the April 18 bombing of the American embassy. While there had been a car bombing the previous October and human intelligence regularly warned of such attacks, the destruction of the embassy illustrated the sophistication and capability of hostile forces. Later, on April 28, two men driving a green Mercedes were captured as they attempted a drive-by shooting outside the British/American embassy. One week later, Colonel Mead's helicopter was hit by small arms fire causing little damage but again offering a sign of the fight to come.[60] The following day, Druze artillery positions opened fire on the USS *Fairfax County,* patrolling nearby waters. The ship was not hit, but the success of previous attacks and the lack of a substantial response to past attacks clearly emboldened the MNF's adversaries.

Just as attacks against the marines began to increase, the 22nd MAU was relieved by the 24th MAU. Aware of the increasing fire, the relieving force continued to operate under highly restricted rules of engagement. Initially, BLT 1/8 improved the defensive positions they manned at the airport. Over half a million sandbags, 1,000 engineering stakes, and 10,000 feet of concertina wire were utilized to provide a level of safety appropriate for what was essentially a peacekeeping mission.[61] As attacks against marines at BIA increased, the reinforced positions provided a good measure of protection against small arms fire and the few artillery rounds that landed inside the American sector.

As the summer wore on, however, neighborhoods patrolled by the marines became increasingly hostile. Young children showed overt hostility throwing rocks at patrols and hurling insults such as, "Khomeini good; America no good."[62] In one instance, a Navy corpsman on patrol found a teen bearing down on him when he turned and knocked the teen to the ground, stepping over the boy and continuing on patrol.

When the marines at BIA returned fire for the first time on August 10, 1983, it was clear that humanitarian aid, intimidation, and neutrality had failed. Then, when BLT 1/8 and Alpha Company found themselves under sustained fire on August 29, peacekeepers were still operating under restricted rules of engagement. The marines were permitted to return fire on positions firing on them, but never to preempt an attack. When Amaal fighters shifted to new positions, walking in the open with their weapons hidden under their clothing, marine snipers could only watch and wait until coming under fire again. In the wake of the August 28–31 attacks on BIA, Colonel Geraghty suspended patrols in Beirut.[63] Doing so emboldened Amaal and Druze fighters, further encouraging them to continue their attacks on marine posts in and around the airport.

On September 8 the USS *Bowen* opened fire on Druze artillery positions southeast of the airport, yet the marines did not use naval gunfire support to their advantage, acting aggressively to maneuver around and eliminate Amaal and Druze firing positions. Instead, they remained in their combat posts awaiting the next attack. Passive response to continuing harassment was not taken because the marines of the 24th MAU lacked the qualities of two centuries of marines. The rules of engagement and the MNF mission prohibited aggressive action. No one in the chain of command ever realized that the early advantages (aid, intimidation, and neutrality) possessed by the MNF had disappeared. Leaders in London, New York, Paris, Rome, and Washington were unwilling to take back the initiative.

As casualties slowly mounted throughout the summer and early fall, Colonel Geraghty and Lieutenant Colonel Gerlach relaxed the rules of engagement allowing BLT 1/8 marines the freedom to engage targets that posed a threat. In an early September situational report Colonel Geraghty explained, "All ops in this report were protective in nature, either passive, building or reinforcing positions, or active; locating hostile weapons firing on the BIA. Marines returned the fire where appropriate." He went on to say, "The increasing involvement in direct and more frequent combat actions has tasked the MAU assets to their fullest."[64]

Although the MAU brought artillery, attack helicopters, mortars and tanks into the American sector, harassment continued.[65] Additional firepower brought little relief. As long as Amaal and Druze forces viewed the Americans as weak and unable or unwilling to leave their defensive positions, there was little hope of ending the attacks. The Government of Lebanon understood the Amaal and Druze perception of the United States.

In an effort to promote peace and end the attacks against American forces, President Gemayel urged President Reagan to flex American muscle and increase the size of forces in Lebanon while acting more aggressively to defeat anti-American factions.[66] The United States' failure to respond effectively after the March ambush, April embassy bombing, May-September artillery attacks, and August-September small arms fire emboldened Syria as well. Lebanon's ambassador to the United States, Abdullah Bouhabib, explained the Syrian view saying, "Syria looks at the United States and they see this dormant giant...So there is no deterrent for them."[67] As long as the United States failed to take aggressive action, Syria would wait out the United States while providing training and material to those inflicting casualties on American forces. Iran's position was very similar.

While BLT 1/8 faced almost daily artillery and small arms attacks (September-October), the marines' closest ally, the LAF, was engaged in a hard-fought battle to control the villages abandoned by the IDF in the first week of September. With the LAF performing poorly and the United States unwilling to leave its defensive positions at BIA, opponents of the United States viewed America as little more than a paper tiger.[68] Thus, attacks continued against the BLT throughout September and October.

In the aftermath of the October 23 bombing, Commandant of the Marine Corps Paul X. Kelley testified before the Senate Armed Services Committee that "only extraordinary security could have met the massive and unanticipated threat.''[69] He pointed out that since June 1, 1983, intelligence reports warned of possible car bombings on over 100 occasions. Prior to the October 23 attack, there had never been a suicide attack against the United States. In previous car bombings, vehicles were detonated remotely or the vehicle's driver fled before the explosion. This gave American troops time to act before an explosion and made deterrence less difficult.

Just four days prior to the BLT Headquarters bombing, Colonel Geraghty was nearly killed when his jeep passed a parked vehicle, which exploded.[70] For Colonel Geraghty and Lieutenant Colonel Gerlach, two issues played a pivotal role in the success of the October 23 attack. First, neither officer conceived of a suicide attack. Second, it was the mission of the marines to restore a sense of normalcy to Beirut. Had the airport become a virtual fortress, their presence would have failed to serve this purpose.

As volunteers cleared the rubble in a desperate search for survivors, the airport became the very thing Colonel Geraghty sought to avoid. In the hours after the bombing, Senator Sam Nunn appeared on *Meet the Press* saying, ''We are no longer a deterrent force in Lebanon. Our marines are hostages.''[71] The inaccuracy in Senator Nunn's remarks was in failing to point out that the marines effectively became hostage in the early days of September.

Soon Congress entered the fray calling for an increased presence in Beirut to provide added protection for the force that remained.[72] With the 22nd MAU's diversion to Grenada, the 24th MAU remained in Beirut longer than expected and continued to come under fire daily. As with previous attacks against American interests, the United States failed to respond credibly to the attack which killed 241 marines and sailors. Failing to respond emboldened Amaʾal fighters further and on November 7 Alpha Company was withdrawn from forward combat posts at the Lebanese University as more than 100 fighters amassed for an attack on Alpha Company.[73] One 18-year veteran of the Marine Corps described the situation around him: ''We have everything going against us. There are a lot of folks who don't want us here, and they use guns to say so. We are on the low ground, exposed on all fronts. We are here only to show the flag and to support the Lebanese government. We're not proper peacekeepers.'' He added, ''This is a no-win situation.''[74]

The United States also found Syria and Iran emboldened by the lack of an adequate response to the October 23 bombing.[75] Syria no longer found it necessary to participate in peace talks.[76] For Syria and Iran, Lebanon became a waiting game. Signals from Washington led the Syrians to believe that the United States would soon pull out of the MNF. Hunkered down in reinforced positions at BIA, the small American force was protected by the 16-inch guns of the USS *New Jersey* and Navy fighter bombers. This protection was not absolute as the shooting down of two American fighters over Syrian positions in the Chouf-weakened air cover afforded the remnants of the 24th MAU.[77]

Despite President Reagan's insistence that an American presence was needed in Beirut, Congress increased pressure on the president to pull the embattled marines out.[78] France, which lost 50 men in a similar car bombing on October 23, began reducing the size of its contingent in early January. [79] By February the United States followed suit.[80] It would, however, require an additional five months and the completion of the new American embassy before the last marines left Lebanon.

The failure to successfully combat the asymmetric means employed by those that opposed the American presence in Beirut lies with decision makers at the highest levels of the chain of command, not the marine rifleman huddled in a sandbag bunker in Beirut. The rules of engagement denied the marines the freedom to effectively neutralize those who sought to force the United States from Lebanon. Whether the blame belongs with President Reagan, Congress, or senior officers will continue to be a point of debate. What is clear, however, is that the passive American presence in Lebanon proved inadequate for the task it was given. As later peacekeeping operations have shown, the inability or unwillingness to aggressively maintain peace is viewed as weakness by those who would seek to destroy the prospects for lasting stability.[81]

WERE AMERICAN OBJECTIVES ACHIEVED?

When President Reagan announced the United States' offer to provide safe conduct to the PLA fighters trapped in Beirut on July 6, 1982, American involvement in the Lebanese crisis was about to begin.[82] The role played by the United States in the months and years that followed taxed not only the Reagan administration, but American foreign policy in the Middle East. And, while there were some successes, the broader mission failed when 241 marines and sailors died on October 23, 1983.

American intervention in Lebanon can be broken into three phases. Although these phases are, to a degree, arbitrarily denoted, they provide useful insight into the 18-month American intervention in Beirut. First, and unquestionably the most successful phase, began with the arrival of the 32nd MAU on August 25, 1982.[83] Marines landing at the port of Beirut were tasked with providing safe conduct to Palestinian fighters trapped in Beirut by the advancing IDF. Their objective was clear: establish checkpoints at the entrance to the port, escort disarmed PLA fighters to the *Sol Georgious* docked at the port, and accomplish this without incident. Colonel Mead's men were to ensure that fighting did not break out as crowds of supporters gathered to see off armed men, women, and children making their way to the port and aboard ship.

By the end of the initial phase, over 6,000 Palestinians made their way through marine checkpoints and aboard ship.[84] While there were moments of tension as heavily armed fighters were forced to relinquish their weapons before passing marine checkpoints, the mission was an overwhelming success. Within weeks of entering Beirut, marines achieved their objective and returned to ships of the Sixth Fleet.

Before the 32nd MAU could complete its Mediterranean deployment, however, Colonel Mead and his men found themselves returning to Beirut in the wake of President-elect Bashir Gemayel's assassination and the retaliatory Phalange massacre at the Sabra and Shantilla refugee camps, which again destabilized Lebanon in mid-September. With Amin Gemayel chosen to replace his brother, the new president-elect requested the United States return to Lebanon as part of a multinational force necessary for the stabilization of Lebanon, which threatened to spiral into internecine violence. Thus began the second phase of the American intervention in Beirut as the 32nd MAU began arriving on September 29,1982.[85]

Serving as a force of interposition, the marines' objective was to secure Beirut International Airport and adjacent neighborhoods, while providing needed security to civilians at the airport and in the remainder of the American sector.[86] As discussed above, the initial response to the American presence was positive. Marines succeeded in clearing mine fields surrounding the airport, returning BIA to full operation. Patrols in the adjacent neighborhoods offered impoverished Shiites a level of security long since absent. American forces controlling the airport also succeeded in separating the IDF from Druze and Shia militias, which reduced the level of conflict in the area. Had the second American intervention in Lebanon ended before heavy fighting began August 29, 1983, it would have generally been considered a success. For a period of 10 months the marines succeeded in suppressing conflict at BIA, Lebanese University, and in the Bourj-al-Bourajiniah suburb of Beirut.

Foreign intervention was, however, never popular with many elements engaged in the ongoing conflict and, as the United States became more closely associated with the Government of Lebanon, the American presence declined in popularity. Attacks against American assets began to increase in the wake of the April 1983 American embassy bombing. Failing to aggressively respond to mounting attacks may have led to the dramatic decline in the security of the American sector. Amaal fighters began openly carrying weapons in the neighborhoods adjacent to the airport, and the threat of Druze artillery attacks forced the closure of BIA to commercial aircraft.[87]

The daily attacks faced by marine combat posts marked the beginning of phase three. When attacks began August 29, BLT 21/8 found itself unable to respond with aggressive force. This left the marines little choice but to return fire from their sandbagged positions. Fighting in this manner provided no long-term solution to the men facing an adversary who fought by a very different set of rules.

Colonel Geraghty and the men of the 22nd MAU found themselves in a precarious position. As a peacekeeping force, aggressive action was outside their mission and contrary to American objectives in Lebanon. Promoting stability and the disengagement of warring factions was clearly contrary to an aggressive American response to early attacks. Yet, by late August, the marines found themselves embroiled in heavy fighting. Not only did the White House and Pentagon cede the initiative to America's adversaries in the spring of 1983, they placed a Marine Amphibious Unit in a tactically indefensible position. Colonel Geraghty's termination of patrols after the August 29 attacks failed to send a credible signal to Washington that the small marine force must be augmented or withdrawn. The administration and the Pentagon failed to account for the changing situation in which the MAU found itself.[88]

The October 23, 1983, bombing and the subsequent American withdrawal from the MNF were the most overt examples of a mission that ended in failure. With the Reagan administration's failure to understand the difficult nature of peacekeeping operations, the mission may have been doomed from the start. Among administration officials, Secretary Weinberger was alone in his ardent opposition to American involvement in any peacekeeping operation in Lebanon. According to then Assistant Secretary of Defense for International Security Affairs Francis J. West, "The Department of Defense didn't want our troops going in at all in that kind of situation." He added, "There wasn't a military mission...We could understand why people might want us there as a symbol and guarantee, but a symbol and guarantee of what? It wasn't peacekeeping; there wasn't really a peace to keep. It wasn't taking out some hostiles. It didn't strike us as being an appropriate mission to use American military force."[89] Secretary Weinberger lost the fight to keep American forces out of Beirut but was proven correct in the end.

Despite the small American force's initial success, it will be the deaths of 241 Americans that will forever be remembered. Had that culminating event never taken place, it is likely that American intervention in Lebanon would have been all but forgotten in much the same fashion as the deployment of 10,000 troops 25 years earlier was. That did not happen. And, in the decades since, the United States has struggled to successfully manage conflict around the globe.

WHAT LESSONS DID THE UNITED STATES LEARN FROM ITS EXPERIENCE?

On November 7, 1983, the secretary of defense convened the DoD Commission on Beirut International Airport Terrorist Act, October 23, 1983. Commonly called the Long Commission, senior military officers spent six weeks investigating what went wrong on that fateful October morning and with the broader American mission in Lebanon. In their finding released in mid-December, several conclusions and recommendations were offered.

Analysis of the mission concluded "that the 'presence' mission was not interpreted the same by all levels of the chain of command and that perceptual differences regarding that mission, including the responsibility of the USMNF for the security of Beirut International Airport, should have been recognized and corrected by the chain of command."[90] This rather damning remark, directed toward the leadership of Colonel Geraghty and Lieutenant Colonel Gerlach, suggests that both commanders were negligent in the security posture set at BIA. While failure must ultimately rest on the shoulders of a commanding officer, the MAU and BLT commanders' actions were consistent with the rules of engagement, which required American forces rely on the LAF for security, and White House objectives.[91]

In analyzing the decision to expand the original mission, the Commission stated that "these decisions may have been taken without clear recognition that these initial conditions had dramatically changed and that the expansion of our military involvement in Lebanon greatly increased the risk to, and adversely impacted upon the security of, the USMNF."[92] More specifically, it is important to note that leaders in Washington failed to recognize that the more closely the United States was associated with the Government of Lebanon, the greater were the number and intensity of attacks. Escalation was also due to the failure of the United States to respond effectively to Amaal and Druze attacks. The small marine force protecting BIA was neither large enough nor equipped to respond to the asymmetric conflict in which they found themselves. Policy makers left American forces in Lebanon unprepared for urban combat and failed to alter mission objectives when surrounding circumstances changed. A careful examination by senior civilian and military leaders of the mission's deteriorating position may have led to significant changes in American participation in the MNF and the Middle East peace process. This did not take place, which left the 22nd MAU in a deteriorating position with a lack of mission clarity.

The "lack of effective supervision of the USMNF security posture prior to 23 October 1983" illustrates the poor command and control of senior leadership.[93] While the Long Commission placed blame for the attack squarely on the shoulders of Colonel Geraghty and Lieutenant Colonel Gerlach, decision making at a much higher level was responsible for the mission's failure. When the situation on the ground no longer fit the president's original objectives, change became necessary. It did not, however, occur. By early September, Colonel Geraghty was operating under mission objectives wholly inappropriate for the conditions present in Beirut. With continuous visits to Beirut by senior military leaders, administration officials, and members of Congress, the changing conditions in Beirut were no secret in Washington or to the throng of reporters covering daily events.

In a finding that easily could have come from the 9/11 Commission, the Long Commission found "that although the USMNF commander received a large volume of intelligence warnings concerning potential terrorist threats prior to 23 October 1983, he was not provided with the timely intelligence, tailored to his specific operational needs, that was necessary to defend against the broad spectrum of threats he faced."[94] Inaccurate and poorly sourced intelligence proved to be one of the United States' greatest weaknesses in Lebanon. While signals intelligence was excellent, human intelligence proved highly unreliable.

Two decades later, in the wake of the September 11, 2001, attacks, internal CIA inquiries, two Senate committees, and the 9/11 Commission would again find human intelligence lacking.[95] Beginning with the limitations placed on the CIA by the Church Committee in the mid-1970s and the Clinton administration's policy of cutting ties to CIA operatives and informants suspected of human rights abuses, human intelligence has often been limited.[96] The unsavory activities an intelligence agency must undertake to gather relevant human intelligence are inherently difficult for democratic states to accept and the United States in particular, as the Church Committee illustrates. Thus, the United States has placed primacy on technological development and collection of signals intelligence, which has proven a mistake for more than 20 years. During the United States' intervention in Lebanon, the CIA failed to penetrate the terrorist organizations responsible for attacks against American forces.[97]

In the Long Commission's final conclusion, it found that "state sponsored terrorism is an important part of the spectrum of warfare and that adequate response to this increasing threat requires an active national policy which seeks to deter attack or reduce its effectiveness. The Commission further concludes that this policy needs to be supported by political and diplomatic actions and by a wide range of timely military response capabilities."[98] The Long Commission's assessment of terrorism and its recommendations remain useful to combating terrorism two decades later. Contrary to the current perception of terrorist networks as entities independent of the nation-state for financial and material support and training, they remain dependent on states for safe harbor and other forms of assistance. Much as Syria and Iran were leading supporters of terrorist organizations in Lebanon, evidence suggests they support insurgents attacking American troops in Iraq.[99]

The United States' experience in Lebanon was marked by the progressive intensification of action against American assets in Beirut. Attacks were designed to test marine defenses and, most importantly, America's response. President Reagan's failure to effectively respond, and the negative consequences of such failure, is perhaps the single greatest lesson to be learned from Lebanon. As the globe's most powerful state for more than five decades, the United States is watched by friend and foe alike with each carefully searching for apparent weakness. Failure to aggressively respond to terrorist attacks against American interests is viewed as weakness by adversaries of the United States. Although President Reagan learned this lesson too late for Lebanon, his response to the April 1986 La Belle discotheque bombing is often credited with the subsequent reduction in terrorist attacks against American assets.[100]

Contrary to the Long Commission's findings, which laid blame for the mission's failure at the feet of ground commanders, American failure in Lebanon was a failure of political leadership. As the great Prussian general and theorist Carl von Clausewitz once wrote, "War may have a grammar of its own, but not its own logic."[101] The logic of war is left for political leaders to determine. It is when they fail to accurately judge their own abilities and the abilities and intentions of an adversary that defeat is suffered. This is made all the more difficult when an adversary is a non-state actor who relies on deception for success. The United States learned this lesson the hard way in Lebanon and would do so again in similar conflicts.

CONCLUSION

It would be a decade before the United States found itself embroiled in the domestic instability of a failed state. Somalia, however, began as a peacemaking operation in which 30,000 marines and soldiers protected relief supplies and ended the clan warfare raging in the country before their arrival. But, as often happens, initial success was followed by failure. Mistakes made in Lebanon were repeated in Somalia.

The chapter that follows examines the American experience in Somalia between the initial deployment of marines to Somalia in December 1992 and the final withdrawal of American forces in 1994. Similar to the analysis of Lebanon, the case of Somalia follows the same question format. The two cases share a number of similarities and, ultimately, have a similar conclusion. Although the missions in both Lebanon and Somalia were failures for the United States, early success in Somalia offers a model of peacemaking success never present in Lebanon. The greatest variation in results will be found in the analysis of Afghanistan, however, where the United States altered its previous policy significantly. And, as may be expected, the results differ substantially from those of Lebanon and Somalia.

4

Somalia (1992–1994): Into the Post-Cold War Era

In the three phases of American involvement in Somalia, the United States experienced success and failure as the United Nations-backed mission undertook the first attempt at nation-building in the post-Cold War era. No longer was preventing the two superpowers from engaging one another in large-scale conflict a primary concern. The fear of the recent past was gone and it became possible for the United Nations, with the assistance of the lone superpower, to turn attention to other matters. With the collapse of Siad Barre's regime in 1991 and widespread starvation setting in by 1992, Somalia was the first opportunity for the United Nations to fulfill the grand designs of its creators.

American involvement in Somalia, much like Lebanon, was an attempt by the United States to restore stability to a country in desperate need. For American troops, peacekeeping turned into a conflict for which they were unprepared and was contrary to mission objectives. And, what began as a short-term solution to an immediate need turned into a protracted conflict in which the United States would ultimately pay a price that was not worth the effort.

When the United States withdrew from Somalia in March 1994, an overwhelming majority of Americans were unsupportive of the president's humanitarian action. After winning the Cold War, Americans wanted little to do with conflict in unknown lands. Congress was also quick to denounce American intervention in Somalia. The crush of public opinion and a critical Congress was more than President Clinton was willing to bear and the

United States unceremoniously withdrew from Mogadishu. The experience and lessons of Somalia fill the pages of this chapter.

WHAT WERE THE ECONOMIC, MILITARY, AND POLITICAL CONDITIONS IN SOMALIA PRIOR TO AMERICAN INTERVENTION?

Settled in the first century AD, Somalia has long been home to hearty clansmen known for their warlike ways and fierce independence. Perched on the Horn of Africa where the Red Sea and Indian Ocean meet, Somalia is a land of heat and vast tracts of arid land fit for little more than the migratory cattle grazing that dominates the nomadic life of many Somali clans.[1] Used as a center for commerce by Arab traders until the seventeenth century, Mogadishu, the hub of Somali civilization, and other coastal cities have long played a central role in the ebb and flow of Somali civilization. Although the clan system, which led to conflict and chaos in the 1990s, did not form until the fourteenth century, it has played a dominant role in society since.

For much of the recent past, Somali history is marked by the domination of successive foreign powers. Beginning with Ethiopia in the fifteenth and sixteenth centuries, followed by the Ottoman Empire (1728–1850), Britain (1875–1944), France (1875–1940), and Italy (1875–1941), Somalia's strategic location at the southern entrance to the Red Sea has made an otherwise unattractive land highly desirable.[2]

The success of foreign invasion can be placed firmly at the feet of Somali clan factionalism and a nomadic way of life dominated by a "cattle culture" and a rejection of the sedentary (unwarrior-like) lifestyle, which reinforced traditional styles of combat and left Somalis technologically backward. Britain and Italy, from the late nineteenth century until Somali independence, played the primary role in the development of what were known, until unification at independence, as British and Italian Somaliland.

By the 1920s, Britain found Somaliland to be of little use and sought to pull out of the troublesome region. Italian dictator Benito Mussolini's invasion of Ethiopia (1935) and his demand that Britain leave Somaliland proved a convenient pretext for British abandonment of a rebellious colonial possession. An Italian-dominated Horn of Africa became unacceptable, however, with the onset of World War II and Britain's need to protect the Suez Canal and the important refueling port of Aden, just across the Red Sea from Somaliland. Thus, in 1941, British forces evicted Italy from Africa once again becoming the dominant power in the region.

In the decade that followed, Somali governance was split between the Italian Trusteeship Administration (*Amministrazione Fiduciaria Italiana della Somalia*) in the south and the British protectorate in the north. For both European nations, the goal was to rapidly establish free and functioning

Somali governments. In the immediate postwar years neither Britain nor Italy could afford to rebuild and administer backward Somali cities, towns, and provinces. Although British Somaliland suffered greater economic deprivation than Italian Somaliland, both suffered from underdeveloped infrastructure, limited social capital, and little wealth, which was desperately needed to pay for construction of power plants, roads, schools, sewage treatment facilities, and waterworks. For many Somalis, however, the future seemed bright as impending independence presented a chance to unite all Somalis into "greater Somalia." This would mean uniting British and Italian Somaliland, Djibouti, and parts of Ethiopia and Kenya into one nation. Pan-Somali dreams would, however, never be realized. Unfortunately, the conflict that plagues Somalia to the present day would soon begin.[3]

During the period in which British and Italian Somaliland moved toward independence (1954–1960), a system of highly stratified politics developed. Largely based on clan ties, political parties rarely offered solutions broadly accepted across clan lines, setting the stage for later conflict. On June 26, 1960, leaders from the north and south met and agreed upon unification. Thus, the Somali Republic was born on July 1, 1960.

Integration, however, did not proceed smoothly. For the Isaaq, the largest clan in the north, integration led the less numerous Daarood to unite politically with the Dir of the south. This loss of power did not sit well with the Isaaq and other clans which experienced a loss of power in other parts of the newly independent state. As the Somali clan system with Daarood, Dir, Gadabursi, Hawiya, Isa, and Isaaq clans became dominated by the Isaaq and Daarood, clans and sub-clans experiencing degraded conditions began to withdraw support from the fledgling government.[4] The confluence of violence began in October 1969. Citing the poor treatment of his sub-clan, a bodyguard of President Abdirashid Ali Shermaarke assassinated the Somali leader, setting off a chain of events which brought Major General Muhammed Siad Barre to power in an army-led coup d'état.

In the immediate aftermath of the coup, the Somali Revolutionary Council (SRC), largely made up of army officers, was established. General Barre's effort to establish "scientific socialism" would lead to the establishment of a new order in Somalia, if the general succeeded. General Barre and the SRC sought to destroy the clan system, minimize the role of Islam in Somalia, and develop a socialist economic system. To achieve this the general turned to the Soviet Union and his secret police. Soviet advisors provided technical assistance and military training while the secret police eliminated all opposition. Progress was made in Somalia during the early years of the Barre regime, but poverty, backwardness, and violence persisted. The nation was, in fact, united under a central government for the first time and Somalia experienced a level of internal stability it desperately needed.

Much as it had always been, Somalia remained poor, maintaining a subsistence economy and depending on Soviet aid for the construction of needed infrastructure and internal improvements.[5] Soviet support soon disappeared when General Barre backed the Western Somali Liberation Front's effort to win back the Ogaden in 1977. After Mengistu Haile Mariam and the Derg led a successful communist coup in Ethiopia (1974), supported by the Soviet Union, the centuries-old nemesis of Somalia became the nation's socialist brother. For Siad Barre and the Somali people, this was an unacceptable state of affairs.[6] Forced to choose between Ethiopia and Somalia, the Soviets chose the former.[7]

After losing the Ogaden War (1977–1978), Barre faced an attempted coup and found it more difficult to govern Somalia in the years that followed. Defeat in combat was, in Somalia's warrior culture, a sign of weakness and an opportunity to supplant a weakened leader. Along with the general's high-handed tactics and persecution of opposition clans, resistance to Siad Barre steadily grew.

With the loss of Soviet aid, Barre turned to the United States for assistance, signing an agreement with the Carter administration for access to the port of Berbera.[8] Throughout the 1980s American support for Barre continued. Financial aid, weapons, and training trickled into Somalia. For the Reagan administration, Siad Barre was the lesser of two evils. A Soviet-supported Ethiopia could not be left to dominate the Horn of Africa. President Franklin Roosevelt's response to criticism of American support for Nicaraguan President Anastacio Somoza rang true once again: "He may be a son of a bitch, but he's our son of a bitch."

Barre's continuing crackdowns on dissent and scientific socialism's failure to provide improved living standards left the Somali regime increasingly isolated and unpopular among Somalis.[9] Repression of the Majerteen and other clans led to the formation of cross-clan opposition groups, determined to overthrow Barre. The Somali Patriotic Movement in the south, Somali National Alliance (SNA) in the center of the country, United Somali Congress (USC) in Mogadishu, and Somali Democratic Alliance in the northeast began forming in the 1970s and 1980s as groups seeking to overthrow General Barre.[10] By 1989, Somalia found itself on the brink of civil war.

Seeing the writing on the wall, President Barre attempted to buy time by calling for a national election at the end of 1990. Barre's effort was unsuccessful. By August 1989, Somalia was spinning out of control. SNM success in the north led other groups to take action. In November 1989 the Fourth Division of the Somali Army mutinied, but was put down by Muhammed Said Masalah. Barre's success was, however, short lived. Opposition groups turned into rebel armies and began slowly advancing on Mogadishu.[11] After more than a year of fighting, President Barre offered to resign if the rebels would agree to a cease fire. They did not and on January 27, 1991, Barre fled Mogadishu for Kismayu. With the taste of victory in their mouths, rebels (General Muhammed Farah Aidid and the USC) chased Barre's forces out of Kismayu and largely out of Somalia.[12]

USC forces, commanded by General Aidid, played the dominant role in the defeat of Siad Barre and his military commander, General Muhammed Hersi Morgan. With Barre in exile in Nigeria, titular head of the USC, Ali Mahdi, and General Aidid turned on one another. Mahdi made the first move by declaring himself president of Somalia on January 29, 1991.[13] This move served to split the USC and turned Mogadishu into a battle ground as supporters of Aidid and Mahdi fought for control of the streets of Mogadishu. Technicals, popularized in media accounts of the conflict, were most often Toyota trucks with large caliber Soviet machine guns or recoilless rifles mounted in the bed. They roamed the streets of Mogadishu as young men high on khat and armed with AK-47s fought for control of Mogadishu's slums.[14]

The reason behind the Aidid/Mahdi split was a simple one. As commander of USC military forces, General Aidid believed it was he who had defeated Siad Barre. Thus, Ali Mahdi, by declaring himself president, usurped the general's right to rule Somalia. Anticipating General Aidid's move to power, Ali Mahdi acted while Aidid was still pursuing Barre. In the aftermath of the Aidid/Mahdi split, Mogadishu and much of Somalia became a battle ground infested with gangs of heavily armed young men who spent their days and nights raping, robbing, and murdering innocent Somalis.[15] As the fighting degenerated into chaos, regionally based resistance groups supplanted the leadership of local elders with the rule of roving gangs.[16] Those who resisted the marauding bands were murdered where they stood.

The fighting taking place south of Mogadishu in the Jubba and Shebeelle Valleys led to the mass exodus of the Rahanwein farmers who had long fed much of Somalia's population with their agricultural products. As Morgan and Aidid chased one another across southern Somalia, crops were destroyed and planting seasons came and went without farmers returning to their land to grow the food Somalis depended on.[17] Warring factions also killed the livestock of rivals, further reducing the food supply. With destruction on such a wide scale, famine was sure to follow, and it did.[18]

From November 1991 through February 1992, the city of Mogadishu was utterly destroyed. The city's limited infrastructure was decimated. Electricity was available only to those who owned generators. Businesses were looted. Homes and shops were destroyed. Thousands of Somalis lay dead. No clear victor emerged, however, as a tenuous truce was reached in the spring of 1992 between Aidid and Mahdi.[19] Aidid and his Somali National Alliance controlled south-central Somalia, while Mahdi, militarily weaker than Aidid, was left with little more than the northern half of Mogadishu and its suburbs.[20]

General Aidid brought a level of stability to the territory he controlled. Death rates among Somalis declined from September to November 1992, aid groups returned to Somalia, and the only bandits robbing foreign aid workers and Somalis were members of the SNA.[21] While such a state of affairs offered little consolation, it was a dramatic improvement over the recent past. Farmers in the Jubba and Shebeelle Valleys were finally able to return to their farms, although starvation had already set in.

As the presence of foreign aid organizations in Somalia rapidly increased, the opportunity for warlords to exploit the lack of security across the country increased as well. For many of the aid organizations in Mogadishu and the cities of southern Somalia, their single largest expenditure were bribes to local gangs who provided "security."[22] In Somalia, security meant simple extortion. Without payments reaching $1,000 per day (per organization and location), CARE, Irish Concern, UNICEF, and other aid groups would be gunned down and robbed by the very men they were paying to protect them. On occasion, guards who were replaced, "underpaid," or high on khat, robbed and/or murdered the aid workers for whom they worked.[23] Providing aid to needy Somalis was anything but safe.

Media coverage of the humanitarian disaster in Somalia began to increase during the summer of 1992. Major news organizations from around the globe posted reporters to Somalia and Kenya to cover the crisis. With heightened media coverage, non-governmental organizations began to pressure the United Nations, United States Congress, and the Bush administration to take action to end the death and destruction.[24] Chairman of the Joint Chiefs of Staff General Colin Powell ardently opposed intervention. The United States had recently (1991) won the first major post–Cold War conflict, Gulf War I, and American military leaders sought to prevent the United States from wandering into a seemingly losing conflict. General Powell had only recently released the Powell Doctrine, which laid down a strict set of criteria for future American intervention abroad.[25]

For General Powell and the Joint Chiefs of Staff (JCS), these criteria were not met in Somalia. In a series of interagency meetings, the Joint Chiefs cited several reasons the United States should not intervene. First, Somalia's conflict was fueled by age-old inter-clan rivalry. Second, the heavily armed combatants were indistinguishable from the general populace, making American force protection impossible. Third, Somalia's terrain presented tactical and logistic difficulties for American forces.[26] Senior military leaders also pointed out that the United States had no national interests at stake in Somalia. With the collapse of the Soviet Union and the crumbling regime in Ethiopia, there was little reason to risk American lives in the Horn of Africa.

Early on, President Bush sided with the Joint Chiefs choosing to provide food instead of American troops. As the crisis deepened, pressure in Washington began to mount as media coverage, UN lobbying, NGO cries for aid, and calls to act from Senators Paul Simon (D-IL) and Nancy Kassebaum (R-KS) further increased pressure on President Bush.[27] Officials within the federal government also pressured the administration. Andrew Natsios of the Department of State's Office of Foreign Disaster Assistance publicly lamented the situation in Somalia drawing comparisons to the famine that struck Ethiopia in the 1980s.[28]

Division in the State Department was, however, evident. While many at Foggy Bottom supported intervention in Somalia, Assistant Secretary of State John Bolton, the highest-ranking American official to visit Somalia, led those who did not support American intervention. According to Secretary Bolton, sending *any* foreign forces into Somalia would be "premature until there is an effective ceasefire." Secretary Bolton also added that an aide to General Aidid warned, "If the UN sent in 50 military observers, they might as well send in 50 coffins too."[29]

At the United Nations, Secretary General Boutros Boutros-Ghali continued to watch events in Somalia unfold. According to former American Ambassador to Somalia (1984–1988) and Special Envoy to Somalia (1991–1994) Robert B. Oakley and Deputy to the Special Envoy John L. Hirsch, "Throughout 1991, the perspective at UN headquarters was that in responding to Somalia's civil war, the main job of the international community should be limited to delivering humanitarian relief supplies."[30] Oakley and Hirsch also point out that Aidid was a vociferous critic of the United Nations and any effort to intervene in Somalia. Aidid was not only a nationalist seeking to keep foreign forces out of Somalia, but he also considered the United Nations a threat to his rise to power. Perhaps of equal significance, General Aidid maintained old animosities toward Secretary General Boutros-Ghali. Prior to becoming secretary general of the United Nations, Boutros-Ghali served as minister of state for foreign affairs in his native Egypt. During that period, Egypt strongly supported the rule of Siad Barre, the man who had imprisoned and tortured Aidid for more than five years, which General Aidid now held against the secretary general.[31]

On January 23, 1992, the United Nations Security Council passed Resolution 733 calling for increased aid to Somalia.[32] Three months later, the Security Council established the United Nations Operations in Somalia (UNOSOM I) with the passage of Security Council Resolution 751. Respected Algerian diplomat Mohamed Sahnoun was dispatched to Somalia by Boutros-Ghali to act as his eyes and ears. American diplomat Joseph Jonah was also working in Somalia, but to gain a cease fire between Aidid and Mahdi. As the militarily weaker of the two, Ali Mahdi welcomed UN intervention while Aidid sought to finish off his rival.

Throughout Sahnoun and Jonah's time in-country, food continued to pour into Somalia. Relief organizations, however, soon discovered that the food they were distributing at an increasingly high cost rarely made it from relief convoy to the mouths of starving Somalis. In one instance, a woman carrying a bag of rice was returning from an aid distribution site when a militiaman shot her in the back killing the woman. Upon approaching his victim, the militiaman realized he had just murdered his own wife for a bag of rice he intended to steal.[33]

Soon after the April 24, 1992, passage of Security Council Resolution 751, 500 Pakistani peacekeepers arrived in Mogadishu to secure the port, safeguard food stores, and escort relief convoys.[34] Much as in past peacekeeping operations, the Pakistanis were allowed to fire only when fired upon and in immediate self-defense. For the Pakistani peacekeepers, the strict rules of engagement and their limited firepower would prove disastrous before the mission in Somalia was complete. Efforts to create a perception among Somalis of a UN peacekeeping force which did not favor one side over another in the Somali conflict proved as unattainable as it had for the marines in Lebanon a decade earlier. As the events of June 1993 proved, the United Nations was alone in believing it was working for the betterment of *all* Somalis.

Sahnoun did not remain at his post long. As the United Nations lead men on the ground, Sahnoun immediately began urging change among the UN relief agencies. After being rebuffed by the secretary general when he did not clarify Sahnoun's position in Somalia, the Algerian diplomat resigned. He was replaced by veteran Iraqi diplomat Ismat Kitanni on November 8, 1992. Sahnoun had proven the United Nations' most effective voice in Somalia. Kitanni did not have such success.

Throughout the summer and fall of 1992, the United States continued its massive relief effort working with the International Committee of the Red Cross, UN relief agencies, and other aid organizations. By the fall of 1992 the United States was responsible for 57 percent of all aid to Somalia. Not only did the American government provide food, but it spent tens of millions of dollars providing a continuous airlift of supplies into Kenya for distribution into Somalia.[35] Congressional, NGO, UN, and media pressure continued despite the massive relief effort and, as they had in the past, the Bush administration and the Joint Chiefs continued to resist pressure to deploy American forces.[36]

While it is unclear what led President Bush to ultimately change his mind in late November 1992, his defeat in the presidential election may have played an important role in the administration's policy reversal. Concerns for a legacy are often suggested as a rationale for undertaking such actions and with little more than three months left in his presidency, George H. W. Bush had little time left to act.

Reports suggest that the momentum building toward intervention in the fall of 1992 eventually convinced key players in the Pentagon (Secretary of Defense Dick Cheney, Chairman of the Joint Chiefs of Staff General Colin Powell, and CINCCENT General Joseph Hoar) and White House (National Security Advisor Brent Scowcroft) that the ad hoc approach taken in the previous 12 to 18 months must end and a comprehensive plan be developed.[37]

Throughout the second half of November 1992 the National Security Council (NSC) Deputies Committee met on a number of occasions to discuss Somalia. During that same period, the Pentagon and Central Command were also hard at work developing a workable solution to the crisis in Somalia. On November 21, JCS Vice Chairman Admiral David Jeremiah stunned the Joint Chiefs and the NSC saying, "If you think U.S. forces are needed, we can do the job."[38]

Somalia was in the area of responsibility (AOR) of Central Command (CENTCOM), which was also responsible for contingency planning for any and all events that might require American forces. CENTCOM had recently won Gulf War I and was riding high. General Hoar, as CINC-CENT, was in agreement with General Powell when it came to avoiding involvement in Somalia. But, when tasked with developing a plan for ending the crisis in Somalia and leading American forces into Somalia, General Hoar was confident of success. When Operation Restore Hope was given the green light, General Hoar turned to Lieutenant General Robert B. Johnston to serve as his ground commander. Tasked to provide forces for Restore Hope were the 1st Marine Division commanded by Major General Charles Wilhelm and the 10th Mountain Division under the command of Major General Steve Arnold. Air Force and Navy units would primarily provide logistic support. UN peacekeepers would come from a number of states in Africa, Asia, and Europe. The United States, however, provided the single largest contingent with more than 20,000 Americans providing assistance and stability to south and central Somalia.[39]

Operation Restore Hope fell under the auspices of the United Nations with the United States serving as the dominant partner in the mission.[40] On November 27, 1992, the operation was approved by the UN General Assembly, which supported the mission with $108 million in aid. The Security Council officially endorsed Restore Hope on December 3 when it passed Resolution 794.[41] With support from the United Nations and the incoming Clinton administration, the White House set Restore Hope in motion with a marine amphibious landing set for the first week of December.

Along with authorizing Restore Hope, Security Council Resolution 794 created the United Nations Intervention Task Force (UNITAF) led by General Johnston. For Boutros-Ghali, Somalia was the United Nation's first attempt at nation-building. The success of Gulf War I and the end of the Cold War emboldened the secretary general and President Bush to undertake such an unprecedented mission.[42] It proved to be a mission for which neither the secretary general nor the new Clinton administration was prepared. Secretary General Boutros-Ghali and Presidents Bush and Clinton expected Somali warlords to cower at the sight of American forces and blue-helmeted peacekeepers. They were wrong and unprepared for the resistance General Aidid and other Somali factions presented.[43]

WHAT WERE AMERICAN OBJECTIVES?

In the fall of 1992, American commanders developed a plan for operations in Somalia consisting of four distinct phases. Phase I began with an amphibious landing by marines on the beaches outside Mogadishu. Their objective: establish control of the port, harbor facilities, and airfields. Once accomplished, air assets were designated to bring the 10th Mountain Division into airfields throughout southern Somalia, thus beginning phase II. Here, American forces were to work together and establish control over areas inland of Mogadishu. During phase III, American forces were slated to continue south and establish control over the major southern city of Kismayu and the hinterlands of the Shebeelle Valley. Finally, in phase IV, UNITAF was to hand over operations to UNOSOM II, commanded by Turkish General Cevik Bir and retired American Admiral Jonathan Howe.[44]

With the first marines landing in early December, the United States entered what may be considered the second phase of the broader American involvement in Somalia, which had four distinct phases of its own. Phase III came with the hand off of relief and nation-building operation to UNOSOM II. It would be during this phase that Task Force Ranger would suffer casualties during the Battle of Mogadishu. Finally, phase IV began with the pullout of American forces from Somalia in March of 1994, and their eventual return in 1995. This analysis, however, ends with the American withdrawal in the aftermath of the Battle of Mogadishu.

Marines coming ashore near Mogadishu found themselves surrounded by reporters gathered to cover the arrival of American forces. The marines did not, however, find themselves facing General Aidid's militia. For reasons of his own, the General relented in his insistence that no foreign forces intervene in Somalia. Joseph Jonah's diplomacy and that of Ambassador Kittani were, perhaps, enough to sway General Aidid. It is also possible that the general viewed an American presence as imminent regardless of his acquiescence and perceived that there may be a benefit in supporting the Americans. As the United States and United Nations entered a new era of post–Cold War internationalism, opinion was divided among the many observers following the progress of Restore Hope and UNITAF.[45] Although an ambitious effort to turn Somalia into a vibrant state was beginning, few of the key players in the months and years ahead could foresee the difficulties nation-building would present.

With the initial deployment of marines to the airport and port on December 7–8, Ambassadors Oakley and Kittani with General Johnston met Mohamed Ali Mahdi and General Aidid on December 11, 1992, to discuss initial efforts to resolve factional conflict and to ensure that militiamen under their control did not clash with arriving UNITAF forces. In the weeks following initial agreement between UNITAF and the Somali warlords there was relative peace throughout the country, with relief operations experiencing limited interference.[46] Logistics proved the greatest problem for UNITAF. With more than 30,000 American and UN troops in Somalia, efforts to provide food, water, and other essentials to UNITAF personnel proved daunting.[47] Roads were in poor condition, Somalia was without electricity, and airport facilities needed to bring in food and equipment were often unserviceable for large aircraft. Despite the difficulties presented, UNITAF succeeded in rapidly eliminating hunger across the country.[48]

By December 14, 1992, Andrew Natsios, USAID's (United States Agency for International Development) senior man in Somalia, was already discussing the transition from feeding starving Somalis to rebuilding a crippled country.[49] As the 1st Marine Division successfully achieved its objectives in phase I, leading elements of the 10th Mountain Division began arriving in Baledogle during the second week of December. Interestingly, one field grade officer commented, "I soon learned that although there was privation in Wanwaylen, there were no people in the pitiful state of starvation that we had seen on television prior to deployment."[50] To the contrary, the Somalis were well fed from relief supplies and quick to make every effort to "rent" the 10th Mountain the debilitated and burned out buildings they occupied at prices that would make real estate magnate Donald Trump blush with envy. By the end of December American forces controlled much of southern Somalia and were able to provide an unprecedented level of security to the towns and villages they patrolled.

Bandits (SNA militiamen) continued to set up check points in the middle of the night where they robbed buses loaded with passengers and other vehicles. With an extensive network of observers watching American troop movements it was difficult to stop banditry outright. After American forces ambushed bandits on several occasions, capturing and killing a number of SNA militiamen, banditry decreased but persisted.[51] In agreements with UNITAF, Ali Mahdi and General Aidid removed "technicals" from cities and rural areas. They were taken to staging areas where UNITAF could ensure that the two factions were complying with the cease fire agreement. What remained a significant problem was UNITAF's unwillingness to disarm combatants. For Somalis it was a catch-22, disarmament meant bandits alone would be armed.[52] Yet, without disarmament, Somali militiamen would continue fighting. Disarming the country also proved problematic for General Johnston because it would mean a dramatic redefinition of UNITAF objectives.[53] From General Johnston's perspective, UNITAF's central objective was to "secure routes for humanitarian relief and to pave the way for a United Nations peacekeeping program."[54]

Within the United Nations, UNITAF was viewed as a means to weaken Ali Mahdi and General Aidid and thus eliminate them from UN nation-building efforts set to follow Restore Hope. According to one senior UN official, "The factions will be weakened by this military intervention, so the creation of a new force—with UN assistance—might work."[55] For many in the UN bureaucracy, reestablishing the Somali national police, a respected institution, was the key to successfully reestablishing long-term order. The failure of international officials to understand the underlying animosities among the Somali tribes and the enduring support for General Aidid was a serious weakness that played a major role in the ultimate failure of nation-building efforts. American commanders were also reluctant to escalate the role they played. Despite the decision to enter Somalia, senior commanders expressed a desire to limit Restore Hope to a short duration with limited objectives.

Serving as the dominant partner in UNITAF, the Americans viewed their mission as one largely independent of other UN forces. Cooperation with Belgian troops in Mogadishu, Canadian troops moving through 10th Mountain positions, and other forces was excellent, but American troops operated with objectives that varied from the longer-term objectives of the United Nations.[56] Realities on the ground, however, forced the United States to alter its original objectives.

For American commanders, the old adage "no battle plan survives first contact with the enemy" proved true once again. Initial mission objectives included securing major port facilities, controlling airfields in southern Somalia, providing security to relief convoys, and securing towns and villages south of Mogadishu. By the end of December, it was clear that stability would not be possible until Somalia was disarmed.[57] This not only included crew served weapons, but also the small arms used by militiamen at the makeshift road blocks where many Somalis were robbed and murdered. The crackdown began in earnest in early January 1993.[58] Weeks earlier, American forces confiscated artillery, mortars, and large caliber machine guns for the first time. By January, the armed factions responsible for intimidating the populace found themselves under fire from UNITAF.[59]

The first American casualty, Private Domingo Arroyo, was killed on January 14, 1993, when an ambush was sprung on marines near Mogadishu's airport.[60] From the death of Private First Class Arroyo forward, marines acted more aggressively when possible threats arose. American forces enjoyed rules of engagement that were far more aggressive than those issued to UNOSOM I forces and that would be exercised by the Pakistanis of UNOSOM II. Stronger rules of engagement also provided American forces more freedom to act than the ROE of marines in Beirut a decade earlier. Much to the credit of the 1st Marine and 10th Mountain Divisions, aggressive rules of engagement and the willingness of American troops to search out and destroy weapons stockpiles played a major role in the success of Restore Hope. General Wilhelm, operations director, issued a warning in early 1993 indicative of the elevation of hostilities at the time saying, "If we're not careful we will start thinking that we're at war and we may forget that our mission here is one of peace and humanitarian assistance."[61]

General Johnston and other American commanders found mission objectives slipping further away from simple relief operation when elements of the 10th Mountain were tasked with reestablishing town councils in Marka and similar villages throughout southern Somalia.[62] During the years of warlord rule and anarchy, the town councils, composed of clan elders, were supplanted by SNA or USC militiamen. If an area were to switch hands, control would fall to the militia leader controlling the area. The stability provided by a respected town council and police force was the bane of militiamen whose goal was temporary gain. In addition to restoring town councils to authority, UNITAF began an effort to restore the national police force to its former position of respect. Throughout the Barre regime, the national police remained above clan politics, retiring from public service when Somalia fell into chaos.[63] Although a lack of cultural awareness hampered UNITAF's efforts, American commanders and diplomats understood that many factions were biding their time until UNITAF left and clan warfare could resume.[64] This made a national police all the more important for future stability.

Throughout the spring of 1993, UNITAF successfully ended hunger in Somalia, brought stability to the country, and made substantial progress toward broader nation-building. As early as January 1993, 850 marines from the 3rd Battalion 9th Marine Regiment left Somalia.[65] With more than 35,000 troops in-country, UNITAF succeeded beyond the best hopes of all involved.[66] The problem of when to turn over operations to UNOSOM II remained. There was little respect for the United Nations among Somalis. Additionally, the UN was proving unable to cobble together a force of sufficient size. For these and other reasons American commanders lacked confidence in UN peacekeeping efforts.[67] Persistent criticism of the United Nations and its ability to restore Somalia began with the UN's earliest intervention in the war-ravaged nation and continued throughout the various missions.[68]

In early March 1993, Secretary General Boutros-Ghali proposed that a peacekeeping force of 28,000 replace American-led forces and begin nation-building efforts.[69] The UN relied on the United States to provide the backbone of the peacekeeping force and ostensibly much of the funding.[70] The nation-building effort of the United Nations in Somalia was unprecedented, making this the first mission of its kind.[71]

UNOSOM II personnel began arriving in Somalia during the month of March with UNITAF set to hand over control on May 1. From the beginning it was clear to many of the key figures involved that the UN was unprepared for the economic, military, and political mission it would soon undertake. Not only would UNOSOM II face the task of providing security throughout Somalia, but it would have to complete the restoration of the national police, return Somalia to agricultural self sufficiency, rebuild destroyed infrastructure, continue national reconciliation, and much more.[72] Rebuilding the Somali economy was itself a daunting task.[73] The objectives of UNOSOM II were broadly defined as "maintaining peace between 15 clan factions by deploying troops throughout Somalia, disarming Somali factions, and rebuilding civil institutions."[74]

On May 4, 1993, General Johnston handed control to General Bir and UNOSOM II.[75] A majority of American troops returned home, but Major General Thomas M. Montgomery and 4,000 soldiers of the 10th Mountain remained in Somalia as a quick reaction force (QRF) for UNOSOM II. With Admiral Howe, a retired American naval officer, leading UNOSOM II General Montgomery reported directly to a fellow American. Senior military officers and the public would not allow American soldiers to serve under foreign commanders, which left Admiral Howe in command of the American contribution to UNOSOM II.

Prior to the May 4 turnover, General Johnston and newly appointed Special Envoy Bob Gosende met with Admiral Howe, General Bir, and General Montgomery to discuss the probability that General Aidid would challenge UNOSOM II in the near future. As General Johnston predicted, Aidid soon began testing UN resolve. In one early meeting designed to develop consensus among the clans, SNA militiamen detained representatives from rival clans in the Olympic Hotel. According to Hirsch and Oakley, it was at this point that Admiral Howe concluded that General Aidid would not be satisfied with compromise.[76] The first real test of UNOSOM II came on June 5, 1993, when SNA militiamen ambushed Pakistani peacekeepers killing 24.

In the month prior to the June 5 ambush, General Aidid slipped his heavy weapons back into Mogadishu and went on the offensive. Admiral Howe understood that UN objectives could not be accomplished if heavy weapons were deployed in the streets of Mogadishu, and UNOSOM II proved unable to provide security and stability to Somalia. Not only would civil war return, but all efforts to disarm the factions would disintegrate. Thus, action was necessary. On June 4, General Aidid was informed that peacekeepers would inspect and inventory SNA weapons depots the following day. When Pakistani troops were dispatched to carry out inspections, they were ambushed on October 21 Road and elsewhere in the city. By that afternoon the QRF and Italian forces were dispatched to end the fighting. When fighting subsided, 24 Pakistanis were dead and many more wounded. The bodies of dead Pakistanis were mutilated and carried through the streets.[77]

With 24 peacekeepers dead, the Security Council passed Resolution 837 on June 6 condemning the premeditated attack. This had little effect as less than two weeks later, SNA militiamen attacked Moroccan peacekeepers. The Moroccans suffered heavy casualties with many wounded. That same day Admiral Howe placed a $25,000 bounty on the head of Muhammad Farah Aidid. For both sides, this meant war. By June 14, U.S.-led strikes against SNA positions were responsible for the destruction of General

Aidid's radio station, a cigarette factory used for troop and weapons staging, several weapons depots, technicals, and other heavy weapons.[78]

Despite the American-led onslaught, General Aidid refused requests from Habr-Gidr leaders, Ethiopia, and Eritrea to enter exile. Instead, he turned to former President Jimmy Carter in an attempt to have the bounty on his head removed. In a letter beseeching Carter to intervene, the General explained why he did not deserve the treatment he was receiving. The letter was promptly turned over to President Clinton who largely relied on National Security Advisor Anthony Lake and Secretary of Defense Les Aspin to handle affairs in Somalia. Remaining in Mogadishu, General Aidid taunted Admiral Howe who was determined to capture or kill Aidid. No longer were UNOSOM II objectives focused on nation-building. Instead, catching General Aidid and destroying his militia became the number one objective of the 28,000-man peacekeeping force.[79]

Throughout the summer of 1993, strikes continued against General Aidid and his supporters with a July 12 attack on a meeting of Habr-Gidr leaders serving as perhaps the deadliest of all American attacks.[80] As the effort to capture General Aidid proved fruitless, Admiral Howe began requesting special operations forces (SOF). General Powell opposed SOF to Somalia, but Admiral Howe proved unrelenting and his friendship with Anthony Lake eventually played a role in General Powell's acquiescence.[81]

The Clinton administration was aware of the deteriorating UN mission in Somalia. On August 27 Secretary Aspin spoke to the Center for Strategic and International Studies suggesting that objectives in Somalia should be scaled down to a narrower, more achievable, nation-building program. Secretary General Boutros-Ghali was informed of the modified American position by Secretary of State Warren Christopher. As may have been expected, the secretary general rejected American advice stating that the policy stemming from Security Council Resolution 837 should remain intact.[82] For the United Nations, scaling back the ambitious program designed for Somalia would signal to the world that the organization lacked the capacity to fundamentally improve the plight of failed states. In the new post-Cold War era, the United Nations could not begin with failure.

HOW DID THE UNITED STATES COMBAT THE ASYMMETRIC STRATEGY AND TACTICS OF ITS ADVERSARY?

From the earliest days of Operation Restore Hope through the turnover of authority to UNOSOM II, factional forces sought to avoid direct conflict with American and UN forces. When peacekeepers did come under fire, the primary tactic used was the ambush. The absence of any uniformed Somali military left peacekeepers in a very difficult position when attempting to determine friend from foe. Thus, militias maintained an asymmetric advantage American troops and UN peacekeepers were unable to match. General Aidid's June 5 attack on Pakistani peacekeepers is, perhaps, the single best example of its use.

The inability of General Montgomery's conventional force to capture or kill General Aidid may be attributed less to any weakness of the 10th Mountain Division than to the shapeless adversary and nature of conflict in which the 10th Mountain found itself. With the collapse of the Barre regime (1990–1991), Somalia became a classic case of what is known as low intensity conflict.[83] Without the ability to distinguish one Somali faction from another, weak centers of gravity, and the murky objectives of faction commanders, separating warring militias proved extremely difficult. Additionally, peacekeepers faced an adversary that recognized no laws of war, failed to display or wear visibly distinguishable markings, and effectively utilized asymmetric tactics. UNOSOM II peacekeepers were simply unprepared to face an adversary willing to challenge the authority of the United Nations. Thus, Admiral Howe repeatedly beseeched the White House for special operations forces equipped and trained for the very conflict facing UNOSOM II.

Before the end of August, Joint Special Operations Command (JSOC) established Task Force (TF) Ranger under the auspices of Operation Gothic Serpent, with the objective of capturing General Aidid and his top lieutenants. Led by an experienced Delta commander, Brigadier General William Garrison, TF Ranger contained the skills and equipment to finally capture the elusive general.[84] Although TF Ranger's presence in Somalia was due to the requests of Admiral Howe, operational control remained with JSOC at Pope Air Force Base, North Carolina, and with CENTCOM in Tampa, Florida.[85] The highly secretive nature of Special Forces operations led to limited cooperation between UNOSOM II and TF Ranger, with cooperation often consisting of General Garrison informing General Montgomery of upcoming missions.[86]

TF Ranger was composed of special operations forces from the Air Force, Army, and Navy. The Air Force component consisted of a combat search and rescue team and combat air controllers who specialized in rescuing downed pilots and controlling combat air support. A small number of Navy SEALs were also included in the task force. Delta Force assaulters of C Squadron and Rangers of the 75th Infantry Regiment comprised the single largest element of TF Ranger. The Army's 160th Special Operations Aviation Regiment (SOAR), the Night Stalkers, provided the aviation component.

Task Force Ranger's objective was simple: capture or kill Muhammad Farah Aidid. Short of the primary objective, the men were to disrupt General Aidid's ability to conduct combat operations by striking blows to his command and control structure and his logistics network. It was hoped that the swift success of TF Ranger would allow UNOSOM II to return to its primary mission and successfully build a stable and secure Somalia.[87]

In the weeks prior to the Battle of Mogadishu (October 3, 1993), made famous by the book and then movie *Black Hawk Down*, TF Ranger conducted six operations capturing a number of Habr-Gidr leaders and Aidid lieutenants. The success of these raids was apparent and a testament to the success of TF Ranger's ability to combat the asymmetric tactics of General Aidid with surprise raids of their own. With the success of TF Ranger, it became imperative for General Aidid to strike a blow against an American force causing significant losses to the SNA.[88]

On the afternoon of Sunday, October 3, 1993, General Garrison received word from local operatives that key members of General Aidid's inner circle were meeting near the Olympic Hotel in the Black Sea neighborhood of Mogadishu. For General Garrison, intelligence was often poor at best. Unreliable Somali informants proved the best source of intelligence, but often fell short of the expectations and requirements of TF Ranger. Such was the case on October 3. The opportunity to capture key SNA figures offered TF Ranger the chance to strike an additional blow to General Aidid from deep within the Black Sea neighborhood at the center of the Habr-Gidr clan's territory and an Aidid stronghold.[89]

In previous raids, General Garrison relied on surprise as his primary tactical asset. The general exercised his advantage in this area in a number of ways. First, TF Ranger was superior in low light combat, which led to a high number of night missions. Second, surprise was achieved by varying the means of infiltration (infil) and exfiltration (exfil). A third tactic utilized successfully was variation in target selection. General Garrison sought to avoid developing predictable patterns. The General's actions made it difficult for General Aidid to anticipate where TF Ranger might strike next. And, as in previous operations, surprise figured heavily into the plan drafted by the task force prior to the launch of its seventh mission on October 3, 1993.

In a bold daylight mission, assault and security teams lifted off from Mogadishu airport at 15:43 local time with an aerial infil planned for the target building, near the Olympic Hotel. Delta assault teams would fast-rope onto the target while Rangers fast-roped to the streets surrounding the target in order to set up blocking positions to cover the assault. Colonel Gary Harrell, an experienced Delta officer himself, was the on-site commander and remained above the action in his MH-6 Little Bird command helicopter. Lieutenant Colonel Danny McKnight, a Ranger and General Garrison's chief of staff, led the ground convoy, which was set to arrive at the target after assault teams took down the building and were ready to exfiltrate with their prisoners.[90] General Garrison remained in overall command and monitored the raid from his command post at the Mogadishu airport.

Experienced special operations forces were on their seventh mission in less than two months. Previous operations were largely successful and no indications led the task force to believe that this mission would be different. There was, however, concern about flying deep into "Indian country," but doing so successfully had the capacity of showing General Aidid and his supporters that the United States could strike anywhere at anytime. General Garrison and his staff considered the risks worth the gain. Just after 15:30 local time, the men of TF Ranger loaded up and headed for the heart of Mogadishu.[91]

Within minutes word began flowing into Mogadishu that an American operation was underway. Because of the many eyes watching Mogadishu airport it was exceedingly difficult for TF Ranger to leave the airport without General Aidid receiving almost immediate word of troop movements. Taking only minutes to reach central Mogadishu, Delta assaulters began their work. As assault teams rapidly took down the target, problems began to arise. One Ranger fell nearly 60 feet while fast-roping to the street below. Minutes later, the first of two Black Hawks was shot down by RPG fire.[92] Simultaneously, Lieutenant Colonel McKnight's convoy found itself fighting its way through burning roadblocks and heavy small arms fire. The conditions facing the small force were rapidly deteriorating.[93]

For General Aidid, this was an opportunity to strike a decisive blow to TF Ranger, which he had thus far failed to do.[94] The Americans were now pushing toward his stronghold. Using handheld radios and messengers, Aidid's informants were keeping SNA commanders updated as to the Americans' progress through the tangled web of streets and the air overhead.

After the first Black Hawk crash, the mission began to rapidly evolve and difficulties, absent in previous operations, began presenting themselves. Speed and surprise were keys to success, but with the first and then second helo crashes, wounded Rangers, heavily defended roadblocks, Somali ambuscades, and a complete lack of street signs for navigation, speed and surprise were lost. An all-out brawl was the consequence. The superior training of the special operations forces, close air support, and the poor command and control and training of SNA militiamen and Habr-Gidr clansmen kept a dramatically outnumbered American force from suffering complete annihilation. When the two-hour mission ended the following morning, more than 70 men were wounded and 16 were dead. Mike Durant, pilot of the second downed Black Hawk, was severely wounded and in the custody of General Aidid.

Although the Battle of Mogadishu proved to be America's bloodiest day since the bombing of the marine barracks in Beirut, the mission objective was achieved as key Aidid lieutenants were captured. Public perception and media coverage in the United States, however, viewed the operation as a disaster. News footage of dead American servicemen drug through the streets of Mogadishu by crowds of cheering Somalis proved to be the beginning of the end for American involvement in nation-building efforts in Somalia.[95]

In the immediate aftermath of the Battle of Mogadishu, the M1-A1 Abrams Main Battle Tanks, Bradley Fighting Vehicles, and AC-130 Spectre Gunship previously requested by General Montgomery were rapidly deployed to Somalia.[96] The American effort to confront an asymmetric adversary utilizing special operations forces was at an end. If General Aidid wanted a direct confrontation with the United States, he would face conventional forces equipped with heavy armor and devastating air support. President Clinton found the risks of employing the United States' highly skilled asymmetric forces in major operations a risk not worth taking.

WERE AMERICAN OBJECTIVES ACHIEVED?

Examining the success and failure of American intervention in Somalia is unquestionably complex. It is perhaps simplest to individually examine the three phases of American intervention analyzed above.[97] Phase I began with President Bush's initial provision of aid in the summer of 1992 during Operation Provide Relief and throughout the duration of UNOSOM I. Phase II began with the December 1992 deployment of UNITAF during Operation Restore Hope and ended with the transfer of power to UNOSOM II in May 1993. Phase III began with American activity in UNOSOM II during Operation Continued Hope and ended with the withdrawal of American forces from UNOSOM II in March 1994.

Feeding hungry Somalis was the president's primary objective when he initially ordered aid flown to Somalia.[98] It is also likely that efforts to end famine in Somalia were viewed as a method to avoid direct military intervention, which was unfavorably looked upon by General Powell and the Joint Chiefs. In order to accomplish this objective, 10 C-130 aircraft flew 48,000 tons of food and medical supplies to Kenya, where relief agencies then trucked the aid to hungry Somalis.[99] Warring factions soon came to view aid as a weapon of mass starvation and began efforts to deny rival clans the relief necessary to keep dieing populations alive. While relief did make it to many hungry mouths, much of it was stolen or extorted by militiamen of the various factions.

Although estimates vary widely, many thousands of Somalis were saved by the aid provided by the United States during Operation Provide Relief. When warlords began utilizing a tactic similar to that of Joseph Stalin against the Ukraine (starvation), the effectiveness of aid diminished significantly, reducing President Bush's ability to end the disaster in Somalia before direct military intervention became inevitable. Thus, American objectives were in part successful; many thousands of Somalis were kept alive by the aid provided. In part American objectives were not achieved; 38,000 peacekeepers, led by the United States, took control of Somalia beginning in December 1992 as part of Operation Restore Hope.

Phase II, in which the American-led UNITAF force conducted security and limited reconstruction efforts, accomplished its original objectives rapidly, leading President Bush and Secretary General Boutros-Ghali to expand mission objectives well beyond their original scope. The ability of UNITAF to rapidly eliminate security issues related to aid distribution allowed the force to begin stability operations, which were underway when UNITAF turned over Somalia to UNOSOM II on May 4, 1993. Although General Johnston and Bush administration officials felt UNOSOM II was unprepared to assume control over a country that remained unstable, UNITAF clearly met and exceeded its objectives.

Understanding the United States' failure to achieve its objectives during UNOSOM II requires a greater level of detail than that provided in the discussion of American objectives in phases I and II. This is of particular importance because it was not the casualties sustained during the Battle of Mogadishu that signaled the failure of American objectives, but the domestic response from Congress, the media, and the American public. Immediate and widespread demands for withdrawal of American forces placed President Clinton in a difficult position. Deploying the American military when there is not a clear threat to the interests of the United States was, and remains, a difficult proposition. Photographs and news footage of dead American servicemen being drug through the filthy streets of a third world capital most Americans could not locate on a map made it impossible.

In the days and weeks after the Battle of Mogadishu, Secretary of State Madeline Albright's "assertive multilateralism" came under increased scrutiny by Congress as support for assistance to Somalia plunged.[100] Where Somalia had been a back burner issue for President Clinton as he pursued an ambitious domestic agenda, it became a distraction and an embarrassing failure. Congressional hearings and calls for the United States to withdraw served to vindicate those who opposed entering Somalia from the beginning.[101] Having won an election with 43 percent of the vote, Bill Clinton lacked the national mandate to pursue military operations the American public opposed.

Soon after the Battle of Mogadishu, an ABC News poll showed that 74 percent of respondents disapproved of American involvement in Somalia.[102] Senate Majority Leader George Mitchell (D-ME), however, continued to support the president's decision to intervene, but the damage was already done and the prospect of achieving operation objectives had vanished. Among President Clinton's political opponents, the president took a daily pounding, much as President Reagan had in the aftermath of the Beirut bombing.[103] Public disapproval fueled congressional criticism of the president's Somalia policy as members of both houses sought to play to the interests of their supporters.

Congressional activity began within weeks of the October battle. Highly critical of the president's foreign policy, influential members of Congress called for the United States to withdraw from Somalia immediately. Media coverage also proved critical, making it difficult for a president sensitive to public opinion and media coverage to sustain an unpopular Somalia policy.[104] Little more than a week after the Battle of Mogadishu,

President Clinton went before the nation to explain American policy in Somalia. He began, "These tragic events raise hard questions about our efforts in Somalia. Why are we still there? What are we trying to accomplish? How did a humanitarian mission turn violent? And when will our people come home?"[105] The president answered these questions saying, "Let's start by remembering why our troops went to Somalia in the first place. We went because only the United States could help stop one of the great human tragedies of this time."

President Clinton then announced that he would increase American troop strength prior to a March 1994 withdrawal. The president described the mission of American forces in the following manner:

> Their mission, what I am asking these young Americans to do, is the following: First, they are there to protect our troops and our bases. Second, they are there to keep open and secure the roads, the port and the lines of communication that are essential for the United Nations and the relief workers to keep the flow of food and supplies and people moving freely throughout the country so that starvation and anarchy do not return. Third, they are there to keep the pressure on those who cut off relief supplies and attacked our people. Not to personalize the conflict, but to prevent a return to anarchy. Fourth, through their pressure and their presence, our troops will help to make it possible for the Somali people, working with others, to reach agreements among themselves so that they can solve their problems and survive when we leave. That is our mission.[106]

With the departure of American forces announced, the minimal deterrent effect of UNOSOM II disappeared. By early November, clan violence was on the rise and despite the efforts of Ambassador Oakley, who returned to Somalia at the request of President Clinton, there was little to be achieved outside the return of Chief Warrant Officer Michael Durant.[107] With Ambassador Oakley's successful negotiation of the return of Michael Durant in early November, the bounty on General Aidid was lifted.[108] Aidid supporters captured by TF Ranger were also released in the months that followed. Although the Battle of Mogadishu did not mark the last American casualty in Somalia, General Aidid and other faction leaders were careful to avoid major conflict with American forces in the months prior to their March 1994 departure.

When American forces departed Somalia, President Clinton's objectives for the mission lay in ruins. General Aidid's early testing of UNOSOM II left the warlord with little doubt that UN peacekeepers preferred to remain inside their bases than in the streets of Mogadishu. The subsequent ambushes of Pakistani and Moroccan peacekeepers and Admiral Howe's inability to capture the general further emboldened factions opposed to the foreign presence. Continued violence prevented UNOSOM II from rebuilding a devastated country. TF Ranger's mission to capture General Aidid and disrupt the SNA's ability to conduct sustained combat operations also failed to achieve its objective. While TF Ranger was highly successful during individual missions, General Aidid remained at large until the United Nations lifted the $25,000 bounty offered for his capture.

Little more than a year after the 10th Mountain Division, TF Ranger, and other American elements withdrew from UNOSOM II, the United Nations pulled out of Somalia leaving the war-ravaged country in the hands of competing warlords. Chief among them, Muhammad Farah Aidid declared himself president of the Republic of Somalia, only to die in factional fighting August 1, 1996. More than a decade after American and UN withdrawal from Somalia, the East African nation remains highly unstable and a breeding ground for terrorists.

WHAT LESSONS DID THE UNITED STATES LEARN FROM ITS EXPERIENCE?

In the immediate aftermath of the Battle of Mogadishu, General Garrison took full responsibility for the failure of TF Ranger in a letter written to President Clinton in which he outlined the events and failures of October 3, 1993.[109] At the same time, intense scrutiny of UNOSOM II led the House and Senate to begin investigating American participation in the operation, with the Senate Armed Services Committee holding formal hearings in May 1994.[110] Within the American military, an effort was launched to develop an understanding of American operations in Somalia and how they went from highly successful to public relations nightmare. Analysis produced several insightful lessons, some of which are similar to those learned in the wake of the October 23, 1983, bombing of Beirut International Airport. Others, however, offer new insight into the difficulty of attempting to reorder a failed state.

When the American-led UNITAF force turned control of Somalia over to Admiral Howe and UNOSOM II on May 4, 1993, the United Nations, with the assistance of the United States, began an unprecedented attempt to rebuild the economic, political, and social infrastructure of a country in chaos. Without the benefit of prior experience, nation-building proved far more difficult than first expected. Among the earliest lessons learned was the need for peacekeeping forces that understood the dynamics of the economic, political, and social situation in which they were being inserted.[111] To achieve such understanding, United Nations peacekeepers needed specific training in Somali history, culture, and language. This lack of knowledge led Admiral Howe and TF Ranger to overlook the dominance of the warrior culture in Somalia and the readiness with which Somali clansmen would give their lives to protect General Aidid and for the honor of fighting the United States.[112]

Poor understanding of local conditions generated the need for increased high value intelligence, which was often lacking. Poor relations between

UNOSOM II and the Somali people left both UNOSOM II and TF Ranger with limited and unreliable intelligence. Alternatively, it was General Aidid who was able to maintain an excellent intelligence network consisting of Somalis in the employ of UNOSOM II and TF Ranger, local boys, area residents, and militiamen tasked with observing the foreign forces.[113] General Montgomery's lack of intelligence concerning the location of General Aidid led to multiple failed attempts to catch or kill the Somali war-lord, which endeared and empowered General Aidid while also decreasing the respectability of UNOSOM II. Although TF Ranger was successful in its seven missions, General Garrison was unable to locate General Aidid and restore respectability to UNOSOM II. In conjunction with a poor knowledge of Somalia, limited and often inaccurate intelligence played a major role in the events leading up to the Battle of Mogadishu.

UNOSOM II found itself in a position very similar to that of the American-led Multinational Force in Beirut a decade earlier. Inserted into a failed state in the midst of factional violence, American forces and their UN partners were to act as peacekeepers and nation-builders. This implies that there is peace, which was not the case in either Lebanon or Somalia. As a noncombat force the perception is that there is little need for heavy weapons. It is the maintenance of peace and the return to civil government that is the objective. Heavily armed American troops rolling through the streets of Beirut or Mogadishu on the tops of tanks creates the perception of ongoing combat for the citizenry and the world. Thus, there is a desire to insert lightly armed peacekeepers, which then became targets of Somali factions seeking to change the status quo.

For the United States the lesson was twofold. First, intervening forces must possess the appropriate firepower to defeat potential adversaries, while also serving as a deterrent to possible challengers.[114] Second, passive security dramatically reduces the effectiveness of an intervention force, and the respect and support of local factions.[115] The consequences of passive security were evident in the wake of UNITAF's departure. Rather than continuing active and aggressive patrols throughout Somalia, UNOSOM II retreated to its bases where peacekeepers tended to remain, even as the security situation worsened. This created a perception of fear in the minds of faction commanders who had previously been unwilling to challenge UNITAF.[116]

President Clinton and the Joint Chiefs learned two additional lessons, which have remained relevant to the present day. For President Clinton, Somalia fundamentally altered his approach toward foreign policy.[117] Much like his predecessor George H. W. Bush, Bill Clinton expected the United States to play an active role in the world. As the United States' first major military operation in the post-Cold War era, Somalia proved to be a public relations disaster. It also served as a central reason for President Clinton's modification to the Weinberger/Powell Doctrine to which the president added two requirements. First, operations must be completed rapidly.

Second, casualties must remain low.[118] Perhaps the single greatest lesson learned by the Joint Chiefs of Staff and President Clinton was the sheer difficulty of nation-building. As Major Alan G. Hendrickson writes, "Nation-building, if it is possible at all, is a monumental task, taking a huge toll in manpower, money and time."[119]

In the post-operation analysis undertaken in the years after the failure of UNOSOM II, the asymmetric strategy and tactics employed by General Aidid have played a minor role in shaping the lessons learned by the U.S. military. Instead, a consensus was reached that the United States should avoid nation-building operations. Not until the War in Afghanistan presented difficulties similar to those of a decade earlier did many analysts view Somalia as a precursor to the asymmetric conflict the United States now faces.[120] As Somalia continues to experience a resurgence of interest among analysts, the lessons of UNOSOM II and TF Ranger will continue to yield useful insights for American military planners.

CONCLUSION

Somalia remains a relevant case for military analysts for a number of reasons. As a Muslim country with a history of oppressive government, extremist elements, factional conflict, and third world status, Somalia shares many of the characteristics of Afghanistan and Iraq. These similarities and the Battle of Mogadishu's presence in living memory places Somalia at the top of many lists when attempting to draw analogies between the United States' current conflicts and those of the past. When turning to Afghanistan in the next chapter, the limits to which Somalia and Afghanistan are analogous is made clear. And, while the two cases share a number of characteristics, there are a number of significant idiosyncrasies that separate the two.

The analysis of the American experience in Afghanistan highlights some continuing weaknesses in the American approach to asymmetric conflict while also illuminating American successes. With Afghanistan serving as the final case study, the broader lessons of the American experience begin to be drawn together before being fully explored in the final chapter. It is also in this final case that lessons relevant to Iraq are explored and the unique attributes of each case are highlighted in an effort to illustrate the need for a distinctive approach to future conflicts in which the United States finds itself engaged.

5

Afghanistan (2001–2004): Winning Wars of Asymmetry

Few nations have experienced foreign invasion as frequently or by so many as Afghanistan. In the fifth century BC Cyrus the Great, founder of the Persian Empire, invaded Afghanistan making his way to the Hindu Kush. Cyrus would later die in a fierce battle against the Massegatae near the Jaxartes River. Alexander the Great invaded Afghanistan two centuries later only to be followed by the Scythians, Parthians, Persians, Huns, Arabs, Turks, and Mongols in the 1,500 years that followed.[1] Throughout much of the nineteenth century, Great Britain and Russia focused their attention on Afghanistan as they played the "Great Game."[2] Although one of the world's most remote nations, Afghanistan has played a major role in the downfall of more than one empire.

At times Afghanistan fades from the consciousness of the world, but events never fail to return attention to this arid and mountainous region of Central Asia. The long and storied past of this remote and unforgiving land plays an important role in the present. Rather than offering three millennia of Afghan military history, this analysis begins with the events leading to the Red Army's December 24, 1979, invasion of Afghanistan and progresses to the current day.

Five questions serve to focus the analysis of the War in Afghanistan (2001-present). First, what were the economic, military and political conditions in Afghanistan prior to American intervention? Second, what were American objectives? Third, how did the United States combat the asymmetric strategy and tactics of its adversary? Fourth, were American objectives achieved? Fifth, what lessons did the United States learn from its experience?

In answering these questions, a picture of the War in Afghanistan develops offering insights into the manner in which the United States might respond to conflict in the coming years. It is through a focus on the asymmetric nature of conflict that variables of greater interest to the future of warfare come to light. The "lessons learned" of the War in Afghanistan also offer useful insight into the difficulties the United States faces in Iraq and the intractable nature of many conflicts.

WHAT WERE THE ECONOMIC, MILITARY, AND POLITICAL CONDITIONS IN AFGHANISTAN PRIOR TO AMERICAN INTERVENTION?

After four decades on the throne, King Muhammad Zahir Shah was overthrown by his cousin and former prime minister, Muhammad Daoud, on July 17, 1973. Daoud blamed the king for government corruption and the poor condition of the Afghan economy. Long a progressive who favored modernization and a more liberal view toward the role of women in society, Daoud quickly established the Republic of Afghanistan (1973) and began an ambitious seven-year plan to revitalize the country.[3] Because Afghanistan's primary source of aid was the Soviet Union, Daoud allowed the quasi-Marxist People's Democratic Party of Afghanistan (PDPA) to develop and play a significant role in politics despite signs that President Daoud might one day be a target of the PDPA.[4] As feared, members of the PDPA, with the aid of the military, began a bloody coup on April 28, 1978, which left the president and his family dead. In the purge that followed, thousands of Afghans lost their lives as the newly formed Marxist regime sought to eliminate all who might challenge the sweeping reforms it began implementing. PDPA Secretary General Nur Muhammad Taraki emerged as the president of the Revolutionary Council and prime minister of the new Democratic Republic of Afghanistan (DRA).[5]

The brutal "reforms" initiated by Taraki led to the outbreak of an insurgency in Nuristan (1978), which soon spread across the country. With instability increasing, former Prime Minister and Minister of Defense Hafizullah Amin launched a palace coup against Taraki in September 1979. Once the shooting ended, Amin was left in control of a country in chaos.[6] Amin quickly moved against his enemies in the PDPA, plunging the country into further distress. Along with internal chaos, Afghanistan found itself in conflict with its Soviet benefactor as Prime Minister Amin and his inner circle refused the advice of Soviet advisors.

Under the auspices of a joint operation, Red Army paratroopers began landing in Kabul on December 24, 1979. By December 26, Prime Minister

Amin lay dead and Babrak Karmal, exiled leader of the Parcham faction, returned to Kabul as leader of the Democratic Republic of Afghanistan. The following day the Red Army rolled across the Amu Darya into Afghanistan. During the first years of the Soviet-Afghan War (1979–1989), Mujahideen suffered severe losses as Soviet and DRA forces maintained complete air supremacy, which they used to maul Muj fighters. By 1982 the Mujahideen were at a low point. Concerned that the Soviet Union might win the war, the CIA, with the assistance of Saudi Arabia and Pakistan, began a covert operation providing the Mujahideen with badly needed weapons including shoulder-launched antiaircraft rockets, such as the Stinger missile and its predecessor.[7] The operation was successful as a stalemate ensued in the mid-1980s with neither side capable of defeating the other.

In 1988 Afghanistan and Pakistan, with the United States and Soviet Union participating, signed the Geneva Accords in which they called for an end to Soviet and American intervention in the internal affairs of the two nations. The peace accord included a plan for the return of refugees and a timetable for Soviet withdrawal from Afghanistan.[8]

With Soviet withdrawal complete by February 15, 1989, Mujahideen commanders then turned their efforts against an isolated DRA led by President Muhammad Najibullah. Despite more than a decade of Soviet aid to the DRA, the communist government collapsed in August 1992.[9] Peace did not prove to be the result. Between 1992 and 1996, competing Mujahideen commands fought for control of the country. The death and destruction wrought by internal fighting opened the way for the rise of an extremist religious and political movement near the major southern city of Kandahar led by little known cleric, Mullah Muhammad Omar.[10]

The story behind the rise of the Taliban is rather unexceptional, but worth brief description.[11] In the summer of 1994 a provincial strongman raped several young girls. Local inhabitants turned to the local mullah for assistance. In turn, he sent a number of his religious students to capture and execute the strongman. The students then responded to the pleas of others suffering under the hand of unjust men throughout the area. The Talibs (students) increased in number and sought to bring stability to the region.[12] Success led Pakistan to support the Taliban in October (1994) after Taliban forces successfully recovered a Pakistani convoy captured by an Afghan warlord. Prime Minister Benazir Bhutto and the Interservice Intelligence Agency (ISI) soon began providing aid to the Taliban in the hope that the group might finally bring stability to the country, which was in the interest of Pakistan.

Through the fall of 1994 the Taliban overran the 12 southern provinces of Afghanistan, defeating Mujahideen warlords piecemeal. In January 1995, Gulbuddin Hekmatyar, leader of Hezb-e-Islami and a client of Iran, was defeated by the Taliban at Ghazni.[13] Continuing north and east the Taliban soon controlled 70 percent of Afghanistan with Kabul falling on September 26, 1996. General Ahmed Shah Massoud, leader of the Northern Alliance (NA), held the remainder of Afghanistan. Composed of ethnic minorities such as Uzbeks, Tajiks, and Hazaras, the Northern Alliance fought the Taliban to a stalemate with the NA controlling the northeastern provinces of Afghanistan.[14] From 1996 until the American invasion of Afghanistan in October 2001, the stalemate continued as the Taliban and Northern Alliance proved incapable of defeating one another. Pakistan continued to support the Taliban while Russia, in an effort to prevent a fundamentalist regime from forming to its south, supported the NA. Thus, in a nation devastated by two decades of war, conflict continued.

Afghanistan's poverty is not solely the product of warfare, however. Throughout its history, Afghanistan has been a nation of inhabitants struggling against an inhospitable land for survival. Two decades of warfare served to exacerbate those difficulties. Prior to the 1979 Soviet invasion, Afghans depended upon a complex irrigation network for much of the water that supplied their fields and orchards. The land surrounding Kabul was among the country's most productive agricultural lands with lush apple and apricot orchards providing the city's inhabitants fresh fruit. Irrigation ditches and apple trees also proved to be excellent camouflage for Mujahideen fighters. This led the Red Army to destroy the orchards and irrigation system surrounding Kabul. In addition to the destruction of Afghanistan's infrastructure, the country's limited resources were spent on the war effort rather than internal improvements desperately needed by an impoverished Afghan people. Already a country lacking substantial natural resources and access to the ocean, so important for trade, two decades of warfare stifled the free flow of goods in and out of Afghanistan.

During the 1990s many Afghans ceased producing consumable agricultural products and turned the country's limited arable land into poppy fields for the production and export of heroin. For the Afghan farmer, a successful poppy harvest increased annual income from $300 to $6,500.[15] Poverty and the Afghan farmer's attempt to ameliorate it turned Afghanistan into an international drug exporter and a nation dependent upon the drug trade for sustenance. In a highly volatile international drug trade, Afghanistan suffered further economic loss as it proved unable to maintain a stable export regime, even an illicit one. Thus, the downward economic spiral continued as Afghans suffered from international isolation, crumbling infrastructure, import dependence and a Taliban regime determined to isolate the country from the influences of the outside world.[16]

It was into this morass that Osama bin Laden entered in May 1996. After first joining the Mujahideen in 1982 and spending much of the next decade supporting Afghan efforts to evict the Red Army, bin Laden went on to play a major role in the creation of al-Qaeda. Throughout the early 1990s bin Laden spent much of his time in the Muslim nations of Africa, but when he was asked to leave the Sudan in 1996, bin Laden returned to Afghanistan. Struggling to sustain Afghanistan, the Taliban welcomed the wealthy Saudi's return. The Taliban had a number of reasons for doing so. First, bin Laden shared the Taliban's religious fundamentalism, which was prevalent in the Saudi-supported Madrassahs along the Afghan-Pakistani border from which Talibs were drawn. Second, the multimillionaire Saudi was known for his willingness to support religious fundamentalism. At a critical time in the Taliban's war against the Northern Alliance, bin Laden's connections and support could prove critical. Third, several thousand experienced al-Qaeda fighters followed bin Laden to Afghanistan where they could provide military assistance to the Taliban.[17]

In addition to aiding the Taliban in its fight against the Northern Alliance, bin Laden and al-Qaeda used Afghanistan as a training ground for new recruits, who came from all over the world to receive training in small arms, demolitions, biological and chemical warfare, and urban combat. Among the most prominent training camp was Karnak Farm where bin Laden maintained his family and where many senior al-Qaeda leaders also lived. From this and other locations in southeastern Afghanistan, al-Qaeda planned a number of attacks against the United States and its assets including the 1998 American embassy bombings, the 2001 bombing of the USS *Cole* (DDG-67) and the attacks of 9/11.[18]

At the time of bin Laden's reemergence in Afghanistan (1996), American intelligence agencies were still piecing together the scope and size of al-Qaeda. There was by this time clear evidence that Osama bin Laden was a major player within Islamic fundamentalism and the international terrorist networks developing at the time. In the wake of the World Trade Center bombing (1993), links between bin Laden and international terrorism became apparent.[19] It was not, however, until the summer of 1997 that the Bin Laden Unit was established within the CIA's Counterterrorism Unit. This was, in part, due to growing concerns raised by CIA operations officers responsible for the capture of Mir Amal Kasi, the Pakistani man who opened fire on CIA employees leaving Agency headquarters on the evening of January 25, 1993.[20] The pursuit of Kasi led the CIA to develop a team of Pushtun operatives, code named "Trodpint," which it used to track Kasi in Afghanistan and Pakistan and later to conduct intelligence gathering operations against bin Laden.[21]

One of the most significant problems faced by the CIA and other intelligence agencies working to capture bin Laden was the Clinton administration's view of terrorism. President Clinton sought to capture bin Laden, but as an attorney who had been an antiwar activist during the Vietnam Conflict and had never served in the military, the president saw the bin Laden problem as a criminal matter and was reluctant to use the military or covert operatives of the CIA to capture or kill the terror mastermind. National Security Advisor, Sandy Berger, an attorney without prior experience in intelligence or the military, also favored criminal prosecution as the primary method of pursuing bin Laden. Thus, when CIA operatives offered, on several occasions, a plan to capture or kill bin Laden and other top al-Qaeda leaders at Tarnak Farm and elsewhere, President Clinton rejected such requests on the grounds that civilians (bin Laden's family) might be killed and because of questions over international law.[22]

Because of past resistance to suggested covert operations to capture bin Laden, Director of Central Intelligence (DCI) George Tenet did not recommend long-prepared covert actions to the president in the wake of the August 7, 1998—American embassy bombings in Kenya and Tanzania. Attorney General Janet Reno openly opposed assassinating bin Laden as the president's top attorney sought to handicap covert operations. In an effort to overcome persistent resistance to covert operations, White House counterterrorism coordinator, Richard Clarke, developed the Delenda Plan (1998), which recommended the use of diplomatic approaches, financial disruption, covert action and military strikes.[23] The plan offered a combination of legal and military options to the president, which Clarke believed to be in keeping with President Clinton's approach to terrorism. Rather quickly, the Delenda Plan was rejected as the administration maintained the course of the previous three years.

During the Clinton administration the U.S. military played a minor role in efforts to capture bin Laden. The Navy was responsible for the 1998 cruise missile strikes against al-Qaeda training camps in Afghanistan, but played a minor role in the daily pursuit of bin Laden and al-Qaeda. Reasons for the military's diminished role are unclear, but it is reasonable to suggest that the administration's limited use of military assets was in keeping with its view of terrorism as a criminal matter rather than an act of war, as Clinton's successor, George W. Bush, would view it.[24]

From the August 7, 1998, terrorist attacks in Kenya and Tanzania until the September 11, 2001, attacks on the Pentagon and World Trade Center, bin Laden continued to expand al-Qaeda in Europe, Southeast Asia, and the United States. Afghanistan served as a hub where cells were formed and members trained before returning through Pakistan, to Britain, Germany, the United States, and elsewhere.[25] While al-Qaeda continued to expand its network internationally, it also expanded its training camps in Afghanistan and its influence within the Taliban. For the average Afghan, al-Qaeda and the Taliban were inextricably linked and unpopular.

Despite its claim to religious purity, the Taliban became a key international supplier of unprocessed opiate. Along with the aid provided by Pakistan through the ISI and al-Qaeda, Taliban rule brought about a decline in the already poor standard of living for the average Afghan.[26] In addition to the almost universal unpopularity of the Taliban and hatred of the "Arabs," the United States continued to maintain loose ties with its Mujahideen allies from the Soviet-Afghan War (1979–1989). This enabled

American intelligence officers to quickly begin preparations for large-scale combined operations with the Northern Alliance and Pushtun clans of southern Afghanistan in the weeks following September 11, 2001. Between 1996 and 2001, General Massoud, commander of the Northern Alliance, received little aid from the United States despite repeated efforts to gain American support, relying instead on inconsistent aid from Russia.[27]

For the Clinton administration, providing continued aid to Massoud hearkened back to the Cold War and the bloody struggle between the United States and Soviet Union in the third world. Trouble was also brewing elsewhere and the president allocated resources to end civil war in Haiti, ethnic cleansing in Bosnia-Herzegovina and Kosovo, and a number of other hot spots. Fortunately for the United States, ties with Mujahideen commanders were not completely abandoned in the years following the Soviet-Afghan War. Thus, when the Northern Alliance received the call it had long been waiting for, they were ready. Despite al-Qaeda's successful assassination of General Massoud on September 9, 2001, American intelligence officers and the special operations forces that soon followed were able to rapidly establish trust and rapport with their Afghan allies.[28]

WHAT WERE AMERICAN OBJECTIVES?

During a March 19, 2004, speech President George W. Bush explained American objectives in Afghanistan saying, "For years, the Taliban made Afghanistan the home base of al-Qaeda. And so we gave the Taliban a choice: to abandon forever their support for terror, or face the destruction of their regime. Because the Taliban chose defiance, our coalition acted to remove this threat." He went on to add, "And now the terror camps are closed, and the government of a free Afghanistan is represented here today as an active partner in the war on terror."[29]

Eighteen months after the United States launched its first attacks against the Taliban, President Bush's statement describes the broader objectives of the Global War on Terror and those of Operation Enduring Freedom. The specific objectives of Enduring Freedom are more complex. In the immediate aftermath of the September 11, 2001, attacks, there was rapid analysis of the day's events and a tentative conclusion was reached among senior civilian and military leaders that Osama bin Laden was responsible. He had already played a role in the bombing of the World Trade Center (1993), American embassy bombings (1998), Millennium Plot (2000), and the bombing of the USS *Cole* (DDG-67).[30] As General Tommy Franks, commander in chief of Central Command (CINCCENT), writes in his memoir, it was immediately clear that bin Laden was behind the attacks against the United States. He further adds, "Now I understood the reason for Massoud's assassination. Having anticipated American retaliation in Afghanistan, bin Laden had taken preemptive action to cripple the Northern Alliance."[31]

As CINCCENT, General Franks's area of responsibility included Afghanistan: bin Laden's known location. Thus, General Franks immediately ordered the development of a plan for sustained conflict in Afghanistan sufficient to topple the Taliban.[32] Central Command's Deputy Commander in Chief, Lieutenant General Michael DeLong, was tasked with putting together a number of options for General Franks, which he would then present to Chairman of the Joint Chiefs of Staff General Hugh Shelton and Secretary of Defense Donald Rumsfeld.

During this early stage of planning, which General Franks estimated would take seven to ten days, many objectives were still in the formative stage.[33] There was a clear desire to overthrow the Taliban and destroy al-Qaeda, but military capabilities remained in question. Those assets in the region, however, were alerted within hours of the 9/11 attacks and prepared for strikes against Afghanistan. This included ordering Vice Admiral Willie Moore to cancel all port calls for ships in Central Command's AOR and moving ships armed with Tomahawk missiles into position to launch strikes.[34]

Following his original schedule, General Franks presented three options to General Shelton and Secretary Rumsfeld. According to General DeLong, "We came back to Shelton and Rumsfeld with three initial options. The first was a cruise missile strike. We had ships, submarines and aircraft that could hit al-Qaeda training camps, with cruise missiles. The upside was instant retaliation and little risk; it was the sort of option the Clinton administration had favored."[35] The downside was significant. Cruise missile attacks would not destroy al-Qaeda and the Taliban, nor would they enable the Northern Alliance to defeat their adversary. General DeLong went on to add, "The second option was option one plus manned bombers (B-52s and B-1s) to take out al-Qaeda camps and Taliban military bases in a three-to-ten day air-war."[36] An air campaign, while increasing the effectiveness of American military action, could not guarantee the toppling of the Taliban or the destruction of al-Qaeda. Battle damage assessment in the immediate aftermath of the NATO air campaign in Kosovo and Serbia offered a rosy picture supported by airpower advocates, but upon closer examination the air campaign turned out to be less effective than originally thought.[37] An air campaign in the rugged mountains of Afghanistan would likely prove less effective than that of the Kosovo War (1999).

Thus, General Franks and his deputy supported option three, which General DeLong described in the following way, "The third option, which we favored, packaged cruise missiles and bombers with 'boots on the ground,' using Special Forces and possibly other army and some marine units. We would need at least ten to twelve days to get our forces in-country. If the administration wanted instant retaliation, this was not the way to go. If they wanted substance and a real campaign, this was the best option."[38] Secretary Rumsfeld, after discussing options with President Bush, gave General Franks the green light to pursue option three. The president added two objectives for consideration when developing and implementing Central Command's plan. First, the campaign must not alienate the Arab world. Second, it must minimize damage to Afghanistan's limited infrastructure so that the country's reconstruction can be completed more rapidly.

During this same period the CIA was implementing its own plan in which paramilitary officers would fly into Northern Alliance held territory and connect with General Muhammad Fahim Khan, General Massoud's replacement, in order to arrange for the Panjshir Valley to be used as a base of operations for the Special Forces. A-Teams would then spread out among General Fahim's commanders where they would assess the overall condition of NA forces, provide financial assistance, utilize GPS (global positioning system) mapping equipment to establish the position of Taliban and Northern Alliance lines, and offer material assistance to NA commanders when possible.[39] The CIA paramilitary officers of "Jawbreaker" flew into the Panjshir Valley in the last week of September aboard antiquated Soviet helicopters, purchased in Uzbekistan and refurbished for upcoming operations.[40]

In the four weeks between the attacks of September 11, 2001, and the beginning of American air strikes in Afghanistan, President Bush applied significant pressure on Pakistan's president, Pervez Musharraf, to end his country's support of the Taliban, which he did.[41] President Bush also focused on developing an international coalition to begin a new Global War on Terror, with the War in Afghanistan serving as the first battle in this global conflict. Among the president's strongest supporters was British Prime Minister Tony Blair who possessed one of the few militaries in the world with the technological capability needed to fight alongside the United States. The president also sought to garner support around the world with particular emphasis placed on Muslim countries. President Bush was well aware of the Soviet experience in Afghanistan. Thus, preventing a second jihad in Afghanistan was a primary objective of the administration, requiring the United States to gain the support of leaders in the Islamic world.

After American diplomats successfully negotiated the support of a number of Muslim world leaders or, at a minimum, the moderation of criticism, Special Forces operators began entering the Panjshir Valley from secret bases in Uzbekistan and Tajikistan on October 15, 2001.[42] Prior to the insertion of Operation Detachment Alpha (ODA) teams, the CIA paramilitary officers of Jawbreaker produced much of the data needed by the air force for target selection and acquisition. The CIA also provided the Northern Alliance with $70 million in badly needed funds.[43] This early financial and tactical assistance proved critical for both the success of the Northern Alliance and the United States as they began pushing the Taliban south in the latter half of October.

In addition to air strikes designed to weaken Taliban front line positions and destroy limited command, control, and communication capabilities,

American C-17 cargo aircraft began a massive effort to provide relief supplies to impoverished Afghans. Initial difficulties arose, however, with such an effort as relief supplies were dropped into remote regions at high altitudes.[44] Afghans were often leery of receiving supplies dropped from aircraft high overhead. Not only did relief supplies fall into mine fields on occasion, but Taliban propaganda claimed that the United States was attempting to poison Afghans in the food packets that were dropped.[45] During the Soviet-Afghan War (1979–1989) the Soviet Union failed to win the hearts and minds of the Afghan people. Instead, it sought to impose communism through mass violence as the Red Army did in Russia two generations earlier. American military planners were well aware of Soviet shortcomings and unwilling to make the same mistakes. Providing effective relief was a key element in the broader objective of turning Afghan support toward the United States and away from the Taliban.[46]

Military objectives were simple. As Secretary Rumsfeld said, "The military role will be over when the Taliban and al-Qaeda [bin Laden's network] are gone. That's what this is about."[47] The president's broader objectives, however, required the United States and its Coalition partners to rapidly establish a multi-ethnic government, end terrorism, provide an alternative to opium production, and establish basic human rights.[48] The speed of success in the ground campaign took the administration and military commanders by surprise. The three-pronged attack of the ground campaign, which sought to take Mazar-i-Sharif in the north before shifting American air power to the Takhar front where the forces of Bariullah Khan would break out and move to capture Talaquan worked well. Pressure would then be put on Kunduz, which fell before the Northern Alliance and Special Forces teams took Kabul.[49] Kabul was in Coalition hands by November 14, 2001.

General Franks describes American operations in Afghanistan as having four phases. In the first phase, the USS *Kitty Hawk* (CV 63) served as a "lily pad" for Special Forces and the 160th SOAR as they began operating in Afghanistan. The second phase began with initial combat operations and continued through follow-on operations. Phase III consisted of "decisive" combat operations with the United States adding Coalition partners during this phase. Finally, phase IV, which may be considered the current phase, is dedicated to the development of Coalition capabilities designed to prevent the reemergence of terrorism.[50]

HOW DID THE UNITED STATES COMBAT THE ASYMMETRIC STRATEGY AND TACTICS OF ITS ADVERSARY?

The War in Afghanistan (2001-present) and the Soviet-Afghan War (1979–1989) differ dramatically in a number of ways. Where the Soviet

Union deployed large-scale ground forces into Afghanistan to support an unpopular regime and establish an economic and social system foreign to Afghans, the United States relied and continues to rely on experienced Mujahideen with the aid of American air power and Special Forces to defeat an unpopular fundamentalist regime supported by an even less popular foreign presence (al-Qaeda).[51] Sensitive to the mistakes made by the Red Army, American military planners sought to mitigate many of the problems incurred by the Soviets by limiting the number of American forces used in ground operations, mollifying clan animosities, and providing tangible aid to Afghans.[52]

The initial ground campaign also differed significantly from the Soviet experience. In the wake of the Taliban's successful capture of 70 percent of Afghanistan by 1998, Taliban and Northern Alliance units established stationary lines in a fashion similar to the Western Front of World War I. Entrenched and fortified lines limited the maneuverability of both the Taliban and Northern Alliance. Neither possessed the strength to penetrate the other's lines. It was under this condition that a stalemate was reached prior to the beginning of American air strikes on October 7, 2001.[53]

A look at Afghanistan in the weeks prior to American intervention reveals little at the strategic or tactical levels that may be considered asymmetric. In fact, the situation was exactly the opposite. The lack of basic military training on both sides of the Takhar front serves as a key explanation for the entrenched positions that would come to spell the doom of the Taliban. For the Taliban, troops were poorly trained religion students, with the aid of slightly better trained al-Qaeda fighters. Neither was experienced with nor prepared for large-scale American air strikes, which tore massive holes into Taliban lines, disorienting commanders and breaking the will of front line troops. For the Taliban and al-Qaeda, defeat in Afghanistan was a result of an inability to adapt to massive air strikes, called in by A-Teams, followed by the charge of Northern Alliance troops on foot or horseback.

The combination of A-Teams, air strikes, and Northern Alliance cavalry and infantry attacks rapidly rolled up Taliban positions while pushing escaping troops south toward Kabul and Kandahar. Once air strikes began, Taliban commanders transformed the provinces they controlled for total war.[54] But, rather than reverting to the asymmetric tactics that proved successful against the Red Army, the Taliban continued to wage conventional warfare in which they sought to prevent the Northern Alliance from making territorial gains in the wake of American air strikes. This strategy proved disastrous for the Taliban and quickly silenced President Bush's critics who claimed the United States was stumbling into another Vietnam-style "quagmire."[55] Between the opening of the air campaign on October 7 and the fall of Kandahar, exactly two months later, the Coalition with its Afghan, American, and British forces applied asymmetric means with great success.[56] Coalition troops utilized superior aviation capabilities with audacity, mobility, and superior training to cut off and outflank an adversary that often outnumbered the combined Coalition force five and ten to one. An estimated 31,000 Taliban and al-Qaeda fighters perished during combat operations.[57]

Between the launch of the first major ground offensive against Mazar-i-Sharif and the collapse of the Taliban 32 days later, the Coalition captured: Mazar-i-Sharif on November 9, Kabul on November 14, Kunduz on November 26, and Kandahar on December 7.[58] The remnants of the Taliban abandoned Zabul Province on the Pakistani border two days after the fall of Kandahar leaving the Coalition in effective control of Afghanistan.

With major combat operations complete, the Coalition shifted its focus to rebuilding Afghanistan into a viable multi-ethnic democracy and eliminating remaining Taliban and al-Qaeda fighters, including Osama bin Laden, who were believed to be hiding in a remote eastern region of Afghanistan known as Tora Bora.[59] Well aware of the Soviet Union's fatal mistakes, the Coalition immediately began massive efforts to rebuild Afghanistan and improve the living standard of Afghans. This not only included improving health care, education, agriculture and infrastructure, but repatriating refugees, empowering women, rebuilding the Afghan Army and working with Pushtun, Hazara, Tajik, and Uzbek leaders to bring about a meeting of the Loya Jurga.[60] The Coalition effort was substantial and greatly mitigated the former appeal of the Taliban. One key element of defeating a weaker opponent in an asymmetric conflict is denying his ability to draw protection and support from the local populace.[61] The Coalition's nation-building efforts were designed to do just that.[62]

Among Coalition partners many areas of responsibility were divided by the Afghan Reconstruction Steering Group, which dispersed security responsibilities as follows:

- National Army—United States (DoD/CENTCOM)
- National Police—Germany
- Judicial Reform—Italy/European Commission
- Counter-narcotics—Great Britain
- Demobilization—United Nations[63]

In the aftermath of major combat operations more than two dozen countries participated in substantial nation-building programs. The United Nations and other multinational organizations were particularly interested in playing a major role in nation-building efforts. Although the United Nations, European Commission, and other international organizations participating in Afghan reconstruction did not fight alongside the United States in combat operations, past nation-building failures across Africa in Bosnia-Herzegovina, Haiti, Somalia, and elsewhere drew these organizations to Afghanistan where they sought to overcome the failures of the past.[64]

While reconstruction efforts increased in size and scope, Coalition forces searched for Osama bin Laden, Mullah Omar, and concentrations of al-Qaeda and the Taliban. Tora Bora remained a primary target for American commanders. By mid-December human intelligence from local Afghans and signals intelligence from the National Security Agency (NSA) led General Franks and other commanders to believe that bin Laden was hiding in the caves of Tora Bora.[65] The decision was made to destroy the vast network of caves and kill or capture all al-Qaeda fighters in the area. One major concern was the potential for creating ill will among the tribes living in the region. Afghans in eastern Afghanistan, along the border with Pakistan, received substantial support from bin Laden in recent years and were considered sympathetic to the Saudi millionaire. In order to mitigate these difficulties, Coalition forces created a force specifically designed for combat at Tora Bora. As General DeLong points out, "So, instead, using CIA, our Special Forces, and friendly Pushtun generals, we created 'Eastern Alliance' forces. The plan was to force al-Qaeda and the Taliban from the high ground of the mountains and into the caves, and then bomb the hell out of the caves." He adds, "Tora Bora began as a ground campaign (not, according to popular belief, as an air campaign)."[66]

Task Force Dagger, composed of Special Forces operators from the Air Force, Army, Navy, and their Afghan allies, established blocking positions east of Tora Bora in order to prevent fleeing al-Qaeda fighters from making it across the border into Pakistan. Combat operations began in late December and lasted several weeks with cave-clearing operations continuing well beyond the end of combat operations.[67] Conservative estimates of 300 al-Qaeda killed in action and the destruction of major weapons, munitions, and supply caches suggest Tora Bora was a success for the United States with one major exception, the escape of bin Laden.[68] Exactly how he slipped past the numerous blocking positions designed to prevent just such an occurrence is unclear, but it is believed that bin Laden and other fleeing al-Qaeda fighters were able to buy safe passage from local Afghans and Afghan soldiers of the Eastern Alliance. The failure to capture bin Laden was a disappointment for all involved in the Tora Bora operation.

In the weeks and months after the fall of Tora Bora, Special Forces teams from Task Force 11 spread across Afghanistan hunting the remnants of the Taliban and al-Qaeda. Simultaneously, reconstruction efforts continued at a vigorous pace as more than two dozen countries began providing substantial assistance. As Afghans developed confidence in the permanent demise of the Taliban, warlords, tribal leaders, and Afghan activists began jockeying for position in the interim government, which took office in December.[69] Hamid Karzai, leader of the Southern Alliance and a Western-educated Pushtun, was chosen as interim president. He immediately went about the difficult task of uniting the various Afghan tribes by dividing positions in government among the warlords, providing Coalition-sponsored assistance across the country and appealing to Afghans tired of two decades of warfare.[70]

Karzai was dependent upon the Coalition and, most importantly, the United States for his position and the support necessary to carry out presidential responsibilities. For the United States, President Karzai's success was a key element in mitigating and eliminating possible asymmetric adversaries.[71] Should the United States send large numbers of troops into Afghanistan to hunt down al-Qaeda, anti-American sentiment would grow. With Hamid Karzai at the helm in Afghanistan working alongside the United States to eradicate Taliban and al-Qaeda remnants, while also protecting the welfare of the Afghan people, a Soviet-style debacle could be prevented. There was a clear expectation that this would indeed be the case.[72]

Between December 2001 and February 2002, intelligence suggested an al-Qaeda presence in a remote region of southern Afghanistan known as the Shah-i-Kot Valley, southeast of Gardez. A steady stream of human and signals intelligence confirmed the suspicions of CIA, TF Dagger, and Advanced Force Operations (AFO) personnel that the Shah-i-Kot was an area al-Qaeda had chosen to reestablish itself inside Afghanistan. Colonel Mulholland, commander of TF Dagger, and Lieutenant Colonel Blaber, AFO commander, realized the significance of the Shah-i-Kot and placed the valley at the top of their target list.[73] Central Command quickly began Operation Anaconda. According to General Franks, "As the name implied, the mission of Anaconda was to encircle and squeeze into extinction an al-Qaeda and Taliban force whose strength was estimated to be as many as 2,000 well-armed Arabs, Afghans, Chechens, Uzbeks, and Pakistanis. The enemy were survivors who'd escaped the Coalition offensive that had liberated most of Afghanistan in November and December. Many of these terrorists had been pushed south out of Tora Bora into the steep Shah-i-Kot Valley; surrounded by towering snowy ridges, the area bristled with trenches, bunkers and mortar pits, as well as caves and tunnels that had been used by fighters like them for years."[74]

General Frank's portrayal of the valley and men defending it is descriptive of the difficult fight the United States would face.[75] In order to cleanse the Shah-i-Kot of al-Qaeda, the United States would, for the first time, deploy conventional forces alongside Special Forces teams and Afghan militiamen. Task Force Rakkasan, composed of just over 2,000 troops from the 10th Mountain and 101st Airborne Divisions under the command of Major General Buster Hagenbeck, was tasked with cutting the trails that ran east and south out of the valley. TF Hammer, led by the A-Teams of Glenn Thomas and Matthew McHale were to approach the Shah-i-Kot from the west with 300 to 400 Afghan militiamen under militia commander Zia Lodin. Task Force K-Bar's mix of Special Forces was to form an outer ring of security. Task Force 64, with its men from the Australian Special Air Service (SAS), accepted the task of watching the area south of the Shah-i-Kot. Finally, Task Force 11's Delta operators were placed on standby at Bagram Air Base.[76]

Operation Anaconda began March 1, 2002, as Zia Lodin and his Afghan militiamen loaded into their trucks along with their A-Teams and began moving to the Shah-i-Kot from Gardez. The move to contact brought about first contact in the early morning hours of March 2 when al-Qaeda fighters opened fire on the approaching force. These attacks were followed by American air strikes, which came over the next seven days from AH-64 Apache Attack Helicopters, AC-130H Spectre Gunships, F-14A Tomcats, B-52 Stratofortress Bombers, and B-1 Lancer Bombers.[77] The combination of air strikes and ground forces slowly destroyed a well-entrenched al-Qaeda force. Coalition casualties were among the highest of any operation in Afghanistan with a number of Afghan militiamen, Special Forces, Army Rangers, and American soldiers either killed or wounded.[78]

After more than a week of intense air strikes, mortar attacks, and small arms fire, al-Qaeda remaining in the Shah-i-Kot fled to Pakistan. Estimates of al-Qaeda casualties suggest 520 fighters were killed during Anaconda.[79] The operation's success came at a price but again illustrated that a small and highly mobile ground force supported by air power can defeat a well-entrenched adversary. Al-Qaeda's failure to adapt to the speed and mobility of Coalition forces proved deadly in the Shah-i-Kot as it had in the initial ground campaign and at Tora Bora. The lessons of the Takhar front failed to be appreciated by al-Qaeda reconstituting in the Shah-i-Kot.

WERE AMERICAN OBJECTIVES ACHIEVED?

Four years have passed since Operation Anaconda, offering sufficient time to examine the success and failure of American objectives in Afghanistan. Operation Enduring Freedom's original objectives focused on ending Taliban rule, destroying al-Qaeda training camps and facilities, eliminating al-Qaeda fighters, providing humanitarian relief to Afghans, preventing civil war, and establishing a multi-ethnic democracy. President Bush also sought to kill or capture Osama bin Laden and his lieutenants while destroying al-Qaeda's ability to strike the United States and its allies in the future.

Toppling the Taliban was the United States' first objective. Combat operations began October 7, 2001, with a week-long air campaign, which utilized fewer than 400 CIA officers and American Special Forces personnel. In fewer than 60 days, the last remnants of the Taliban were fleeing their final stronghold and birthplace, Kandahar, for the safety of Pakistan.[80] In recent months the Taliban has attempted to regain control of Kandahar and other southern provinces from Coalition and Afghan forces.[81] Terrorist attacks against soft targets still occur, which serves as an illustration of the Taliban's lack of strength as it attempts to establish an insurgecy and pose a sustained threat to Hamid Karzai's government.[82] October and November of 2006 were particularly difficult months for the new government and the Coalition as Taliban ambushes killed a number of civilian and military personnel.[83] Should Coalition troops exit Afhganistan it is unknown whether the Karzai government can defeat a resurgent Taliban.

During major combat operations, the U.S. Air Force began a major relief operation in areas controlled by the Northern Alliance followed by Taliban-controlled regions.[84] As the Coalition pushed the Taliban south, relief supplies flooded into liberated areas. Already familiar with the net-work of relief organizations responsible for providing assistance during previous crises, Afghans, with some exceptions, accepted aid from Britain, America, the United Nations, and NGOs. Everything from food to medical care was provided to impoverished Afghans as the bitter Afghan winter approached. The success of relief efforts not only alleviated suffering but also played an equally important role in promoting cooperation with Coalition forces while siphoning support away from the Taliban. While it is difficult to determine the exact effect of relief efforts in this area, anecdotal evidence suggests that relief played an important role for many Afghans in persuading them to support or, at a minimum, tolerate Coalition forces. These efforts have not ceased as aid and reconstruction continue to the present day with American-led efforts to rebuild Afghanistan.[85]

Although Special Forces operators continue to hunt al-Qaeda fighters in Afghanistan and the Afghan-Pakistani border region, the country has experienced minimal al-Qaeda activity since Operation Anaconda eliminated the last substantial al-Qaeda force in Afghanistan. Much of the Coalition's lasting success may be due to its early efforts to destroy al-Qaeda training camps and facilities during the opening air campaign and the extensive efforts of American Special Forces to locate al-Qaeda fighters and eliminate them. In the first weeks of the ground campaign, Army Rangers launched night raids behind enemy lines in attempts to kill or capture key al-Qaeda and Taliban leaders.[86] Special Forces teams conducted similar raids eliminating al-Qaeda fighters in Afghanistan and the Pakistani border region. No accurate al-Qaeda casualty reports are available, making it difficult to determine the extent to which Coalition Special Forces reduced the capacity of al-Qaeda to strike again in the future. This is made more difficult because estimates of the total number of al-Qaeda operatives and the number of persons trained in al-Qaeda camps remains classified. What is certain, however, is that al-Qaeda lost Afghanistan as a base of operations, which was a primary objective of Operation Enduring Freedom.

One key objective military planners and the Bush administration placed at the top of the Coalition's list was preventing a large-scale domestic insurgency. Military planners were familiar with the Soviet experience in Afghanistan and the price paid by the Soviet Union for alienating Afghans.

Large-scale relief was one element of preventing such an insurgency, which might take the form of a widespread dispersal of al-Qaeda and Taliban forces supported and protected by local populations.[87] A second element of this objective was the utilization of a small number of American ground forces in combat operations. Enduring Freedom relied on Afghans for the bulk of ground forces. A minimal foreign presence was thought to create less animosity toward Coalition objectives. For this reason, there were fewer than 400 American combat troops in Afghanistan during the ground campaign.[88]

Current troop levels are significantly higher than during the initial campaign with 20,000 American troops in Afghanistan at the current time. Many of these troops are, however, involved in security, reconstruction, and other support efforts.[89] In a country significantly larger than Germany, it is interesting to note that the number of American troops in Afghanistan today stands at approximately 1/30 the troop level of postwar Germany (1945).[90] The Bush administration's strategy has seen some success. Anecdotal evidence from Afghanistan suggests many Afghans desire higher numbers of American troops so that they can provide greater security and stability in the country.[91] Some Afghans, however, are disappointed with the progress made in the last four years and are turning to the Taliban for assistance.[92]

The final objective of the Bush administration was establishing a Western-oriented democracy in Afghanistan. As former CIA Officer Gary Schroen points out, Hamid Karzai was selected early on to serve as the leader of the new government, at least until the first presidential election in Afghan history could be held.[93] President Bush and the Department of Defense were deeply concerned about the Tajik- and Uzbek-dominated Northern Alliance sweeping into Kabul and across Pushtun provinces and sparking a civil war. For this reason, Hamid Karzai's Southern Alliance was created and given the task of defeating Taliban forces in southern Afghanistan. Ethnic balance in the postwar era was a key to the creation of a successful democracy.[94]

After the Bonn meetings, held in early 2002, Hamid Karzai was selected to lead the new Afghan government. Unlike past governments formed after one faction's victory in combat, the government installed on June 24, 2002, was the result of the Northern Alliance (Tajik and Uzbek), Rome Group (loyal to King Zahir), Cyprus Group (Iran-backed), and Peshawar Front (Pushtun) agreeing on the establishment of a multi-ethnic government with ministries divided among the various ethnic groups.[95]

On October 9, 2004, Hamid Karzai was elected president of Afghanistan in the country's first presidential elections. This was followed a year later by provincial and parliamentary elections.[96] With four years of experience under their collective belts, the members of Afghanistan's government are experiencing remarkable success. Participation in elections is significant and the willingness of Afghanistan's warlords to cooperate with the central government, while far from complete, is a substantial improvement over the past 30 years of instability. Karzai's success is a positive result for the Bush administration and the broader objective of establishing a multi-ethnic democracy in Afghanistan. How long this success may continue is unknown. The long-standing ethnic and tribal conflict responsible for much of Afghanistan's past instability is unlikely to disappear simply because the central government includes members of major factions. The true test of success for President Bush will come when Coalition troops withdraw. In the meantime, however, democracy is proving remarkably successful in Afghanistan. This does not suggest that the government in Kabul will ever experience the degree of support or exercise the same control as the U.S. government. Three thousand years of fierce independence from central control by Afghan tribes makes it unlikely that Afghans will suddenly acquiesce to the wishes of the Kabul government. Some modicum of peace and national unity is, however, possible.

WHAT LESSONS DID THE UNITED STATES LEARN FROM ITS EXPERIENCE?

The United States' experience with asymmetric conflict over the past two decades illustrates the difficulties of fighting an adversary unwilling to stand his ground and be annihilated by a superior force. The War in Afghanistan is, without exception, the most successful major American military operation since the end of the Second World War. This is due, in large part, to the Taliban's failure to modify its tactics when the United States joined Northern Alliance efforts to topple the Taliban. Thus, it was the Taliban's inability or unwillingness to revert to asymmetric tactics that led to its defeat in the ground campaign. Stephen Biddle suggests the Taliban's poor morale, training, and tactical knowledge is responsible for its failure to adapt to the Coalition offensive.[97] This failure alone does not explain Coalition success, however.

The combination of American air power, Special Forces, and Northern Alliance ground troops presented a powerful triumvirate. In a coordinated effort, American air power, guided by American Special Forces, tore holes in Taliban lines, which Northern Alliance cavalry then exploited. Key to Coalition success was the flexibility and adaptability of the Special Forces A-Teams fighting with the Northern and Southern Alliances. Where conventional forces face limitations on freedom of action, Special Operations Forces are highly capable of adapting to an ever-changing set of circumstances. This made fire and maneuver, a traditional tactic of conventional forces, a tactic utilized by the Coalition with devastating success. Rather than employing artillery, highly trained A-Teams relied on air power to provide direct fire, which enabled ground forces to move rapidly on the battlefield increasing the speed, mobility, and versatility of combat troops.[98]

In addition to the tactical elements listed above, there are several lessons the Coalition learned as it achieved broad political success in Afghanistan. First, the Taliban's oppressive rule made the regime extremely unpopular. This led many Afghans to stay out of the fight altogether and many others to work with the Coalition in overthrowing the Taliban. From its inception, Mullah Omar's support was geographically isolated to the Kandahar region. Outside his home base, cooperation with the Taliban was purchased through coercion. Second, the Taliban relied on al-Qaeda for much of its financing, tactical expertise, and morale.[99] Many Afghans considered al-Qaeda fighters to be arrogant foreigners disrespectful of Afghan customs. The dislike of al-Qaeda by the majority of Afghans undercut the ability of bin Laden to assist the Taliban as it sought to hold its ground against the Coalition.

Afghan military culture is also unique in its widespread acceptance of defection in warfare. Afghans have long accepted switching sides in the middle of a conflict as a norm in warfare. It carries with it little or no stigma and is part of the pragmatic nature of Afghan culture. During the Soviet-Afghan War, warlords frequently shifted alliances and sides. In the years after the Soviet-Afghan War, the Kabul government's composition frequently changed as factions supported or opposed Burhanuddin Rabbani's government from 1992–1996. As the Taliban campaign (1995–1996) began to succeed, warlords previously opposed to the Taliban began to defect when it appeared the Taliban would succeed.[100] When Coalition forces demonstrated that the demise of the Taliban was inevitable, a number of Taliban commanders switched sides once again, leaving Mullah Omar with significant holes in his defensive position.[101]

Although Afghanistan's culture of defection played an important role in the defeat of the Taliban, it is idiosyncratic in nature. Few of the world's countries share this Afghan tradition and none are prospective adversaries of the United States. This culture of defection along with the Coalition's ability to exploit divisions within the Taliban and the poor condition of Taliban forces, the regime's unpopularity, and relative isolation may all prove idiosyncratic of Afghanistan and less useful in drawing broader lessons.[102] This is of particular importance when attempting to apply an Afghan model to Iraq or other future conflicts which may differ from Afghanistan in important ways.

One lesson of Afghanistan, which the American experience in Lebanon and Somalia also illustrates, is the United States' inability to deter adversaries in weak or failed states.[103] President Bush's September 20, 2001, speech before a joint session of Congress urged the Taliban to turn Osama bin Laden over to the United States clearly explaining that the United States would invade Afghanistan if al-Qaeda continued to receive safe harbor.[104] When the Taliban did not act the president issued a second warning on October 2 and a third on October 6.[105] The Taliban offered to release foreign aid workers it held, but refused to turn over bin Laden or expel al-Qaeda. The Taliban's tenuous grip on power and inexperience in world affairs led the regime to miss the significance of President Bush's threats. A stable regime is unlikely to have missed the clear message the president was sending and would have recognized the strength of the United States.

Although the War in Afghanistan presents the United States with a number of positive lessons, there are also lessons learned from the weaknesses in the Coalition plan and its execution. Much as it did in Lebanon (1983) and Somalia (1993), poor human intelligence proved to be a significant weakness of the Coalition. The failure of American air power to eliminate key al-Qaeda and Taliban personnel during air strikes and the failure of Special Forces to locate, capture, or kill Osama bin Laden, Mullah Omar, and other key targets exemplifies the poor quality of intelligence the United States relied upon. In several instances, air strikes were authorized when it was believed that bin Laden or Mullah Omar was at a specific location. In each instance intelligence was incorrect leading to strikes that failed to kill either man.[106] Special Forces teams operating out of Camp Rhino, a secret special operations base behind Taliban lines early in the war, found the intelligence they depended on for covert missions inaccurate and outdated. The failure to capture Mullah Omar at Karnak Farm is one example of the poor quality of intelligence the United States utilized.[107]

In addition to poor human intelligence the United States relied on 6- or 12-man Special Forces A-Teams to accomplish missions requiring a significantly larger force.[108] While the Special Forces are the best at what they do, in order to seal off escape routes from Tora Bora or the Shah-i-Kot Valley, for example, it takes large numbers of American boots on the ground.[109] The number of American troops needed to accomplish interdiction operations fell well below the numbers needed during key battles and in the aftermath of the ground campaign. Anthony H. Cordesman suggests the shortage of American troops may be to blame for the escape of bin Laden and Mullah Omar.[110] The attempt to limit the American "footprint" in Afghanistan was effective in many ways, but its single greatest drawback was in limiting the United States' ability to place sufficient troops where they were needed.

Afghanistan's tribal society and the long-standing animosities between those factions within the Coalition led the United States to inadvertently choose sides among the loosely allied Afghans. In one instance, an Afghan faction within the Coalition had American aircraft bomb a village, which was said to hold enemy fighters but proved to be the village of a rival faction.[111] This type of Coalition fratricide occurred on several occasions and could have presented significant problems for General Franks and the Coalition. These events offer an important lesson for the United States: Know your enemy and your allies.

Following similar lines, the United States must pay careful attention to who prospective winners and losers will be in the aftermath of American action. Those areas in southern Afghanistan where support for the Taliban and al-Qaeda remain the highest are experiencing the least material improvement. Conditions in Afghanistan were bleak for all segments of society under the Taliban, which has played an important role in mitigating resistance to Hamid Karzai's government, but, as Iraq illustrates, when a major group (Sunnis in Iraq and Pushtuns in Afghanistan) sees a diminution of its position resistance is likely.[112]

Perhaps the most important lesson of the war is one for senior military commanders, academics, and journalists. The war in Afghanistan is not Vietnam. The circumstances that came together during the decade and a half of American intervention in Vietnam are unlikely to be repeated again. Future wars may share similarities to the Vietnam Conflict, but all wars share similarities. As General George S. Patton once said, "Warfare has not changed since time immemorial." Keeping in mind the similarities of warfare and the unique set of circumstances that the United States will face in future conflicts should provide civilian and military leaders with a sense of perspective, which is easily lost.

CONCLUSION

As this analysis illustrates, the War in Afghanistan is, in some ways, illustrative of the mode of warfare adversaries of the United States are likely to utilize when American military might is employed abroad. This is particularly true of a resurgent Taliban. Beginning with air power, the United States is likely to continue its reliance on technological superiority rather than large-scale force deployment in combat. Troop levels in Iraq are an ever present reminder of this. It is also likely that military planners will internalize the lessons of Afghanistan as they prove relevant to the Global War on Terror. As the past has shown, however, mistakes tend to be repeated.

Whether the War in Afghanistan is viewed as the first of a new generation of conflicts or an idiosyncratic war has yet to be answered. The perceived value of the American experience is largely dependent upon who is listening as the current debate over fourth generation warfare illustrates. Long-term relevance may depend upon the success of democracy in Afghanistan. Should the country relapse into civil strife, few are likely to look at the War in Afghanistan as a model for future combat and postwar operations. If, however, Afghanistan succeeds, military planners may see Afghanistan as a model to follow. What is perhaps most likely is that Afghanistan will be overshadowed by the War in Iraq.

As this brief look at Afghanistan suggests, it has remained a locus of conflict for more than two millennia. The American experience is only the latest in a long succession of conflicts in the area. Whether the United States succeeds, where Alexander and the Soviets could not, will remain an unanswered question for years to come. Only after American troops withdraw from Afghanistan will we know the strength of the regime put in place by the Coalition. Early analysis suggests moderate success, but success will surely evolve in the years ahead. As history illustrates, when the United States maintains broad public support for its military policies, success is the outcome. When, however, public support is lost, as it was in Vietnam, American objectives become increasingly difficult to achieve. Afghanistan illustrates the importance of public support once again as the United States and its allies struggle to defeat a resurgent Taliban and disaffected warlords.

Conclusion: The Lessons of War and Implications for Iraq

Nations are often said to fight today's war as they did the last. In recent memory, Britain, France, and Germany attempted to utilize first generation warfare from 1914–1919 despite the revolution in arms of the late nineteenth century that signaled the move to the second generation.[1] Why did European military commanders fail to recognize the changing face of warfare? Europe's previous conflict, the Franco-Prussian War (1870–1871), was fought with the linear tactics of the first generation, similar to those utilized in the American Civil War. It was to this model that commanders naturally returned. Thus, when the Schlieffen Plan did not lead to the rapid defeat of France in 1914, warfare degenerated into headlong infantry assaults that chewed up a generation of Europe's young men.[2] World War II offers a second example. Buoyed by its victory in World War I, France constructed the Maginot Line expecting a future conflict with Germany to look much like the last.[3] France's failure to adapt to the development of mechanization and third generation warfare, exhibited in the *Blitzkrieg*, led to its defeat in 1940.

European powers are not alone in "refighting the last war." The Korean War (1950–1953) was an attempt by General Douglas MacArthur and President Harry Truman to refight the Pacific Campaign.[4] Both men failed to see the new dynamics established at the onset of the Cold War and were ill prepared for General Peng Dehuai's "volunteers" as they crossed the Yalu River into North Korea. Little more than a decade later the United States found itself in a second conflict in Asia; this time fighting experienced guerrillas who had already defeated two of France's most decorated military commanders in General Henri Navarre and General Jean Lattre de Tassigny. Rather than learning from the mistakes of the French, Commander of Military Assistance Command Vietnam General William Westmoreland attempted to wage a conventional war in the jungles of Vietnam.[5] Such a strategy may have been effective in Korea, but it would not work in South-east Asia.

In each of these instances civilian and military leaders failed to recognize the changing face of warfare as they sought to fight the last war once again. As we enter the twenty-first century, a similar opportunity presents itself. Will the U.S. military continue to remain mired in third generation warfare as we wait for the ghost of the Red Army to make its push west or will decision makers boldly move into the fourth generation?[6]

With the September 11, 2001, terrorist attacks against the United States, the dynamics of conflict changed once again. No longer do we face a national army capable of standing toe-to-toe with American forces as the Red Army once could. Instead, we face a loose network of terrorist cells that once maintained a hub in Afghanistan. Defeating this new adversary will require the United States to abandon the "American way of war." Conflicts of asymmetry are conflicts of radical departure from convention and require a level of adaptability, knowledge, and skill absent in current military doctrine.

This study has focused on understanding asymmetric conflict and the variables that play an important role in the success and failure of the United States' last three asymmetric conflicts. Analysis of the American experience in Lebanon (1982–1984), Somalia (1992–1994), and the War in Afghanistan (2001–2003) present seven "lessons learned" that offer the fourth generation warrior insight into the strengths and weaknesses of the American way of war, which should be kept in mind as the United States continues to wage war against an adversary unwilling to utilize conventional strategy or tactics.

LESSONS LEARNED

Human Intelligence

Human intelligence is a persistent weakness. In Lebanon, Somalia, and Afghanistan, poor or inadequate human intelligence played a significant role in the United States' inability to achieve its objectives. In Lebanon, the United States did not maintain a reliable human intelligence capability prior to American intervention. When the marines of Battalion Landing Team (BLT) 2/8 landed on the beaches of Beirut during the summer of 1982, the Marine Amphibious Unit commander was dependent upon unreliable CIA intelligence, which came from poor quality Lebanese sources. As Commandant of the Marine Corps General Paul X. Kelley noted in his testimony before the Senate Armed Services Committee in December 1982, numerous reports of planned attacks and car bombings against marine positions were included in the MAU commander's regular intelligence brief. In each case, intelligence was erroneous.[7] When the marine barracks at Beirut International Airport were destroyed by a "car bomb" on October 23, 1983, intelligence did not indicate a suicide attack was likely.[8]

A decade later, the United States found itself in Somalia with many of the same conditions present as existed in Lebanon. Once again, Americans were without reliable human intelligence. The informants working for the United States frequently failed to provide actionable intelligence, limiting UNITAF, and later, Task Force Ranger's ability to carry out missions against hostile militia forces.[9] Unlike Lebanon, however, UNITAF consisted of more than 20,000 American troops tasked with restoring security to Somalia.[10] This mission enabled the large American force to aggressively pursue its objectives, which included intimidating the gangs responsible for much of Somalia's bloodshed. It was not until UNITAF turned over authority to UNOSOM II in May 1993 and the majority of American troops withdrew that the lack of human intelligence began to prove problematic. Without a substantial American force to prevent internecine violence, the importance of intelligence increased dramatically.[11]

When TF Ranger left Mogadishu Airport on October 3, 1993, for the Black Sea District in central Mogadishu, General Garrison's intelligence sources did not warn of the battle that was to come. There were no indications of a waiting ambush, the concentration of militiamen in Mogadishu, or General Aidid's plan to exact heavy American casualties. Had intelligence indicated a danger, General Garrison may have altered the mission that left 17 of his men dead and over 70 wounded.[12]

The War in Afghanistan, while clearly more successful than American intervention in Lebanon or Somalia, saw poor human intelligence play a significant role in the United States' inability to capture or kill Taliban and al-Qaeda leaders. Throughout the war, American troops were reliant on signals intelligence in a war against an adversary that fought on foot, horseback, and from the bed of Toyota pickup trucks. The Taliban and al-Qaeda's lack of technological sophistication made human intelligence of greater significance. Thus, four years after the collapse of the Taliban and a manhunt of unprecedented proportions, the United States is still unable to locate Mullah Muhammad Omar, Ayman al-Zawahiri, or Osama bin Laden.[13]

As the United States continues to wage war against a widely dispersed terrorist network with cells maintaining loose ties to one another, the problems presented by inactionable human intelligence will remain ever present. The fact remains: there is no technological substitute for reliable human intelligence.[14] It is on building and rebuilding networks of informants and spies that the United States must concentrate its efforts in the years to come if it hopes to win the War in Iraq and the Global War on Terror.

Force Capability

Intervening forces must be of sufficient size and capability to achieve American objectives. When President Dwight D. Eisenhower ordered

American troops into Lebanon in July 1958, the force consisted of more than 10,000 heavily armed marines and, later, soldiers. The show of overwhelming force by the United States led to the rapid de-escalation of tension in the country, with the restoration of stability and the completion of American objectives taking less than 60 days.[15] Twenty-five years later, however, President Reagan sent a lightly armed force of less than 2,000 men into a country in the middle of a civil war. Without main battle tanks, heavy artillery, or air cover, the small marine force was tasked with stabilizing southern Beirut and keeping the Israeli Defense Force and Muslim militias apart. BLT 2/8 and the BLTs that followed were outmanned and outgunned by the Palestinian Liberation Organization (PLO), Shiite-Amaal, and Druze militias waging war in southern Lebanon.[16] The inadequate size and capability of the American force left the marines in an untenable position, which culminated in the October 23, 1983, bombing of the marine barracks at Beirut International Airport.

A similar mistake was repeated a decade later when UNITAF turned over authority to UNOSOM II in Somalia; withdrawing more than 20,000 American and UNITAF troops, while leaving 4,000 men of the 10th Mountain Division to serve as a quick reaction force for an undersized and lightly armed UNOSOM II peacekeeping force. Admiral Howe and General Bir quickly discovered that General Aidid was no longer intimidated by the dramatically weakened UNOSOM II force, which quickly found itself the target of Somali militiamen.[17] The climax of American intervention came when just over 100 American special operations forces were ambushed by 10,000 to 30,000 Somali National Alliance militiamen and angry Habr-Gidr clansmen.[18] General Montgomery's QRF lacked the necessary firepower to rapidly rescue the trapped men, who struggled to hold out against overwhelming odds for 18 hours while a sufficient rescue convoy could be cobbled together. It was only after the Battle of Mogadishu that American forces received the M1-A1 Abrams Main Battle Tanks, Bradley Fighting Vehicles, and air support requested months earlier.[19]

While the War in Afghanistan has yet to produce combat that the American public finds as shocking as the bombing of the marine barracks or the Battle of Mogadishu, the insufficient size of American forces during the weeks and months following the defeat of the Taliban played a significant role in the United States' inability to capture or kill bin Laden, al-Zawahiri, and Mullah Omar and the failure to capture or kill al-Qaeda and Taliban forces fleeing Tora Bora and the Shah-i-Kot Valley during Operation Anaconda. Coalition efforts to seal Afghanistan's border with Pakistan are proving ineffective because of the limited number of available troops and ineffective participation by Pakistani forces. This, in turn, continues to allow remaining al-Qaeda and Taliban fighters to move back and forth across the border to launch terrorist attacks against Coalition troops and Afghan civilians.

Recent wars in Afghanistan and Iraq illustrate the ability of the United States to rapidly defeat adversaries utilizing conventional tactics with limited combat forces. Technological innovation has proven successful in increasing the combat effectiveness of the individual soldier, sailor, airman, and marine, requiring fewer "boots on the ground."[20] Much of this advantage is, however, lost when conventional combat operations end and an adversary turns to asymmetric means. As Afghanistan and Iraq illustrate, winning the peace often requires a greater number of highly trained troops than winning the war.[21]

Static Defense

Static defense is ineffective against asymmetric adversaries. When Colonel Mead and Lieutenant Colonel Johnston led their men back into Beirut on September 29, 1982, they were tasked with maintaining stability in southern Beirut and separating Muslim factions from the IDF. The mission called on the marines to serve as peacekeepers, a role they were neither trained for nor anxious to perform. During the early months of the marines' deployment, the men were warmly received by the citizens of Beirut. This changed when Muslim factions no longer viewed the United States as an agent of change in Lebanon. When faction leaders realized that the marines sought to preserve the Lebanese government, which they desired to overthrow, the marines were no longer received with smiles and cold Coca-Cola. By March 1983, the situation on the ground began to slowly change as the marines became targets of opportunity when they left the airport to patrol Beirut.[22] When the marines did not respond aggressively to militia attacks more followed. The passive force found itself under frequent and heavy fire by August 1983 when marines returned fire against Amaal militiamen for the first time.[23] Following the rules of engagement and mission objectives, the marines did not pursue an active defense, but "hunkered down" and waited for attacks to cease. On October 23, 1983, a van loaded with 12,000 pounds of explosives drove through marine checkpoints at the airport and into the lobby of the BLT Headquarters. Two hundred forty-one sailors and marines were killed in the explosion. Static defense was a failure.

The United States' experience in Somalia offers examples of success and failure. During the American-led UNITAF mission, the large force actively patrolled trouble areas where troops asserted a dominant presence.[24] General Johnston, UNITAF commander and BLT 2/8 commander in Beirut a decade earlier, did not make the same mistakes in Somalia as were made in Lebanon. The active and aggressive posture of UNITAF successfully brought a return to stability in Somalia. It would fall on Admiral Howe and General Bir to make the mistakes of Lebanon when UNOSOM II took over for UNITAF.

General Bir's UNOSOM II force consisted of 28,000 UN peacekeepers that were neither equipped nor trained for urban combat. This led General Bir to take a passive role in maintaining the stability restored by UNITAF. Well aware of the change in strategy, General Aidid soon began to test UNOSOM II by bringing his militiamen back into Mogadishu and by attacking UNOSOM II convoys and patrols. On June 5, 1993, 23 Pakistani peacekeepers were killed when SNA militiamen ambushed them while on their way to inspect an illegally maintained arsenal. Admiral Howe and General Bir were unable to respond aggressively to this attack. Instead, UNOSOM II ended regular patrols and pulled back from its role in providing security and stability to Somalia. UNOSOM II's passive role in peacekeeping operations left the 10th Mountain Division's QRF and the newly arrived TF Ranger to restore security to Somalia and capture General Aidid.[25] This effort ended in a perceived disaster at the Battle of Mogadishu.

Afghanistan proved to be dramatically different from the previous two American experiences. Rather than focusing on bringing stability to a war-torn country, as was the case in Lebanon and Somalia, the War in Afghanistan was an effort to topple a hostile regime and the terrorist network it supported. The aggressive campaign waged by the United States and the Coalition between October 7, 2001, and the completion of Operation Anaconda in March 2002 bears little resemblance to the Multi-National Force in Lebanon or UNITAF/UNOSOM II in Somalia.

It is in the period after the completion of major combat operations that Coalition actions are relevant to the current discussion. Where the mission of American forces called for static defense in Lebanon and Somalia, Special Operations Forces aggressively pursued Coalition adversaries in Afghanistan. Air power was also used to eliminate targets harassing Coalition troops. This aggressive stance has, as al-Qaeda's "number two" man, Ayman al-Zawahiri, recently stated in a captured letter, led to the defeat of al-Qaeda in Afghanistan.[26] In post-campaign operations, the United States has continued to maintain an aggressive search and destroy policy, which has made the reemergence of the Taliban more difficult.

Nation-Building

Intervention must be accompanied by the reconstruction of infrastructure and the rebuilding of civil society. In all three cases, the infrastructure of each nation was destroyed during the long period of internal conflict that preceded American intervention. Civil society also suffered greatly as leading citizens fled each country for Europe and the United States. The institutions that held society together were often destroyed or forced to withdraw. In Lebanon and Somalia, for example, the military and police remained above ethnic and religious conflict during much of the internecine conflict, but were ultimately drawn into the conflict removing stabilizing institutions within society. Somalia and Afghanistan experienced decay within the tribal system, which played an important role as arbiter of conflict and interpreter of law and custom. In both countries, tribal elders were supplanted by warlords who were concerned with private ambitions rather than the needs of society. Rebuilding these institutions is crucial to American success when it intervenes in states such as Lebanon, Somalia, and Afghanistan. By rebuilding key infrastructure and restoring the institutions of civil society, citizens are given a stake in the success of the United States and are more likely to support American objectives and reject the efforts of America's adversaries.

In Lebanon and Somalia the United States was unable to generate popular support and became a target of domestic and foreign insurgents, supported by a portion of the local population. Afghanistan, however, is a very different experience. This may be because the United States and its Coalition partners have learned from past mistakes. In the immediate aftermath of the Taliban's defeat Coalition countries, international organizations, and NGOs began a massive effort to provide food, health care, jobs, and security to Afghans across the country. Long-term rebuilding projects rapidly began. Tribal councils were reconstituted, along with the Loya Jirga, and every effort was made to restore the social institutions of Afghanistan. These efforts are proving fruitful as a majority of Afghans see the United States as liberator rather than invader.[27] In future conflict, reconstruction of infrastructure and civil society will remain a pivotal factor for American success, given the nature of conflict the United States is likely to face.

Idiosyncrasy

Future conflict is likely to have a number of idiosyncrasies that make its modeling difficult. In each of the three conflicts examined in this study, a number of variables proved idiosyncratic in each case. Lebanon was a nation with a number of competing factions, much like Somalia and Afghanistan, but with external forces intervening in a long-standing domestic conflict. Syrian, Iranian, Palestinian, and Israeli intervention in Lebanese domestic politics created a complex set of circumstances that are unlikely to exist elsewhere as future conflicts may or may not experience intervention of a similar nature. This leaves the United States to discover and attempt to understand the dynamics at play in the area American forces are to be sent. Somalia also presented a unique set of cultural circumstances that are not likely to be seen again. Two variables serve as examples of the unique attributes of the conflict in Somalia. First, Somali militiamen were dependent upon a steady diet of khat, which they chewed throughout the day reducing natural inhibitions. This often led militiamen to act irrationally, making it more difficult for UNITAF and UNOSOM II troops to anticipate the actions of General Aidid's men. Somalia also has a long tradition of a "warrior ethos," which made it difficult for American forces to predict rational action on the part of militiamen. For Somali militiamen, it was better to face certain death at the hands of the Americans than show any sign of cowardice. Drug use and a warrior ethos are not unique to Somalia, but the combination of possible variables and their variation from accepted Western norms are the nexus of idiosyncrasy.

Similarly, Afghanistan presents a number of idiosyncrasies for the United States. Tribal and cultural norms in Afghanistan set it apart from other Islamic societies. Over the past three millennia Afghanistan developed a set of customs and norms that are replicated no where else in the Islamic world. These norms, in combination with the rugged terrain of the country, thwarted Greek, Persian, Mogol, British, and Russian invaders. American forces are now facing these cultural and geographic issues, which they never faced before. Due to Afghanistan's rugged terrain and high elevations, troops and equipment are being tested to their very limits and well beyond that for which they were designed or trained. Earlier discussions of the campaigns in Tora Bora and the Shah-i-Kot Valley illustrate this point. One final Afghan idiosyncrasy is its culture of switching sides in the midst of conflict. Nowhere else in the world is it permissible to shift alliances with such ease as it is in Afghanistan. As the United States continues to find itself engaged abroad, it will intervene in countries requiring a deep understanding of the local culture, language, and people. A one-size-fits-all approach will not succeed.

Asymmetry

Adversaries of the United States will continue to utilize asymmetric strategies and tactics. The War in Afghanistan and the War in Iraq are illustrative of the fact that facing the United States in a conventional conflict is a losing proposition. In both Afghanistan and Iraq the United States suffered a majority of casualties after the completion of major combat operations. As initial combat in both countries illustrates, the military might of the United States is unmatched. Utilizing asymmetry means against the United States is no guarantee of success, however. In contrast to the successful asymmetric strategy in Lebanon and Somalia, Taliban and al-Qaeda efforts to build an insurgency in Afghanistan are failing.[28] American success and failure has not been overlooked by prospective adversaries. Even among major powers, such as the People's Republic of China, significant work is being done to develop new ways to defeat the United States utilizing asymmetric means.[29] America's adversaries are likely to continue developing these capabilities in the future. It will be left to the United States to actively seek to counter them.

Intractable Problems

Internal conflicts in a number of states may prove intractable. More than two decades after American forces withdrew from Lebanon, the small

Mediterranean nation continues to be plagued by endemic violence and a number of the same problems it faced when marines first landed in Beirut in 1982.[30] Unquestionably, the economic, political, and social problems of Lebanon have dramatically improved since the signing of the Taef Agreement (1989). Violence is down, economic growth is up, and many young Lebanese are now rallying behind efforts to oust Syrian forces and intelligence operatives from the country, but problems between Maronites, Druze, Sunnis, Shiites, and other groups continue to plague the country, however, and may burst into violence if the tenuous balance that currently exists is breached. The recent conflict between Hezbollah and Israel is one example of the fragile nature of Lebanon's current state of peace. It clearly demonstrates that the systemic discord among Lebanese factions has not been resolved.

Somalia has proven less successful than Lebanon. The country remains in a state of chaos more than a decade after American troops withdrew from the country. In 2005, President Abdullahi Yusuf leads a transitional federal government which is engaging the numerous factions in talks to form a permanent government. Fighting continues, however, as warlords seek control over the capital and important regions of the country.[31] Somalia continues to be a breeding ground for terrorists as instability and poverty persist with many Somalis suffering from malnourishment and dependence on international aid.[32] Foreign investment in Somalia has failed to materialize because of the continuing conflict, which prevents the Somali economy from experiencing necessary growth, which in turn keeps Somalis among the world's poorest people. The endemic tribal conflicts of Somalia may only cease with the rise of strongmen capable of playing the role Siad Barre once held. More than a decade of conflict and negotiation has proven fruitless, making the prospects for democracy in Somalia bleak.

Afghanistan may likewise prove to be a country with intractable problems the United States cannot solve militarily or with foreign aid. Tribal conflict between Pushtuns, Hazaras, Tajiks, and Uzbeks and between the numerous political factions dates back generations and centuries and is unlikely to disappear with the arrival of American forces. President Karzai will play an important role in mitigating conflict between the tribes, but his success may end when Coalition forces depart, rebuilding efforts cease, and Afghanistan is once again left to its own devices. As illustrated in the case study of the War in Afghanistan, discord between Afghan factions within the Coalition remains high.

Post-Cold War conflict has proven a "mixed bag" for the United States and is likely to prove increasingly difficult as America's adversaries adapt to the tactics employed by American forces in Afghanistan and Iraq. With the United States likely to be drawn into conflict in failing or failed states, the difficulties of intractable problems will be ever present. As the Global War on Terror continues in the years ahead, terrorist networks are likely to move operations to states with governments lacking the capacity to deter and disrupt them.[33] The lack of a stable government is often the result of an inability to solve long-standing problems, which makes the issue of intractability particularly relevant.

Lebanon, Somalia, and Afghanistan present a number of insightful lessons. While the United States repeated mistakes in all three cases, it is clear that with each conflict civilian and military leadership attempted to adapt to changing circumstances. These efforts met with varying degrees of success. As experience illustrates, no plan survives first contact with the enemy and no conflict is free of mistakes. And although the United States is unmatched in conventional warfare, it will continue to struggle with conflicts of asymmetry where an adversary refuses to stand and fight.

PENETRATING THE DECISION CYCLE

In the minds of many readers the analysis presented in the preceding chapters generates a fundamental question. As Vladimir Lenin famously wrote, what is to be done? While a thorough answer to this question is itself a lengthy work waiting to be written, let me end my analysis by briefly offering two places to begin the search for a solution.

As George W. Bush and future American presidents continue to face adversaries unwilling to engage the United States in second or third generation warfare, where America is unrivaled, it becomes imperative that the "American way of war" adapt to the changing face of conflict. More than two decades ago Colonel John Boyd (USAF) predicted the need for change and offered a radical reinterpretation of the nature of conflict, which was rejected while the United States and Soviet Union remained adversaries. With the Cold War at an end and the Global War on Terror in its early stages, understanding Boyd's conception of "moral conflict" is perhaps more appropriate than at any previous point.[34]

While it is Boyd's development of the OODA Loop (observe, orient, decide, act) for which he is best known, Colonel Boyd's doctrine of moral conflict is of perhaps greater value and highly relevant to the analysis of asymmetric conflict offered in the preceding pages.[35] There is little question that the United States finds itself in the midst of fourth generation warfare in Afghanistan and Iraq.[36] While the transformation in warfare that is the hallmark of the fourth generation has been undertaken by America's adversaries, little has been done within the U.S. military to transform doctrine to meet the demands of conflict in the coming decades.[37] Intransigence and a "big box" perspective remain the norm with the exception of SOF and a small cadre of Department of Defense personnel who have long understood the evolving nature of conflict. Rather than fundamentally altering the American conception of warfare, the Pentagon has relied on improved technology to maintain the United States' edge in combat. And although

American forces are the most effective in the world, it is the conception of conflict that has yet to change.

Boyd's moral conflict with its emphasis on factors largely taken for granted in American military doctrine offers an alternative capable of winning current conflicts and those of the future. At the center of Boyd's strategic thinking is his emphasis on penetrating an adversary's OODA Loop. According to Boyd:

> Operate inside an adversary's observation-orientation-decision-action loops, or get inside his mind-time-space, to create a tangle of threatening and/or non-threatening events/efforts as well as repeatedly generate mismatches between those events/efforts an adversary observes, or anticipates, and those he must react to, to survive:
>   thereby
> Enmesh an adversary in an amorphous, menacing, and unpredictable world of uncertainty, doubt, mistrust, confusion, disorder, fear, panic, chaos...and/or fold an adversary back inside himself:
>   thereby
> Maneuver an adversary beyond his moral-mental-physical capacity to adapt or endure so that he can neither divine our intentions nor focus his efforts to cope with the unfolding strategic design or related decisive strokes as they penetrate, splinter, isolate or envelop, and overwhelm him.[38]

The nature of conflict in Boyd's grand tactics fundamentally differs from current military doctrine. Flexibility, a cornerstone of Boyd's doctrine, may better serve American troops as they enter conflicts eerily reminiscent of Lebanon or Somalia in the future. With AirLand Battle Doctrine continuing to appear much as it did during the Cold War, Boyd's notion of conflict is not simply a push for greater technological innovation, but also a view of conflict that enables American troops to attack an adversary utilizing the moral and psychological forces first described by Sun-tzu.

Developing a doctrine that integrates the variables introduced by Boyd is, however, beyond the scope of the analysis offered here. Future work must move toward an integrated doctrine that satisfies "big box" requirements yet offers the flexibility required to win asymmetric conflicts. As knowledge of causal variables in these conflicts improves, doctrine must prove able to integrate learning at a rapid pace currently unseen. In addition to building on the work of Boyd, there is also a need for a greater understanding of the rationality of asymmetric actors. If doctrine is to utilize moral and psychological variables, it is necessary to understand the values and psychological strengths and weaknesses of one's adversary.

RATIONAL CHOICE AND ASYMMETRIC CONFLICT

Although theories of rational choice have failed to offer the predictability that scholars believe necessary to illustrate validity, rational choice theory remains an important theoretical tool for understanding the preferences and actions of friend and foe alike.[39] Theories of rational choice assume individual rationality, personal preferences, ranking of those preferences, and individual action, which enables the development of unified theory and a useful place to begin when attempting to develop an understanding of the actions of an adversary. Such a framework also proves useful when, for example, attempting to understand the Sunni-led insurgency in Iraq.

As the attacks of September 11, 2001, illustrate, Khalid Shaikh Muhammad and al-Qaeda's desire to strike the United States on American soil was underestimated because of a fundamental misunderstanding of Islamic fundamentalism and its adherents. The perception of the United States as a "paper tiger" lacking the will to strike back illustrates a similar misperception on the part of al-Qaeda. The image of weakness American leaders allowed to form and persist was a result of the poor understanding of Islamic culture and values, which future research may assist in reshaping as the United States develops a better understanding of the actions of al-Qaeda, Hezbollah, Hamas, and other groups that may surface as adversaries of the United States.[40] Development of valid rational choice theories may prove invaluable in improving the detection, denial, and deterrence capabilities vital to the United States in its efforts to win the Global War on Terror and future conflicts. Knowledge of al-Qaeda, Hezbollah, or North Korea's dictator, Kim Jong-il's preferences and the risks each is prepared to take to fulfill those preferences can dramatically increase the ability of America to achieve its objectives vis-à-vis these adversaries.

Further research and development of rational choice theories specifically designed for the asymmetric actor is needed.[41] Formal models may prove useful as American decision makers attempt to better understand who it is they may face, their values, and the risks they are willing to take. Rather than simply dismissing Osama bin Laden or Kim Jong-il as madmen, attributing rationality to their actions may prove a more appropriate course of action.[42] The opportunity to expand the limited work done thus far is significant as asymmetry in conflict is certain to continue in relevance for many years to come. When combined with efforts to develop doctrine relevant to fourth generation warfare, the ability of the United States to successfully combat its adversaries stands to see marked improvement. As the analysis above illustrates, mistakes are often repeated and lessons are infrequently learned. Improving the flexibility of military doctrine by reshaping it in a form relevant for today's asymmetric conflicts may improve American success in the future.

Notes

INTRODUCTION

1. "Transcript of President Bush's Address," *CNN.com*, September 20, 2001, http://archives.cnn.com/2001/US/09/20/gen.bush.transcript/ (accessed September 15, 2005).

2. Ibid.

3. Ibid.

4. On Christmas day, 1991, the Soviet Union ceased to exist. The Cold War was over.

5. Among these early advocates of an alternative path were Colonel John Boyd, Ralph Peters, and Bill Lind.

6. Brian Williams, "The Atlantic Wall," Militaryhistoryonline.com, 2000, http://www.militaryhistoryonline.com/wwii/dday/prelude.aspx (accessed February 1, 2004).

7. Perry Biddiscombe, *The Last Nazis* (Charleston, SC: Tempus Publishing, 2000).

8. Charles Whiting, *Hitler's Werewolves* (New York: Playboy Press, 1972).

9. Perry Biddiscombe, *Werwolf! The History of the National Socialist Guerrilla Movement* (Toronto: University of Toronto Press, 1997).

10. From Biddiscombe, *Werwof!*: Higher estimates of the total number of Werewolves suggest that 10,000 Germans participated in *Werwolf* activities of some kind, although command and control of *Werwolf* units began crumbling by April 1945 as Allied forces occupied Germany. The total death count for Werewolves is estimated at 3,500 to 5,000 men, women, and boys. Many were killed in fire fights with Allied troops. A large number were captured and executed for their guerrilla activities; and from Biddiscombe, *The Last Nazis,* chap. 3: American forces executed boys as young as 14 years old for carrying out guerrilla activities.

11. Biddiscombe, *Werwolf!* 36–37.

12. Victor Chuikov, *The End of the Third Reich* (New York: Imported Publications, 1978); and Erich Kuby, *The Russians and Berlin, 1945* (New York: Hill and Wang, 1968). The highest-level casualty of *Werwolf* attacks was

General N. E. Berzarin, Soviet Commandant of Berlin, who was assassinated June 16, 1945.

13. Biddiscombe, *The Last Nazis.*

14. Brian McAllister Linn, *The Philippine War, 1899–1902* (Lawrence: University of Kansas Press, 2002); Diane Preston, *The Boxer Rebellion* (New York: Berkley Publishing, 2001); Max Boot, *The Savage Wars of Peace: Small Wars and the Rise of American Power* (New York: Basic Books, 2002); and Herbert Molloy, *The Great Pursuit* (New York: Smithmark Publishers, 1995).

15. U.S. Marine Corps, *Small Wars Manual* (Manhattan, KS: Sunflower University Press, 1940).

16. See James Chace, *Acheson: The Secretary of State Who Created the American World* (Cambridge, MA: Harvard University Press, 1999); and James Schnabel, "Policy and Direction: The First Year," in *The United States Army in the Korean War* (Washington, DC, 1972). Many scholars and pundits credit Secretary of State Dean Acheson's January 12, 1950, speech before the National Press Club with signaling to the Chinese, North Koreans, and Soviets that the United States would not interfere should North Korea invade the South. When the North did invade the South, American forces fought alongside South Koreans eventually fighting North Korean and Chinese forces to a standstill at the 38th parallel.

17. Ellen D. Collier, "Instances of Use of United States Forces Abroad, 1798–1993" (Naval Historical Center, Department of the Navy, 1993); Zoltan Grossman, "From Wounded Knee to Afghanistan: A Century of U.S. Military Interventions," *Z Magazine* 14, no. 8 (2001). The War in Iraq must be added to the list provided in the two sources listed above to complete the list of American conflicts.

18. Neill MacAuley, *The Sandino Affair* (Micanopy, FL: Wacahoota Press, 1998).

19. Victor Davis Hanson, *An Autumn of War: What America Learned from September 11 and the War on Terrorism* (New York: Anchor Books, 2002).

20. William S. Lind, Colonel Keith Nightengale (USA), Captain John F. Schmitt (USMC), Colonel Joseph W. Sutton (USA), and Lieutenant Colonel Gary I. Wilson (USMCR), "The Changing Face of War: Into the Fourth Generation," *Marine Corps Gazette,* October (1989).

21. See Martin Van Crevald, *Technology and War: From 2000 B.C. to the Present* (New York: Free Press, 1989). Socrates, long before becoming a philosopher, served as a hoplite in the phalanxes of Athens, which looked very similar to the linear formations of Napoleonic warfare more than 2,000 years later. Should Socrates have fought in 1812 AD rather than 371 BC, he would have replaced his spear with a musket but would otherwise have been familiar with the tactics of the day.

22. Victor Davis Hanson, *The Soul of Battle: From Ancient Times to the Present Day, How Three Great Liberators Vanquished Tyranny* (New York: Anchor Books, 1999). Epaminondas, the great Theban military commander, after defeating the Spartans at the Battle of Leuctra (371 BC), followed up his victory by marching into the Peloponnese where he destroyed helotage, thus ending Sparta's ability to exist as a warrior culture. With much the same desire, the attackers of September 11, 2001, sought to strike at the very heart of American civilization in order to destroy the United States's ability to project cultural, economic, and military power around the globe.

23. Alexander L. George and Richard Smoke, *Deterrence in American Foreign Policy: Theory and Practice* (New York: Columbia University Press, 1974).

24. Ibid., 95.

25. See Charles Krauthammer, "The Unipolar Moment," *Foreign Affairs* 70, no. 1 (1990); and Collier, "Instances of Use."

26. See Charles Kindlebarger, *The World in Depression 1929–1939* (Berkeley and Los Angeles: University of California Press, 1974); see also Mancur Olson, *The Logic of Collective Action* (Cambridge, MA: Harvard University Press, 1965); and Duncan Snidal, "The Limits of Hegemonic Stability Theory," *International Organization* 39, no. 4 (1985).

27. See Kamal Salibi, *Modern History of Lebanon* (Los Angeles: Caravan Books, 1996). When looking at the breakdown of order in Lebanon, the influx of Palestinian refugees in 1948, 1967, and 1975 is the single greatest reason this once peaceful country plunged into civil war.

28. "U.S. Missiles Pound Targets in Afghanistan, Sudan," *CNN.com,* 1998, http://www.cnn.com/US/9808/20/us.strikes.01/ (accessed February 10, 2005).

29. Alan Hendrickson, *Somalia: Strategic Failures and Operational Successes* (Marine Corps Command and Staff College, 1995).

30. See Steven Stedman, "International Actors and Internal Conflict," in *Project on World Security* (New York: Rockefeller Brothers Fund, 1999) for a detailed discussion of "internal conflict" in Africa.

CHAPTER 1

1. Berndt Brehmer, "The Dynamic O.O.D.A. Loop: Amalgamating Boyd's O.O.D.A. Loop and the Cybernetic Approach to Command and Control" (Stockholm: Swedish National Defense College, 2004).

2. Herodotus, *The Histories,* trans. George Rawlinson (New York: Alfred A. Knopf, 1997).

3. Thucydides, *History of the Peloponnesian War,* trans. Rex Warner (New York: Penguin Books, 1954).

4. Xenophon, *Anabasis,* trans. Carleton Brownson (Cambridge, MA: Harvard University Press, 1998).

5. Arrian, *The Campaigns of Alexander,* trans. Aubrey de Selincourt (New York: Penguin Classics, 1958).

6. Polybius, *The Rise of the Roman Empire*, trans. Ian-Scott Kilvert (New York: Penguin Books, 1980).

7. Ibid; Livy, *The War with Hannibal,* trans. Aubrey de Selincourt (New York: Penguin Classics, 1972).

8. During the Second Punic War it was Hannibal who was often outnumbered by Roman forces but still managed his greatest victories.

9. Livy, *The War with Hannibal,* 85.

10. Ibid., 101–3.

11. Ibid., 145–50.

12. Julius Caesar, *The Conquest of Gaul* (New York: Penguin Books, 1983); and Caesar, *The Gallic Wars,* trans. H.J. Edwards (Cambridge, MA: Harvard University Press, 2000).

13. Caesar, *The Civil Wars,* trans. A.G. Peskett (Cambridge, MA: Harvard University Press, 1984).

14. Flavius Josephus, *The Jewish War,* trans. G.A. Williamson (New York: Penguin Classics, 1984).

15. The final end of the revolt took place at the citadel of Masada where, in 73 AD, the remnants of the rebellion flung themselves from the citadel walls hours before Legionnaires stormed the gates.

16. Martin Van Crevald, *The Art of War: War and Military Thought* (London: Cassell, 2002), 45.

17. Flavius Renatus Vegetius, *The Military Institutions of the Romans,* trans. John Clark (Westport, CT: Greenwood Press, 1985).

18. Ibid., bk. 1, 1.

19. Al-Qaeda operatives frequently participated in a two-year program of extensive training in explosives, small arms, psychological operations and counter-detection. This system of training was disrupted by the invasion of Afghanistan in 2001, but efforts have since been taken to rebuild al-Qaeda training elsewhere.

20. See J.F.C. Fuller, *Memoirs of an Unconventional Soldier* (London: Nicholson and Watson, 1936); and Vegetius, *Military Institutions of the Romans,* bk. 3, 1.

21. Vegetius, *Military Institutions of the Romans,* bk. 3, 4. Vegetius admonishes the Emperor saying, "But of all precautions the most important is to keep entirely secret which way or by what route the army is to march. For the security of an expedition depends on the concealment of all motions from the enemy."

22. Ibid., bk. 3, 8.

23. In books one and two, Vegetius suggests that the Legions regularly undertake training marches of 20 miles in half a summer day (five hours), as they had in ancient times. This was while carrying a 60-pound pack and fully armed. During the Napoleonic wars, *La Grande Armee,* the speediest army in the world, covered 15 to 20 miles in a full day, making the Roman rate of march significantly faster.

24. Vegetius, *Military Institutions of the Romans,* bk. 3, 8–9.

25. Ibid., bk. 3, 19–20. At the end of book three Vegetius offers a number of maxims. One of which states, "It is much better to overcome the enemy by famine, surprise or terror than by general actions, for in the latter instance fortune has often a greater share of valor. Those designs are best which the enemy are entirely ignorant of till the moment of execution."

26. Ibid., bk. 3, 10.

27. Ibid., bk. 3, 21. In a maxim reminiscent of Sun-tzu, Vegetius says, "To distress the enemy more by famine than the sword is a mark of consummate skill."

28. Ibid., bk. 3, 10.

29. Niccolo Machiavelli, *The Art of War,* trans. Ellis Farneworth (Cambridge, MA: Da Capo Press, 1965).

30. Ibid., 26.

31. Machiavelli, a former official of the Florentine Republic, was deeply concerned with the plight of Florence, which was little more than a pawn in the power politics of his day.

32. Peter Paret, ed., *Makers of Modern Strategy from Machiavelli to the Nuclear Age* (Princeton, NJ: Princeton University Press, 1986), 26–40.

33. Steven Forde, "Varieties of Realism: Thucydides and Machiavelli," *The Journal of Politics* 54, no. 2 (1992).

34. War for the nobility was the apex of preparation and training during the feudal era. While peasants fought as bowmen (artillery), light infantry and support personnel, the heavy cavalry, the position of honor on the battlefield, was reserved for the nobility.

35. Machiavelli, *The Art of War*, 141–44.

36. Ibid., 202–3. In book seven Machiavelli, like Sun-tzu and Vegetius before him, says, "If a general knows his own strength and that of the enemy perfectly, he can hardly miscarry."

37. Hanson, *Soul of Battle*. General William T. Sherman, Commander of the Army of Tennessee, explained his March to the Sea by proclaiming that war is inherently a nasty affair, which should be made as terrible as possible so that those who wage it will do so less frequently.

38. Walter Laqueur, ed., *Voices of Terror: Manifestos, Writings and Manuals of al Qaeda, Hamas, and Other Terrorists from around the World and Throughout the Ages* (New York: Reed Press, 2004), 413–14.

39. Sun-tzu, *The Art of War*, trans. Ralph D. Sawyer (New York: Barnes & Noble Books, 1994), 59.

40. *The Seven Military Classics of Ancient China*, trans. Ralph D. Sawyer (Boulder, CO: Westview Press, 1993).

41. First translated in the West by a French clergyman during the rise of Napoleon Bonaparte, *The Art of War* was read and admired by the future emperor and, later, by leaders of the Nazi regime.

42. Sun-tzu, *The Art of War*, 129.

43. Alastair Johnston, *Cultural Realism: Strategic Culture and Grand Strategy in Chinese History* (Princeton, NJ: Princeton University Press, 1998). Alistair Ian Johnston, in an analysis of Chinese conflict beginning with China's first recorded warfare, finds that Chinese rulers seek the offensive when they possess superior military strength. When weaker, rulers turn to defense. And, when rulers see their position as exceptionally weak, adversaries are appeased with tribute and other concessions. Rarely, however, is Sun-tzu's advice utilized.

44. Sun-tzu, *The Art of War*, 129.

45. Ibid., 167.

46. Ibid., 168–71.

47. Douglas M. McCready, "Learning from Sun-Tzu," *Military Review*, May–June (2003): 86–87.

48. Sun-tzu, *The Art of War*, 179–82.

49. Ibid., 188.

50. Epaminondas's march through the Peloponnese, Sherman's March to the Sea, Rommel's North Africa campaign, Patton's drive to the Rhine, and MacArthur's

island hopping campaign and Inchon invasion demonstrate the application of Sun-tzu's emphasis on *ch'i* and the strategic configuration of power. See Hanson, *Soul of Battle*. See also Archer Jones, *The Art of War in the Western World* (Urbana: University of Illinois, 1987); and J.F.C. Fuller, *A Military History of the Western World: From the Earliest Times to the Battle of Lepanto* (Cambridge, MA: Da Capo Press, 1987).

51. Sun-tzu, *The Art of War*, 245–46.

52. Henry Guerlac, "Vauban: The Impact of Science on War," in *Makers of Modern Strategy* (see note 32), 71. Guerlac describes the development of military theory in the seventeenth century best when he says, "If we ask how these developments are reflected in the military literature of the sixteenth and seventeenth centuries, the answer is simple enough: the volume is, on average, greater than the quality. Antiquity was still the greater teacher in all that concerned the broadest aspects of military theory and the secrets of military genius."

53. During this period conflicts on the Continent arose, but they were significantly less devastating than those during the previous period.

54. Gerhard Ritter, *Frederick the Great: A Historical Profile*, trans. Peter Paret (Berkeley and Los Angeles: University of California Press, 1968). Frederick saw the Prussian army as an instrument of his own will, which must respond to commands with immediate action.

55. See Ian Westwell, *Warfare in the 18th Century* (Austin, TX: Raintree Steck-Vaughn, 1999). See also Jeremy Black, *Warfare in the 18th Century* (London: Cassell, 2002).

56. Frederick Hohenzollern, *Frederick the Great on the Art of War*, trans. Jay Luvaas (Cambridge, MA: Da Capo Press, 1999), 334.

57. R.R. Palmer, "Frederick the Great, Guibert, Bulow: From Dynastic to National War," in *Makers of Modern Strategy* (see note 32), 26–40. For Frederick, desertion was as great a threat to his army as was the enemy. Thus, Frederick was loathe to turn loose soldiers to harass lines of communication and supply for fear his conscripts would desert.

58. Jacques Hippolyte, *Stratégiques, Classiques De La Stratégie* (Paris: l'Hern, 1977). Guibert's conception of the unified state is later called grand strategy by B.H. Liddell-Hart.

59. Van Crevald, *The Art of War*, 90–99.

60. Philip Longworth, *The Art of Victory: The Life and Achievements of Generalissimo Suvorov* (London: Constable and Company, 1965).

61. Ibid., 35–40.

62. Unknown to many in the West, Generalissimo Suvorov was responsible for the capture of Francis Pulawski, Yemelyan Pugachev, and Tadeusz Kosciuszko, hero of the American War of Independence and Polish patriot.

63. Bruce W. Menning, "Train Hard, Fight Easy: The Legacy of A.V. Suvorov and His 'Art of Victory,'" *Air University Review*, November–December (1986).

64. Alan Schom, *Napoleon Bonaparte: A Life* (New York: Perennial, 1998).

65. Jay Luvaas, ed., *Napoleon on the Art of War* (New York: Free Press, 1999), chap. 6.

66. Ibid., 133. See also Yann Cloarec, ed., *How to Make War* (Paris: Ediciones La Calavera, 1998).

67. Napoleon Bonaparte, "Order of the Army No. 14552,"1808, in *Napoleon on the Art of War,* ed. Jay Luvaas (New York: Free Press, 1999), 10.

68. Napoleon Bonaparte, "Correspondence from Napoleon to Eugene," 1805, in *Napoleon on the Art of War,* ed. Jay Luvaas (New York: Free Press, 1999), 14.

69. Luvaas, ed., *Napoleon on the Art of War,* 19.

70. Ibid., 88. See also David G. Chandler, *The Campaigns of Napoleon* (New York: Schribner, 1973).

71. Napoleon Bonaparte, "Napoleon to the Executive Directory," 1796, in *Napoleon on the Art of War*, ed. Jay Luvaas (New York: Free Press, 1999), 65.

72. General Dwight Eisenhower is often considered one of history's great generals, but not because of his success as a combat commander. His strategic and tactical vision was mediocre at best. General Eisenhower's contribution to warfare lay in his ability to keep American, British, French, and other Allied forces united.

73. Van Crevald, *The Art of War,* 100. See also John R. Elting, "Jomini: Disciple of Napoleon," *Military Affairs* 28, Spring (1964).

74. John Shy, "Jomini," in *Makers of Modern Strategy* (see note 32), 144.

75. Antoine Henri de Jomini, *The Art of War* (London: Greenhill Books, 1996), 73. Jomini says, "Indeed, if the art of war consists in throwing the masses upon the decisive points, it will be necessary to take the initiative."

76. Ibid., 69–70.

77. Ibid., 36–38. Jomini does warn against fighting what he calls "double wars." Spain serves as his primary example. The ultimate defeat of France is often attributed to the material and personnel losses and large number of troops kept in Spain fighting guerrillas and Lord Wellington.

78. Ibid., 43–45, 61. Jomini also says of morale, "The first means of encouraging the military spirit is to invest the army with all possible social public consideration. The second means is to give the preference to those who have rendered services to the state, in filling any vacancies in the administrative departments of the governments, or even to require a certain length of military service as a qualification for certain offices." Hezbollah, Hamas, and the PLO have all followed Jomini's maxim as each has fostered a spirit of martyrdom among their constituents, creating a ready supply of homicide bombers and guerrillas.

79. de Jomini, *The Art of War,* 50.

80. Ibid., 50–51. See also Michael Handel, *Masters of War: Sun Tzu, Clausewitz and Jomini* (London: Frank Cass, 1992).

81. See Walter Laqueur, *Voices of Terror* (New York: Sourcebook, 2004). In a number of bin Laden's speeches during the late 1990s, the terror chief explained that the United States would not respond to future attacks because America is a cowardly nation. Evidence also suggests that bin Laden desired an American invasion of Afghanistan after 9/11 so that the United States could be drawn into a Soviet-Afghan War style conflict.

82. de Jomini, *The Art of War,* 91.

83. Van Crevald, *The Art of War*, 109.

84. Alan Beyerchen suggests that the human elements of Clausewitz's work make it eternally valid. Alan Beyerchen, "Clausewitz, Nonlinearity, and the Unpredictability of War," *International Security* 17, no. 3 (1992): 60.

85. Carl von Clausewitz, *On War* (New York: Alfred A. Knopf, 1993), 83.

86. Clausewitz viewed war primarily as a conventional act between state-sponsored militaries. It is his views on conventional conflict and the totality of war that have enshrined the Prussian theorist in Western military thought. His discussion of partisan or people's war generally receives little discussion.

87. Peter Paret, "Clausewitz," in *Makers of Modern Strategy* (see note 32), 191–92.

88. Martin Van Crevald, *The Transformation of War: The Most Radical Reinterpretation of Armed Conflict since Clausewitz* (New York: Free Press, 1991). Among Clausewitz's most articulate critics is Van Crevald who challenges the applicability of Clausewitz in the post–Cold War world suggesting that his conception of total war is inappropriate for the asymmetric conflict of the twenty-first century. Van Crevald adds that Clausewitz's understanding of war, as an elemental act of violence waged by states, is as outmoded as his conception of total war. Gary Ulman also argues that Clausewitz is irrelevant in the twenty-first century because he does not conceive of an enemy whose purpose is the annihilation of a people, as is the case with many asymmetric actors.

89. Clausewitz, *On War*, 578.

90. In his own time, the defeat of France in Spain took many small engagements to slowly destroy French forces. Conventional battles between Anglo-Spanish forces and the French were rare and indecisive. History has also shown that partisan war is won bit by bit rather than "by a single stroke."

91. Clausewitz, *On War*, 580.

92. Ibid.

93. Ibid., 581.

94. Ibid.

95. Arthur K. Cebrowski, "The Small, the Fast and the Many," *Net Defense*, January 15, 2004.

96. John G. Morgan and Anthony D. McIvor, "Rethinking the Principles of War," *Proceedings*, October (2003).

97. See Walter M. Hudson, "The Continuing Influence of Clausewitz," *Military Review*, March–April (2004). Clausewitz recognizes that conventional forces and the asymmetric actors opposing them rely on tactics which are largely diametrically opposite. Where American forces in Iraq, for example, seek to cordon insurgents in Fallujah utilizing mass to overwhelm the enemy, insurgents seek to remain dispersed and prevent themselves from being trapped because they have initiated a tactical defense.

98. Clausewitz, *On War*, 581.

99. Ibid., 582; and Yitzhak Klein, "Long Defensives: Victory without Compellence," *Comparative Strategy* 15 (1996). In his discussion of offensive and defensive warfare, Yitzhak Klein illustrates the difficulty conventional forces have in fighting

the type of war advocated by Clausewitz. As Klein points out, "Military establishments tend to prefer offensives because planning offensives creates an impression of control over the course of events and because successful offensives make things happen in a particular way—they compel."

100. Peter R. Moody, "Clausewitz and the Fading Dialectic of War," *World Politics* 31, no. 3 (1979); and Edward M. Collins, "Clausewitz and Democracy's Modern Wars," *Military Affairs* 19, no. 1 (1955).

101. A. T. Mahan, *The Influence of Sea Power Upon History, 1660–1783* (New York: Little Brown & Co., 1980). The basic premise of Mahan's greatest work is straightforward. Britain won the seventeenth- and early-eighteenth-century contest with France because it gained supremacy of the seas and maintained the free flow of goods between Britain and its colonies.

102. See also A.T. Mahan, *The Influence of Sea Power Upon the French Revolution, 1793–1812* (Boston: Little & Brown, 1892); and A.T. Mahan, *Armaments and Arbitration* (New York: Harper, 1912).

103. Jon Sumida, "New Insights from Old Books," *Naval War College Review* 54, no. 3 (2001).

104. Keith Nielson and Elizabeth Jane Errington, ed., *Navies and Global Defense: Theories and Strategy* (Westport, CT: Praeger, 1995).

105. Mahan, *Influence of Sea Power Upon History*.

106. Mahan's conception of asymmetry was the introduction of the submarine, which he derided in his work.

107. Julian Corbett, *Some Principles of Maritime Strategy* (New York: Longman, Green and Company, 1911).

108. Michael Handel, "Corbett, Clausewitz and Sun Tzu," *Naval War College Review* 53, no. 4 (2000).

109. Ibid., 3.

110. See Stephen W. Roskill, *The Strategy of Sea Power: Its Development and Application* (London: Collins, 1962).

111. John E. Mack, *Prince of Disorder: The Life of T.E. Lawrence* (Cambridge, MA: Harvard University Press, 1998).

112. Maxwell Johnson, "The Arab Bureau and the Arab Revolt: Yanbu to Aqaba," *Military Affairs* 46, no. 4 (1982).

113. T.E. Lawrence, *The Seven Pillars of Wisdom: A Triumph* (New York: Anchor, 1991).

114. Ibid., 192–94. Lawrence expressed his understanding of the Arabs and their Ottoman enemies saying, "Armies were like plants, immobile, firm-rooted, nourished through long stems to the head. We might be a vapor, blowing where we listed. Our kingdom lay in each man's mind; and as we wanted nothing material to live on, so we might offer nothing material to the killing." He adds, "In Turkey things were scarce and precious, men less esteemed than equipment. Our cue was to destroy, not the Turk's army, but his materials. The death of a Turkish bridge or rail, machine gun or charge of high explosive, was more profitable to us than the death of a Turk."

115. T.E. Lawrence, *T.E. Lawrence on Guerrilla Warfare*, http://pegasus.cc. ucf.edu/~eshaw/lawrence.htm (accessed February 15, 2004).

116. Lawrence, *Seven Pillars of Wisdom*, chap. 15.

117. Ibid., 224.

118. Ibid., 225.

119. J.A. English, "Kindergarten Soldier: The Military Thoughts of Lawrence of Arabia," *Military Affairs* 51, no. 1 (1987). Lawrence viewed war as possessing three basic elements: hecastic (geography, weather, railways, etc.), bionomic (wear and tear, life and death, humanity), and diathetic (psychological). All aspects belong to one of these three elements.

120. Van Crevald, *The Art of War*, 204–5.

121. Fuller, *Military History of the Western World;* and J.F.C. Fuller, *Armament and History: The Influence of Armament on History from the Dawn of Classical Warfare to the End of the Second World War* (Cambridge, MA: Da Capo Press, 1998). After retiring from the Royal Army in 1933, Major General Fuller began a prolific writing career which increased his popularity and solidified his place as one of the twentieth century's most influential strategists. These are among his most influential works.

122. B.H. Liddell-Hart, *Strategy,* 2nd ed. (New York: Meridian, 1991).

123. Robert H. Larson, "B.H. Liddell-Hart: Apostle of Limited War," *Military Affairs* 44, no. 2 (1980): 70.

124. Liddell-Hart, *Strategy,* chap. 1.

125. Ibid., 334–36.

126. Ibid., 337.

127. James D. Atkinson, "Liddell-Hart and Warfare of the Future," *Military Affairs* 29, no. 4 (1965). According to Atkinson, technology and the psycho-political aspects of war are central to understanding the success of the indirect approach. For the asymmetric actor, overcoming the technological disadvantage and exploiting the psychological is key.

128. Giulio Douhet, *Command of the Air* (Washington, DC: Office of Air Force History, 1983). See also Michael J. Eula, "The Classical Approach: Giulio Douhet and Strategic Air Force Operations: A Study in the Limitations of Theoretical Warfare," *Air University Review,* September–October (1986). An Italian general and pioneer of air power theory, Douhet suggests in his classic *Command of the Air* that strategic bombing before the use of ground forces can win a war before it starts. By knocking out communications, industry and military facilities, a nation can be so demoralized that it sues for peace. In effect, Douhet advocates an indirect approach utilizing air power to accomplish what Liddell-Hart expected ground forces to accomplish.

129. Liddell-Hart, *Strategy,* 367.

130. Mao Tse-tung, *On Guerrilla Warfare,* trans. Samuel B. Griffith II (Urbana Champagne: University of Illinois Press, 1961). For a more in-depth look at the military thought of Mao, see his collected works: Mao Tse-tung, *Selected Works of Mao Tse-Tung,* vol. 1 (London: Lawrence and Wishart, 1954).

131. Tse-tung, *On Guerrilla Warfare,* 21.

132. Josephus, *The Jewish War.*

133. Tse-tung, *On Guerrilla Warfare,* 33. In his translation of *On Guerrilla Warfare,* General Samuel B. Griffith suggests that it is virtually impossible to defeat a guerrilla movement if it successfully passes through phase I.

134. Leroy Thompson, *The Counter-Insurgency Manual* (London: Greenhill Books, 2002).

135. Historically, the overthrow of an unpopular ruler by an outside power holds wide support early but quickly loses favor the longer an intervening power remains. This was true of the Romans after the battle of Pydna (168 BC), when the Legions removed Macedonian dominance from Greece, but stayed, and has been the case in many other examples since.

136. Tse-tung, *On Guerrilla Warfare.*

137. General Vo, while ultimately victorious, moved to phase III prematurely in 1950 and 1968. Vietminh and, later, Viet Cong forces were obliterated, nearly leading to the collapse of communist efforts.

138. Tse-tung, *On Guerrilla Warfare,* 26.

139. Ibid., 46.

140. Ibid., 48.

141. Ibid., 52, 97–98. Mao also explains that the strategy of the guerrilla is based on tactical offense, tactical speed, and tactical operations on exterior lines of operation. Acknowledging the defensive nature of guerrilla warfare, Mao warns the guerrilla that he must be prepared for protracted operations. Most importantly, Mao warns the guerrilla commander against the use of static defense.

142. Tse-tung, *Selected Works.*

143. Zedong Mao, *The Situation and Tasks in the Anti-Japanese War after the Fall of Shanghai and Taiyuan* (New York: Foreign Language Press, 1956); and Marjorie Dryburgh, *North China and Japanese Expansion 1933–1937: Regional Power and the National Interest* (London: Curzon Press, 2000).

144. Karim Kadim, "Insurgent Attacks Kill 8; Iraqi Official Discourages Protests," *USA Today,* March 28, 2005.

145. Sun-tzu and Mao discouraged the use of terrorism for the very reason mentioned.

146. Anthony James Joes, *Resisting Rebellion: The History and Politics of Counterinsurgency* (Lexington: University of Kentucky Press, 2004).

147. Vo Nguyen Giap, *People's War People's Army* (New York: Bantam Books, 1962).

148. Giap, *People's War People's Army,* 27.

149. Ibid., 68.

150. Ibid.

151. See Donald M. Snow, *From Lexington to Desert Storm and Beyond* (Armonk, NY: M.E. Sharpe, 2000), chap. 1. Snow suggests war is waged for limited or total ends by limited or total means.

152. Vo Nguyen Giap, *How We Won the War* (Philadelphia: Recon, 2001).

153. Ibid., 24.

154. Ibid., 48–49; and see Ali Jalali, *Afghan Guerrilla Warfare: In the Words of the Mujahideen Fighters* (St. Paul, MN: MBI Publishing, 2001). Throughout the American presence in Vietnam, communist forces operated under a strategic and tactical doctrine similar to that of Afghan forces during the Afghan War (1979–1989). Both relied heavily on the ambush to attack unsuspecting patrols and convoys.

They also sought to harass lines of communication and supply. In most instances, attacking forces dispersed before air support could arrive.

155. In other instances he also uses "People's War."

156. Che Guevara, *Guerrilla Warfare* (Lincoln: University of Nebraska Press, 1998).

157. Ibid., 7–9.

158. Ibid., 22.

159. Ibid., 99–100.

160. Ibid., 23.

CHAPTER 2

1. Kenneth F. McKenzie, Jr., "The Revenge of the Melians: Asymmetric Threats and the Q.D.R.," in *McNair Paper* (Washington, DC: Institute for National Strategic Studies, National Defense University, 2000), 2; and Sun-tzu, *The Art of War*, 2.

2. Tacitus, *The Annals of Imperial Rome* (New York: Penguin Classics, 1956), 2. In 7 AD the Goth leader Arminius led the Roman Consul Publius Quinctilius Varus into the muddy and confined space of the *Teutoburger Wald* where he and his Goths turned on Varus, annihilating to the man, the XVII, XVIII, and XIX Legions. For the Roman Empire, it was the greatest defeat they had ever suffered at the hands of
barbarians. For Arminius, it was textbook asymmetric warfare.

3. Lawrence, *Seven Pillars of Wisdom*.

4. Tse-tung, *On Guerrilla Warfare*.

5. Giap, *People's War People's Army;* and Guevara, *Guerrilla Warfare*.

6. William S. Cohen, *Report of the Quadrennial Defense Review* (Washington, DC: Department of Defense, 1997). For an in-depth description of asymmetric warfare, the threats faced by the United States and possible solutions see, McKenzie, "Revenge of the Melians."

7. William S. Cohen, *Annual Report to the President and Congress* (Washington, DC: Department of Defense, 1999), 1–5.

8. McKenzie, "Revenge of the Melians," 2.

9. Bill Clinton, *A National Security Strategy for a New Century* (Washington, DC: White House, 1999), 16.

10. McKenzie, "Revenge of the Melians," 4; David L. Grange, "Asymmetric Warfare: Old Method, New Concern," *National Strategy Forum Review,* Winter (2000): 1; *Asymmetric Warfare,* http://www.fact-index.com/a/as/asymmetric_warfare.html (accessed May 15, 2004); and "Strategic Assessments: Engaging Power for Peace," (Institute for National Strategic Studies, 1998). Grange adds, "Strategists define asymmetric warfare as conflict deviating from the norm, or an indirect approach to affect a counterbalancing force." An additional explanation from *Asymmetric Warfare* suggests, "The idea of asymmetric warfare fuses together many previous and more specific ideas of guerrilla warfare, espionage, atrocity, violent resistance, sabotage, nonviolent resistance, and terrorism. It is a broad and inclusive term coined to recognize that two sides in a conflict may have such drastically different strengths and weaknesses that they resort to drastically different (thus

'asymmetric') tactics to achieve relative advantage—including attacks on 'civilians.'" Finally, from the Institute for National Strategic Studies, asymmetric warfare is called "a version of not 'fighting fair.'"

11. Vincent J. Goulding, Jr., "Back to the Future with Asymmetric Warfare," *Parameters,* no. 4 (2000–2001): 1. As Goulding states, asymmetry is now the term *du jour* for future military operations. Given the fact that no adversary will face the United States in conventional battle, all conflicts are asymmetric.

12. McKenzie, "Revenge of the Melians," 3–5.

13. "Bush Warns Syria, Iran from the Consequences of Interfering in Iraq," *ArabicNews.com,* December 16, 2004, http://www.arabicnews.com/ansub/Daily/Day/041216/2004121607.html (accessed September 15, 2005); and Rafael Epstein, "Iran Accused of Interfering in Iraq," Australian Broadcasting Corporation, April 24, 2003, http://www.abc.net.au/cgi-bin/common/printfriendly.pl?http://www.abc.net.au/am/content/2003/s839157.htm (accessed September 15, 2005).

14. Liddell-Hart, *Strategy,* 322.

15. Larry Elder, "The Battle over Islam," *LarryElder.com,* September 15, 2004, http://www.larryelder.com/islambattle.html (accessed September 15, 2005).

16. "In Full: Al-Qaeda Statement," BBC News Online, October 10, 2001, http://news.bbc.co.uk/1/low/world/middle_east/1590350.stm (accessed September 5, 2004).

17. In describing grand strategy, strategy, and tactics as used by adversaries of the United States employing asymmetric approaches, al-Qaeda is the example chosen. Given that the global war on terror is the current focus of domestic, foreign, and military policy and action, this seems appropriate.

18. "Nature, Structure of al-Qaeda Changing," *USA Today,* March 8, 2003.

19. Liddell-Hart, *Strategy,* 321.

20. Clausewitz, *On War,* 207.

21. Liddell-Hart, *Strategy,* 321.

22. Al-Qaeda is known to be responsible for the following terrorist attacks: World Trade Center bombing (1993), U.S. embassy bombing, Nairobi (1998), U.S. embassy bombing, Dar es Salaam (1998), and the attack on the USS *Cole* (DDG-67) (2000).

23. Thomas C. Greene, "Security Fears Tip Spanish Election," *The Register,* 2004.

24. McKenzie, "Revenge of the Melians," 10.

25. Dennis Drew and Don Snow, *Making Strategy: An Introduction to National Security Processes and Problems* (Montgomery: Air University Press, 1988).

26. Clausewitz, *On War,* 147.

27. Liddell-Hart, *Strategy,* 321.

28. Drew and Snow, *Making Strategy: An Introduction to National Security Processes and Problems,* 13–21. Drew and Snow clarify the differences between strategy and tactics in the five-step "strategy process" they suggest. Step one consists of determining national security objectives. Step two is devoted to formulating grand strategy. Steps three and four divide "strategy" into two parts with the development of military strategy followed by operational strategy. Step five, the final step, is devoted to the development of battlefield strategy or tactics.

29. Clausewitz, *On War,* 146.

30. Roger W. Barnett, *Asymmetrical Warfare: Today's Challenge to U.S. Military Power* (Washington, DC: Brassey's, 2003).

31. Jonathan B. Tucker, "Asymmetric Warfare," *FORUM for Applied Research and Public Policy,* no. 2 (1999).

32. I.F.W. Beckett, *The Encyclopedia of Guerilla Warfare* (New York: Facts on File, 2001). See also Thompson, *The Counter-Insurgency Manual.*

33. David Rooney, *Guerilla: Insurgents, Patriots and Terrorists from Sun Tzu to Bin Laden* (London: Brassey's, 2004), 9–19.

34. Tse-tung, *Selected Works of Mao Tse-Tung.* Mobile guerrilla warfare advances through three progressive stages. In the organizational stage, guerrilla movements develop a base of support. They then move to the guerrilla stage where guerrillas attack government forces. Once the government is sufficiently weakened and unable to defeat a conventional attack the conventional phase begins and the government and its armed forces are defeated. One key aspect of mobile guerrilla warfare is the ability to move forward or backward through each phase as circumstances allow.

35. Donald M. Snow, *Distant Thunder: Third World Conflict and the New International Order* (New York: St. Martin's Press, 1993), 58.

36. Asymmetric conflict and terrorism are not one and the same. The current asymmetric conflict the United States is facing is dominated by the Global War on Terror, but America's asymmetric conflicts of the early twentieth century saw little or no use of terrorism by America's adversaries.

37. Robert Ted Gurr, *Why Men Rebel* (Princeton, NJ: Princeton University Press, 1971).

38. Ibid., chap. 2–4.

39. See Donald M. Snow, *Uncivil Wars: International Security and the New Internal Conflicts* (Boulder, CO: Lynne Rienner Publishers, 1996); Stedman, "International Actors and Internal Conflict"; Max Manwaring, "Internal Wars: Rethinking Problem and Response," (Carlisle, PA: Strategic Studies Institute, 2001); and Jack Goldstone, "State Failure Task Force Report: Phase 3 Findings," (McLean, VA: Science Applications International Corporation, 2000).

40. See S. Mahmud Ali, *The Fearful State: Power, People and Internal War in South Asia* (London: Zed Books, 1993).

41. See Ibrahim Abdullah, *Between Democracy and Terror: The Sierra Leone Civil War* (Dakar: Codesria, 2004).

42. Snow, *Uncivil Wars,* 110.

43. Stephen Ellis, *The Mask of Anarchy: The Destruction of Liberia and the Religious Dimension of an African Civil War* (New York: New York University Press, 2001).

44. Snow, *Distant Thunder: Third World Conflict and the New International Order.*

45. Ed Wheeler and Craig Roberts, *Doorway to Hell: Disaster in Somalia* (Tulsa, OK: Consolidated Press, 2002).

46. *France Bolsters Ivory Coast Peace Force,* British Broadcasting Company, 2003, http://news.bbc.co.uk/2/hi/africa/2728909.stm (accessed September 3, 2004).

47. "Zimbabwe's Mugabe Warns Britain," *CNN.com*, May 2, 2001, http://www.cnn.com/2001/WORLD/africa/05/02/mugabe.threat/ (accessed September 4, 2004).

48. U.S. Congress, *Act to Authorize the Defense of the Merchant Vessels of the United States against French Depredations*, 5th Cong., June 25,1798, 572, 50–51; and Donald M. Snow, *When America Fights: The Users of U.S. Military Force* (Washington, DC: CQ Press, 2000).

49. *Quasi-War with France 1798–1801* (Navy Historical Center, Department of the Navy), 1996, http://www.history.navy.mil/faqs/stream/faq45-3.htm (accessed September 2, 2004).

50. Collier, "Instances of Use of United States Forces Abroad, 1798–1993"; and Grossman, "From Wounded Knee to Afghanistan."

51. The declared wars of the United States are the War of 1812, the Mexican-American War (1846), the Spanish-American War (1898), World War I (1917–1918), and World War II (1941–1945). Undeclared conventional wars include the Civil War (1861–1865), the Korean War (1950–1953), the Persian Gulf War (1990–1991), and the Iraq War (2003).

52. Boot, *The Savage Wars of Peace.*

53. Robert M. Utley and Wilcomb E. Wasburn, *Indian Wars* (New York: Mariner Books, 2002). The nineteenth century was also a century of intermittent war between the federal government and American Indian tribes. Warfare, for the American Indian, was asymmetric. Exceed the white man's cost tolerance and end his westward expansion. Strategically, never face the U.S. Army in open battle. Instead, strike soft targets. Tactically, terrorize the civilian population moving onto Indian lands. The U.S. Army used a mix of conventional strategy and asymmetric tactics as it sought to annihilate resistance through lightening raids.

54. See Joseph Wheelan, *Jefferson's War: America's First War on Terror* (New York: Carroll and Graf, 2003).

55. McAllister Linn, *The Philippine War, 1899–1902.*

56. Stuart Miller, *Benevolent Assimilation: The American Conquest of the Philippines, 1899–1902* (New Haven, CT: Yale University Press, 1984).

57. Snow, *Uncivil Wars,* 80–85.

58. Brian McAllister Linn, *The U.S. Army and Counterinsurgency in the Philippine War, 1899–1902* (Chapel Hill: University of North Carolina Press, 2000).

59. From 1899 to 1941 the United States fought insurgents in the Philippines (1899–1902), Haiti (1915–1934), and Nicaragua. Marines were also engaged in fighting or garrison duty in Cuba, Panama, Nicaragua, and Mexico (1898–1914) during periods of instability and rebellion. The East did not prove a peaceful place either as American forces fought Boxers in China (1900–1901) and communist revolutionaries in Siberia (1918–1920).

60. Robin Moore, *The Green Berets* (New York: St. Martin's Press, 2002). President Kennedy established the Green Berets to combat the communist-supported guerrilla movements forming in the third world. In the War in Afghanistan and the Global War on Terror, the Green Berets play a leading role.

61. Tacitus, *The Annals of Imperial Rome,* chap. 6. Roman legions posted on the empire's frontiers were frequently engaged in asymmetric or guerrilla warfare with

Goths in Germany (9 AD), Celts in Britain (60 AD), and Jews in Judea (70 AD). Britain saw greater asymmetric conflict with such examples as North America (1756–1763, 1776–1783, 1812–1814), South Africa (1880–1881 and 1899–1902), and Malaysia (1946–1963).

62. Cohen, *Report of the Quadrennial Defense Review;* see also Michael E. O'Hanlon, *Defense Policy Choices for the Bush Administration* (Washington, DC: Brookings Institution Press, 2001), 63–65; and *Road Map for National Security: Imperative for Change* (Washington, DC: U.S. Commission on National Security for the 21st Century, 2001), 146.

63. *Joint Vision 2010* (Washington, DC: U.S. Joint Chiefs of Staff, 1996).

64. *Joint Vision 2020* (Washington, DC: U.S. Joint Chiefs of Staff, 2000).

65. Igor Beliaev and John Marks, *Common Ground on Terrorism: Soviet-American Cooperation against the Politics of Terror* (New York: W.W. Norton, 1991).

66. James Ridgeway, "Chinese Army Pushes Cyberwar Barbarians at the Gate," GlobalSecurity.org, November 24, 1999, http://www.globalsecurity.org/intell/library/news/1999/11/991124-ridgeway.htm (accessed September 15, 2005); "China Dragon Bares Its Claws for Cyberwar," *NewsMax.com,* November 17, 1999, http://www.newsmax.com/articles/?a=1999/11/17/45206 (accessed September 15, 2005); "Chinese Plans for Cyberwar Pose a Threat to U.S., Says Pentagon," *Indian Express.com,* November 21, 1999, http://www.indianexpress.com/fe/daily/19991121/fec21059.html (accessed September 15, 2005); "Hacker Attacks in U.S. Linked to Chinese Military: Researchers," Breitbart.com, December 13, 2005, http://www.breitbart.com/news/2005/12/12/051212224756.jwmkvntb.html (accessed December 13, 2005).

67. See Graham Allison, *Nuclear Terrorism: The Ultimate Preventable Catastrophe* (New York: Times Books, 2004).

68. "Iraq Withdrawal Heads Agenda for New Spanish Cabinet," Spacewar.com, April 14, 2004, http://www.spacewar.com/2004/040419164753.rriav7ye.html (accessed December 15, 2005); Sabrina Castelfranco, "Italian PM Announces Phased Withdrawal from Iraq," *Voice of America,* March 16, 2005, http://www.voanews.com/english/archive/2005-03/2005-03-16-voa1.cfm?CFID=6396882&CFTOKEN=13361206 (accessed December 15, 2005).

69. Paul Wilkinson, "The Strategic Implications of Terrorism," 2004, http://biblioteca.upeace.org/masters/documents/Wilkinson%201997.%20The%20media%20and%20terrorism.pdf (accessed May 15, 2004); Ayez Ahmed Khan, "Terrorism and Asymmetrical Warfare International and Regional Implications," *DefenseJournal.com,* 2002, http://www.defencejournal.com/2002/february/terrorism.htm (accessed September 15, 2005); and Charles Kegley, *The New Global Terrorism: Characteristics, Causes, Controls* (New York: Prentice Hall, 2003).

70. See Caleb Carr, *The Lessons of Terror: A History of Warfare against Civilians* (New York: Random House, 2003) for a historical look at terrorism and its long past.

71. See Clark L. Staten, "Asymmetric Warfare, the Evolution and Devolution of Terrorism: The Coming Challenge for Emergency and National Security Forces," Emergency Response and Research Institute, 1998, http://

www.emergency.com/asymetrc.htm (accessed May 15, 2004). Al-Qaeda has been the terror network most responsible for the evolution of terrorist groups from the traditional top-down structure to a far more effective and difficult-to-detect hub-and-spoke network.

72. Brian M. Jenkins, ed., *Countering the New Terrorism* (Santa Monica, CA: RAND, 1998), 8–37.

73. Rowan Scarborough, "Drug Money Sustains al Qaeda," *Washington Times,* December 23, 2003. John Stewart, "Russian Government Blames Chechnya, al Qaeda," Australian Broadcasting Corporation, 2004, http://www.abc.net.au/late line/content/2004/s1193459.htm (accessed September 10, 2004).

74. Jenkins, ed., *Countering the New Terrorism,* 10.

75. See Stephen J. Blank, *Rethinking Asymmetric Threats* (Carlisle, PA: Strategic Studies Institute, Army War College, 2003). Some have suggested that the miniaturization of technology has enabled terrorists to increase the lethality of the bombs used in terrorist attacks.

76. Allison, *Nuclear Terrorism: The Ultimate Preventable Catastrophe,* chap. 1. See Allison's discussion of what he calls "al-Qaeda's Manhattan Project" for a complete discussion of al-Qaeda's efforts to acquire nuclear weapons.

77. Gavin Cameron, et al., "The 1999 W.M.D. Terrorism Chronology: Incidents Involving Sub-National Actors and Chemical, Biological, Radiological and Nuclear Materials," *The Nonproliferation Review,* no. 3 (2000).

78. Ibid., 160.

79. Kyle B. Olson, "Aum Shinrikyo: Once and Future Threat?" *Emerging Infectious Diseases* 5, no. 4 (2000).

80. "Asking for Help," *ABC News,* 2002, http://abcnews.go.com/?lid=ABC COMMenu&lpos=ABCNews (accessed September 11, 2004).

81. Joseph C. Cyrulik, "Asymmetric Warfare and the Threat to the American Homeland," *Landpower Essay Series,* Association of the United States Army, The Institute of Land Warfare, Paper No. 99–8 (November 1999): 5–6.

82. "The Cost of Terrorism," *Daily Policy Digest,* 2002, http://www.ncpa.org/ iss/ter/2002/pd051502f.html (accessed September 11, 2004).

83. The economic and human costs of a large-scale WMD attack largely depend on the tactic used. A nuclear explosion in New York City is expected to kill a million or more Americans and cause an evacuation of all boroughs, Long Island, and Northern New Jersey. A biological or chemical attack will kill far fewer New Yorkers but will have a significant psychological effect.

84. See Matthew Levitt, *Targeting Terror: U.S. Policy toward Middle Eastern State Sponsors and Terrorist Organizations, Post-September 11* (Washington, DC: Washington Institute for Near East Policy, 2003).

85. Bruce MacLachlan, *Operational Art in the Counter-Terror War in Afghanistan* (Newport, RI: Naval War College, 2002).

86. George W. Bush, "Results in Iraq: 100 Days toward Security and Freedom" (Washington, DC: The White House, 2003).

87. Montgomery C. Meigs, "Unorthodox Thoughts About Asymmetric Warfare," *Parameters,* no. 3 (2003): 6.

88. Bruce Berkowitz, "Fighting the New War," *Hoover Digest,* no. 3 (2002).

89. See also Osama bin Laden's comments in Laqueur, ed., *Voices of Terror.*

90. Michel Wieviorka, "French Politics and Strategy on Terrorism," in *The Politics of Counter-Terrorism: The Ordeal of Democratic States,* ed. Barry Rubin (Washington, DC: School of Advanced International Studies, 1990); and Craig R. Whitney, "France's 'Cowboy' Judge: A Relentless Tracker of International Terrorists," *International Herald Tribune,* December 5, 1996.

91. See Jean Bethke Elshtain, *Just War Against Terror: The Burden of American Power in a Violent World* (New York: Basic Books, 2004) for a more detailed discussion of the effects of America's anti-terror policies

92. See Bill Powell, "The Man Who Sold the Bomb," *Time,* February 14, 2005, for a detailed discussion of al-Qaeda's ties to A. Q. Khan, former head of the Pakistani nuclear program.

93. McKenzie, "Revenge of the Melians," 20.

94. PBS, "1 Megaton Surface Blast: Pressure Damage," WGBH, Boston, 2004, http://www.pbs.org/wgbh/amex/bomb/sfeature/1mtblast.html (accessed September 14, 2004).

95. See Lynn Davis, *Individual Preparedness and Response to Chemical, Radiological, Nuclear and Biological Terrorist Attacks* (Santa Monica, CA: RAND, 2002); "Homeland Security Planning Scenarios," GlobalSecurity.org, June 1, 2005, http://www.globalsecurity.org/security/ops/hsc-scen-1.htm (accessed December 15, 2005); and Charles Ferguson, *The Four Faces of Nuclear Terrorism* (New York: Routledge, 2005).

96. Allison, *Nuclear Terrorism: The Ultimate Preventable Catastrophe,* 15.

97. Donald Rumsfeld, *Nuclear Posture Review Report* (Washington, DC: Department of Defense, 2002).

98. R. A. Falkenrath, ed., *America's Achilles Heel: Nuclear, Biological and Chemical Terrorism and Covert Attack* (Cambridge, MA: MIT Press, 1999).

99. Patrick M. Hughes, "Future Conditions: The Character and Conduct of War, 2010 and 2020," in *Seminar on Intelligence, Command, and Control* (Cambridge, MA: Center for Information Policy Research, Harvard University, 2003), 28–32.

100. R. C. Webb, et al., "The Commercial and Military Satellite Survivability Crisis," *Defense Electronics* 24 (1995).

101. Norman Friedman, "Russians Offer E. M. P. Counter," *Proceedings* 123 (1997).

102. Sam Nunn, "Nuclear Terrorism: Unite Against the Gravest Threat," *International Herald Tribune,* May 28, 2003. For more information on the threat of nuclear terrorism visit the Nuclear Threat Initiative's web site at www.nti.org.

103. R. J. Larsen and R. P. Kadlec, *Biological Warfare: A Post Cold War Threat to America's Strategic Mobility Forces* (Pittsburgh, PA: Matthew B. Ridgeway Center for International Security Studies, University of Pittsburgh, 1995).

104. Anthony H. Cordesman, *Military Balance in the Middle East XIV: Weapons of Mass Destruction* (Washington, DC: Center for Strategic and International Studies, 1999).

105. George Tenet, *Global Trends 2015: A Dialogue About the Future with Nongovernmental Experts* (Washington, DC: National Intelligence Council, 2000), 34.

106. Cordesman, "Military Balance," 81.

107. McKenzie, "Revenge of the Melians," 81–85.

108. "Anthrax Reaches the Senate," *Fox News.com,* October 15, 2001, http://www.foxnews.com/story/0%2C2933%2C36527%2C00.html (accessed September 16, 2004); and "Congress to Reconvene Tuesday Despite Continuing Anthrax Tests," *CNN.com,* October 22 2001, http://www.cnn.com/2001/HEALTH/conditions/10/22/anthrax/ (accessed September 16, 2004). Let me point out that Anthrax is a chemical agent not a biological one. The fear and disruption is, however, the same.

109. See Jonathan B. Tucker, *Toxic Terror: Assessing Terrorist Use of Chemical and Biological Weapons* (Cambridge, MA: MIT Press, 2000).

110. "Biotechnology and the Future of the Biological and Toxin Weapons Convention" (Solna, Sweden: Stockholm International Peace Research Institute, 2001). Biological and chemical weapons have long been used in warfare, but not until the Great War were chemical weapons used on a massive scale.

111. Cordesman, "Military Balance," 80–83.

112. Ibid., 82.

113. "City Commission Workshop Fire-Rescue Department Planning" (Fort Lauderdale: Fort Lauderdale City Commission, 2002).

114. McKenzie, "Revenge of the Melians," 81–83.

115. Victor A. Utgoff, *The Challenge of Chemical Weapons* (New York: St. Martin's Press, 1991). To kill approximately 125,000 civilians in a city such as New York, it would take more than 14,000 pounds of VX under dry, low wind conditions. When it is considered that a large capacity crop duster holds 400 pounds of chemicals, it would take 35 flights to disperse enough VX to cause such casualties.

116. Many of the injuries caused in the Aum attack were from rushing to exit the subway.

117. See Eric Croddy, *Chemical and Biological Warfare* (New York: Copernicus Books, 2002). Al-Qaeda did have a crude chemical weapons program in Afghanistan prior to the Taliban's defeat in 2001.

118. Adam Savino, "Cyber-Terrorism," The University of Dayton School of Law, 2004, http://www.cybercrimes.net/Terrorism/ct.html (accessed September 17, 2004).

119. Kim Cragin and Sara A. Daly, *The Dynamic Terrorist Threat: An Assessment of Group Motivations and Capabilities in a Changing World* (Santa Monica, CA: RAND, 2004); and Steven A. Hildreth, *Cyberwarfare* (Washington, DC: Congressional Research Service, 2001), 15.

120. Special Oversight Panel on Terrorism, Committee on Armed Services, *Cyberterrorism,* May 23, 2000.

121. Hildreth, "Cyberwarfare."

122. Qiao Liang and Wang Xiangsui, *Unrestricted Warfare* (Beijing: PLA Literature and Arts Publishing House, 1999).

123. *Cyberterrorism.*

124. Cohen, *Report of the Quadrennial Defense Review.*

125. Bill Clinton, "Presidential Decision Directive/N.S.C.–63" (Washington, DC: White House, 1998).

126. Mark Ward, "Cyber Terrorism 'Overhyped.'" BBC News, March 14, 2003, http://news.bbc.co.uk/2/hi/technology/2850541.stm (accessed September 18, 2004).

127. See Dan Verton, *Black Ice: The Invisible Threat of Cyber-Terrorism* (New York: McGraw-Hill, 2004). Dan Verton, a former intelligence officer and reporter for *PC Magazine,* suggests that cyber-terrorism is a growing threat that will soon supplant WMD as the greatest threat to the United States. Gene Meyers, "Getting to the Fight: Aerospace Forces and Anti-Access Strategies," *Air and Space Power Chronicles,* VII (2001); and Andrew Krepinevich, *Meeting the Anti-Access and Area Denial Challenge* (Washington, DC: Center for Strategic and Budgetary Assessment, 2003).

128. Meyers, "Aerospace Forces and Anti-Access Strategies"; and Krepinevich, *Meeting the Anti-Access and Area Denial Challenge.*

129. "Aircraft Carriers—C.V., C.V.N.," U.S. Navy, 2004, http://navysite.de/carriers.htm (accessed September 13, 2004).

130. McKenzie, "Revenge of the Melians," 43–44.

131. Martin Shaw, "New Wars of the City: 'Urbicide' and 'Genocide,'" University of Sussex, 2000, http://www.sussex.ac.uk/Users/hafa3/city.htm (accessed May 15, 2004).

132. "Iraq Coalition Casualty Count," Icasualties, 2004, http://icasualties.org/oif/Stats.aspx (accessed September 15, 2004).

133. Lind et al., "The Changing Face of War."

134. Ibid., 3.

135. Ibid., 4. Also see Harold Gould and Franklin Spinney, "New Generation of War Changes the Paradigm," *The Virginian Pilot,* October 3, 2001; G.I. Wilson, John P. Sullivan, and Hal Kempfer, *"Fourth Generation Warfare: How Tactics of the Weak Confound the Strong,"* Military.com, September 8, 2003, http://d-n-i.net/fcs/comments/c490.htm (accessed May 15, 2004).

136. Vice Adm. Jack (USN Ret.) Shanahan, Col. Chet Richards (USAF Ret.), and Frank Spinney, "Bury Cold War Mindset: Fourth-Generation Warfare Rewrites Military Strategy," *Defense News,* August 5–11, 2003; and General Anthony Zinni, "4 G.W. & Zinni's Question: What Is Nature of Victory?" (Arlington, VA: Naval Institute Forum, 2003).

137. Thomas P.M. Barnett, *The Pentagon's New Map: War and Peace in the Twenty-First Century* (New York: G.P. Putnam's Sons, 2004). Barnett argues that many military leaders are unwilling to develop a new security rule-set for a post-Cold War world. Instead, as Barnett argues, these leaders prefer to substitute China for the Soviet Union and continue operating with a force structure that is largely prepared to fight a large-scale land battle and a nuclear war from beneath the ocean's surface.

138. See Fareed Zakaria, *The Future of Freedom: Illiberal Democracy at Home and Abroad* (New York: W.W. Norton, 2003).

139. Barnett, *Pentagon's New Map,* 118–19.

140. See David S. Landes, *The Wealth and Poverty of Nations: Why Some Are So Rich and Some Are So Poor* (New York: W.W. Norton, 1999).

141. Barnett, *Pentagon's New Map,* 118–19.

142. See Lawrence E. Harrison, *Culture Matters: How Values Shape Human Progress* (New York: Harper Collins, 2001); and Samuel P. Huntington, *The Clash of Civilizations and the Remaking of World Order* (New York: Simon and Schuster, 1998).

143. Huntington, *Clash of Civilizations*.

144. See Martin Libicki, "Illuminating Tomorrow's War," in *McNair Paper 61* (Washington, DC: Institute for National Strategic Studies, 1999).

145. See Russell W. Glenn, *Marching Under Darkening Skies: The American Military and the Impending Urban Operations Threat* (Santa Monica, CA: RAND, 1998); Martin Libicki, "Rethinking War: The Mouse's New Roar?" *Foreign Policy*, no. 4 (1999); Shaw, "New Wars of the City"; and Daryl G. Press, "Urban Warfare: Options, Problems and the Future" (Bedford, MA: MIT Security Studies Programs, 1999).

146. Barnett, *Pentagon's New Map*, 118–19.

147. See C.J. Dick, "Conflict in a Changing World: Looking Two Decades Forward" (Surrey: Conflict Studies Research Center, Royal Military Academy Sandhurst, 2002).

148. See Tenet, "Global Trends 2015;" Henry H. Shelton, *Joint Vision 2020* (Washington, DC: U.S. Joint Chiefs of Staff, 2000); and Thomas R. Wilson, *The Four Thrusts* (Washington, DC: Defense Intelligence Agency, 2001). C^4ISR is a frequently used military acronym, which stands for command, control, communications, computing, intelligence, surveillance and reconnaissance.

149. Libicki, "Illuminating Tomorrow's War," 1–5.

150. Dennis J. Reimer, "Dominant Maneuver and Precision Engagement," *Joint Forces Quarterly*, no. 4 (1996).

151. Glenn C. Buchan, *Future Directions in Warfare: Good and Bad Analysis, Dubious Rhetoric, and the "Fog of Peace"* (Santa Monica, CA: Rand, 2003), 16–18.

152. John Pike, *Unmanned Aerial Vehicles* (Federation of American Scientists, 2004), http://www.fas.org/irp/program/collect/uav.htm (accessed September 21, 2004).

153. Bruce Berkowitz, *The New Face of War: How War Will Be Fought in the 21st Century* (New York: Free Press, 2003), chap. 8–10. Berkowitz provides a particularly well-explained discussion of the Pentagon's development of information technologies and information warfare capabilities.

154. Ellen Messmer, "U.S. Army Kick-Starts Cyberwar Machine," *CNN.com*, November 22, 2000, http://archives.cnn.com/2000/TECH/computing/11/22/cyberwar.machine.idg/index.html (accessed September 15, 2004); see also Wilson, *The Four Thrusts*.

155. For an explanation of this process, see Graham Allison, *Essence of Decision: Explaining the Cuban Missile Crisis*, 2nd ed. (New York: Longman, 1999).

CHAPTER 3

1. Kamal Salibi, *A House of Many Mansions: The History of Lebanon Reconsidered* (Berkeley and Los Angeles: University of California Press, 1990), 1–5.

2. See Matti Moosa, *The Maronites in History* (Syracuse, NY: Syracuse University Press, 1986).

3. See Steven P. Olson, *Terrorist Attacks: The Attack on U.S. Marines in Lebanon on October 23, 1983* (New York: Rosen Publishing, 2003).

4. The signing of the Ta'if Accord in 1991 officially ended the Lebanese Civil War and guaranteed the president of Lebanon would remain a Maronite, the prime minister a Sunni, and the speaker of the National Assembly a Shiite. Among the poorest of Lebanon's groups, Shiites long felt they were underrepresented despite concessions from Christian and Sunni leaders.

5. Jack Shulimson, *Marines in Lebanon 1958* (Washington, DC: Department of the Navy, Headquarters U.S. Marine Corps), 1–5.

6. Dwight D. Eisenhower, 1958.

7. Ibid.

8. Ibid.

9. Roger J. Spiller, "Not War but Like War: The American Intervention in Lebanon," in *Leavenworth Papers* (Fort Leavenworth, KS: Combat Studies Institute, U.S. Army Command and General Staff College, 1981), 10–23.

10. See H.A. Hadd, "Who's a Rebel? The Lessons Lebanon Taught," *Marine Corps Gazette* 46, no. 3 (1962).

11. Robert McClintock, "The American Landing in Lebanon," *United States Naval Institute Proceedings* 88, no. 10 (1962). During Operation BLUEBAT one American soldier was killed by a sniper and several wounded, but with less than a handful of casualties, the mission was considered an overwhelming success.

12. John Kelly, *Lebanon: 1982–1984* (Santa Monica, CA: RAND Corporation). In 1969 Lebanon's prime minister recognized the PLO and the Palestinian cause, offering Palestinians temporary safety in Southern Lebanon. This action would set the stage for the conflict that erupted in 1975.

13. By 1975 there were over 300,000 Palestinians living in refugee camps in Southern Lebanon. Under the leadership of Yasser Arafat and the PLO, militants staged attacks on Israel from their bases in Lebanon and attacked Lebanese who opposed their activities.

14. Marius Deeb, *Syria's Terrorist War on Lebanon and the Peace Process* (New York: Palgrave Macmillan, 2004), 5–39.

15. *The U.S. Marines in Lebanon* (Wesleyan University Department of Government, August 7, 2001), http://www.wesleyan.edu/gov/ (accessed 2004).

16. Trudy Rubin, "U.S. Marines in Lebanon: A Solution?" *Christian Science Monitor,* July 7, 1982; John Yemma, "Shattered State in the Mideast," *Christian Science Monitor,* February 4, 1983; Daniel Southerland, "U.S. Marines Only One Part of Complex Lebanon Package," *Christian Science Monitor,* July 8, 1982; and Geoffrey Godsell, "'Send in the Marines': Decisive U.S. Action Tends to Favor P.L.O.," *Christian Science Monitor,* July 8, 1982.

17. T. Elaine Carey, "American Marines Meet the P.L.O.," *Christian Science Monitor,* August 26, 1982.

18. Benis M. Frank, *U.S. Marines in Lebanon, 1982–1984* (Washington, DC: History and Museums Division Headquarters, U.S. Marine Corps, 1987), 12–14.

19. Ibid., 13–14.

20. Brad Knickerbocker, "U.S. Looks Beyond Beirut to Future of Palestinians," *Christian Science Monitor,* August 24, 1982.

21. Anne Shutt, "Marines End Beirut Task, Secretary of Defense Says," *Christian Science Monitor,* September 2, 1982.

22. Trudy Rubin, "Knesset Debate on War Likely to Echo across Israel," *Christian Science Monitor,* September 9, 1982.

23. Anne Shutt, "Israeli Planes Hit Lebanon Again," *Christian Science Monitor,* September 14, 1982.

24. Daniel Southerland, "Keeping Peace in Beirut: First Step in Lebanon Recovery," *Christian Science Monitor,* September 21, 1982.

25. Trudy Rubin, "Israel's Bill for War: Less Than Expected," *Christian Science Monitor,* August 26, 1982; Brad Knickerbocker, "Open-Ended Role for U.S. Marines in Beirut Makes Pentagon Brass Edgy," *Christian Science Monitor,* September 30, 1982; and Anne Shutt, "Marines Return to Lebanon," *Christian Science Monitor,* September 30, 1982.

26. Ronald Reagan, "Letter to the Speaker of the House and the President Pro Tempore of the Senate Reporting on United States Participation in the Multinational Force in Lebanon" (American Reference Library, September 29, 1982).

27. Ibid.

28. In numerous instances in which marines intervened in the internal affairs of a war-torn state, it was aggressive tactics and mobility that led to success. Completion of missions in Haiti, the Dominican Republic, Nicaragua, and elsewhere exemplify the tactical doctrine employed by marines. This differed dramatically from the passive-static presence in Lebanon.

29. Eric Hammel, *The Root: The Marines in Beirut, August 1982–February 1984* (Pacifica, CA: Pacifica Press, 1985), 427.

30. Trudy Rubin, "Opening of Airport Gives Beirutis a Psychological Boost," *Christian Science Monitor,* October 1, 1982; and Warren Richey, "All Quiet on Beirut Front: Marines in Lebanon Boost U.S. Image," *Christian Science Monitor,* October 21, 1982.

31. Robin Wright, "U.S. Marine–Israeli Relations Tense," *Christian Science Monitor,* January 26, 1983.

32. Linda Feldmann, "U.S. Officer in Beirut Averts an Israeli Tank Crossing," *Christian Science Monitor,* February 3, 1983; and Joseph C. Harsch, "The Case of Captain Johnson," *Christian Science Monitor,* February 10, 1983.

33. Frank, *U.S. Marines in Lebanon.*

34. Linda Feldmann, "Beirut: U.S. Marines Take Cover after Ambush," *Christian Science Monitor,* March 17, 1983.

35. Laurent Belsie, "Fallout from Beirut Bombing," *Christian Science Monitor,* April 19, 1983.

36. Laurent Belsie, "Schultz Raises Hope in Lebanon," *Christian Science Monitor,* April 29, 1983; and Frank, *U.S. Marines in Lebanon,* 64.

37. Robin Wright, "Marines in Lebanon Facing Increased Danger," *Christian Science Monitor,* August 25, 1983; and Robin Wright, "Fighting in Lebanon Escalates Following Israeli Pullback," *Christian Science Monitor,* September 7, 1983.

38. Robin Wright, "Lebanon: The Politics Behind Gunfire and Kidnapping," *Christian Science Monitor,* August 12, 1983.

39. Robin Wright, "Marines in Lebanon Facing Increased Danger."

40. On August 28, 1983, retired marine lieutenant colonel and President Reagan's special envoy to the Middle East, Ambassador Bud McFarlane, broke off negotiations with Druze leader Walid Jumblatt. It was soon after negotiations ended that Druze guns opened fire on LAF and marine positions in Beirut.

41. Howard LaFranchi, "Two U.S. Marines Killed in Beirut," *Christian Science Monitor,* August 30, 1983.

42. Hammel, *Marines in Beirut.*

43. Ronald Reagan, "Statement by Deputy Press Secretary Speaks on the Death of Two United States Marines in Lebanon" (American Reference Library, August 29, 1983).

44. Robin Wright, "Lebanese Druze Guns Shoot Holes in U.S. Peace Efforts," *Christian Science Monitor,* September 9, 1983.

45. Ibid.

46. Daniel Southerland, "Lebanon Urges More U.S. Muscle," *Christian Science Monitor,* September 9, 1983; Brad Knickerbocker, "Pentagon Begins Offensive to Support Defense Buildup," *Christian Science Monitor,* September 13, 1983; Robin Wright, "Rapid Escalation of U.S. Forces in Lebanon Concerns Allies," *Christian Science Monitor,* September 14, 1983; Brad Knickerbocker, "U.S. Buildup in Lebanon," *Christian Science Monitor,* September 14, 1983; and Trudy Rubin, "Syria Reacts with Threats to U.S. Navy Salvos as 'Defensive' Role of the Marines Expands," *Christian Science Monitor,* September 19, 1983.

47. Ronald Reagan, "Interview with Members of the Editorial Board of the *New York Post* in New York City" (American Reference Library, September 16, 1983); and Ronald Reagan, "Radio Address to the Nation on the Situation in Lebanon" (American Reference Library, October 8, 1983).

48. Frank, *U.S. Marines in Lebanon,* 94.

49. Ronald Reagan, "Address to the Nation on Events in Lebanon and Grenada" (American Reference Library, October 27, 1983).

50. Alan J. Rosenblatt, "Aggressive Foreign Policy Marketing: Public Response to Reagan's 1983 Address on Lebanon and Grenada," *Political Behavior* 20, no. 3 (1998).

51. Ronald Reagan, "Remarks to Military Personnel at Cherry Point, North Carolina, on the United States Casualites in Lebanon and Grenada" (American Reference Library, November 4, 1983); Ronald Reagan, "Interview with Bruce Drake of the *New York Daily News*" (American Reference Library, December 12, 1983); Ronald Reagan, "Question-and-Answer Session with Reporters on Domestic and Foreign Policy Issues" (American Reference Library, December 14, 1983); and Ronald Reagan, "Remarks and a Question-and-Answer Session with Reporters on the Pentagon Report on the Security of United States Marines in Lebanon" (American Reference Library, December 27, 1983).

52. Brad Knickerbocker, "U.S., Syria Flex Muscles in Mideast," *Christian Science Monitor,* November 9, 1983; David Anable, "On Keeping a Great Nation on Course, Rather Than Tacking between Extremes," *Christian Science Monitor,* November 9, 1983; Ned Temko, "Rising Risks for Reagan in Lebanon," *Christian Science Monitor,* December 19, 1983; and Robin Wright, "Beirut Deadlock Keeps Marines Issue Alive," *Christian Science Monitor,* January 13, 1984.

53. Robin Wright, "U.S. Role in Beirut Goes on Despite Exit of Marines from Peace Force," *Christian Science Monitor,* February 27, 1984.

54. Frank, *U.S. Marines in Lebanon,* 10; Knickerbocker, "Open-Ended Role for U.S. Marines in Beirut Makes Pentagon Brass Edgy"; and Daniel Southerland, "Will Lebanon's Peacekeepers Be Domestic or Multinational?" *Christian Science Monitor,* October 26, 1982. By 1982, there were more than 30,000 Syrian troops in Lebanon. The number of Druze, Amaal, and Palestinian forces is more difficult to determine, but each may have maintained several thousand armed guerrillas and conventional forces. When compared to the MNF, which maintained approximately 3,000 peace-keepers, it becomes clear that without the threat of escalation by the MNF nations there was little hope the American, French, and Italian forces could end the conflict in Lebanon.

55. Rubin, "Opening of Airport Gives Beirutis a Psychological Boost."

56. Richey, "All Quiet on Beirut Front: Marines in Lebanon Boost U.S. Image."

57. Frank, *U.S. Marines in Lebanon,* 40.

58. Hammel, *Marines in Beirut,* 70.

59. Feldmann, "Beirut: U.S. Marines Take Cover after Ambush."

60. Laurent Belsie, "U.S. Marine Commander Escapes Injury in Lebanon," *Christian Science Monitor,* May 6, 1983.

61. Frank, *U.S. Marines in Lebanon,* 72.

62. Hammel, *Marines in Beirut,* 109–10.

63. Frank, *U.S. Marines in Lebanon,* 81.

64. Timothy Geraghty, *Situational Report No. 25* (U.S. Marine Corps, 1983).

65. On September 9, 1983, Lieutenant General Ibrahim Tannous, Commander of the Lebanese Armed Forces, formally asked Special Ambassador Robert McFarlane for direct support of LAF forces fighting in the Chouf and around Beirut. This date is considered as having fundamentally changed the mission of the United States in Lebanon.

66. Southerland, "Lebanon Urges More U.S. Muscle."

67. Ibid; see also Rubin, "Syria Reacts with Threats to U.S. Navy Salvos as 'Defensive' Role of the Marines Expands"; and Linda Feldmann, "Shultz Accuses Syria of Blocking Cease-Fire," *Christian Science Monitor,* September 22, 1983.

68. Wright, "Rapid Escalation of U.S. Forces in Lebanon Concerns Allies."

69. Senate Armed Services Committee, "Remarks to the Senate Armed Services Committee of General Paul X. Kelley," October 31, 1983.

70. Hammel, *Marines in Beirut,* 281.

71. Charlotte Saikowski and Daniel Southerland, "Beirut Bombings Lend Urgency to Search for a Settlement in Lebanon," *Christian Science Monitor,* October 24, 1983.

72. Julia Malone, "Congress Calls for Security for Marines Amid Skepticism," *Christian Science Monitor,* October 25, 1983.

73. Hammel, *Marines in Beirut,* 410.

74. Robin Wright, "Can Beirut Forces Be Safe?" *Christian Science Monitor,* November 2, 1983.

75. David Winder, "What's Behind the Major Debate About Foreign Troops in Lebanon?" *Christian Science Monitor,* October 31, 1983.

76. Knickerbocker, "U.S., Syria Flex Muscles in Mideast"; Brad Knickerbocker, "Weinberger: U.S. Blames Syria for Attack on Marines," *Christian Science Monitor,* November 23, 1983; "U.S. And Syria," *Christian Science Monitor,* December 6, 1983; and Daniel Southerland, "Cost to Eject Syrians from Lebanon Has Israel, U.S. Considering Other Options," *Christian Science Monitor,* December 6, 1983.

77. Ned Temko, "Syria Moves to Speed Exit of Marines," *Christian Science Monitor,* January 4, 1984.

78. "Reagan Team Tells Senate Marines Needed in Beirut," *Christian Science Monitor,* January 13, 1984.

79. "France Reducing the Size of Its Beirut Contingent," *Christian Science Monitor,* January 3, 1984.

80. Robin Wright, "As Marine Exit Begins, Pressure Increases on Gemayel to Resign," *Christian Science Monitor,* February 19, 1984.

81. Some scholars suggest the mission in Lebanon was a peacemaking operation rather than peacekeeping. These arguments have merits since the truce between rival factions was tenuous at best.

82. Rubin, "U.S. Marines in Lebanon: A Solution?"; John Yemma, "Hawks Are Overshadowing Diplomats in Besieged Beirut," *Christian Science Monitor,* July 7, 1982; and Godsell, "'Send in the Marines': Decisive U.S. Action Tends to Favor P.L.O."

83. Carey, "American Marines Meet the P.L.O."

84. Frank, *U.S. Marines in Lebanon,* 15.

85. Shutt, "Marines Return to Lebanon."

86. Reagan, "Reporting on United States Participation in the Multinational Force in Lebanon."

87. Hammel, *Marines in Beirut,* 109–15.

88. "How the Marines Fared in Lebanon," *Christian Science Monitor,* February 22, 1984.

89. *The U.S. Marines in Lebanon* (Wesleyan University).

90. *Report of the D.O.D. Commission on Beirut International Airport Terrorist Act, October 23, 1983* (Washington, DC: U.S. Department of Defense, 1983), 7.

91. See Reagan, "Reporting on United States Participation in the Multinational Force in Lebanon"; Ronald Reagan, "Statement by Deputy Press Secretary Speaks on the Situation in Lebanon" (American Reference Library, September 23, 1982); Reagan, "Pentagon Report on the Security of United States Marines in Lebanon"; Reagan, "Domestic and Foreign Policy Issues"; and Reagan, "Interview with Bruce Drake of the *New York Daily News.*"

92. *Report of the D.O.D. Commission on Beirut International Airport Terrorist Act.*

93. Ibid., 9.

94. Ibid., 14.

95. "Transcript: 9/11 Commission Hearing," *Washington Post,* April 13, 2004, http://www.washingtonpost.com/wp-dyn/articles/A9088-2004Apr13.html (accessed June 27, 2005).

96. Stephen F. Knott, "Congressional Oversight and the Crippling of the CIA," George Mason University's History News Network, November 4, 2001, http://hnn.us/articles/380.html (accessed June 27, 2005).

97. PBS, "Target America," in *Frontline,* 120 min., USA, 2001.

98. *Report of the D.O.D. Commission on Beirut International Airport Terrorist Act,* 14–15.

99. "Rice Criticizes Alleged Syrian Support for Terrorists in Iraq," *Assyrian International News Agency,* May 21, 2005.

100. *Background Note: Libya* (Washington, DC: Bureau of Near Eastern Affairs, U.S. Department of State, 2004).

101. Christopher Bassford, *Clausewitz in English: The Reception of Clausewitz in Britain and America* (New York: Oxford University Press, 1994).

CHAPTER 4

1. *The World Factbook* (Central Intelligence Agency, 2005), https://www.cia.gov/cia/publications/factbook/index.html (accessed July, 25, 2005). Somalia is a land dependent upon cattle and the Jubba and Shebeelle Valleys, where Somali agriculture is centered. With less than 2 percent of Somalia suitable for farming, drought or warfare in either the Jubba or Shebeelle can cause mass starvation across the entire country, as it did when civil war broke out in 1991.

2. I.M. Lewis, *A Modern History of Somalia: Nation and State in the Horn of Africa* (New York: Longman, 1980).

3. See Ali Jimali Ahmed, *The Invention of Somalia* (Trenton, NJ: Red Sea Press, 1995).

4. Jack Davies, *Reunification of the Somali People* (Chevy Chase, MD: Davies Consulting, 2001). The Somali clan system is similar to a spider's web of interlacing loyalties. Somalis trace their lineage back to Noah and are considered descendants of the Eastern Cushites. The formation of clans in the previous millennia led to the formation of the six clans mentioned above and to a much greater number of sub-clans. Thus, loyalty has long remained first to the sub-clan and then the clan. The concept of a Somali nation was one introduced in the post-independence era.

5. Martin Stanton, *Somalia on $5 a Day: A Soldier's Story* (New York: Presidio Press, 2001), 64–66.

6. See Kenneth Weiss, *The Soviet Involvement in the Ogaden War* (Washington, DC: Center for Naval Analysis, 1980).

7. Stanton, *Somalia on $5 a Day,* 63–64.

8. For Siad Barre, "scientific socialism" was merely a means to an end. The general was not a dedicated communist. It was power he coveted and if that meant working with the Americans, so be it.

9. Jonathan Stevenson, *Losing Mogadishu: Testing U.S. Policy in Somalia* (Annapolis, MD: Naval Institute Press, 1995), 30–35.

10. Ibid., 32.

11. In 1989, opposition groups began working together to overthrow Barre. This cooperation would break down as the scramble to replace Barre began in the aftermath of his defeat.

12. Stanton, *Somalia on $5 a Day,* 69–70; and Scott Peterson, "Following Dictator's Removal Somalia Is Torn by Tribal Strife," *Christian Science Monitor,* October 22, 1991.

13. "Somalia Chronology," *Christian Science Monitor,* July 22, 1991.

14. Ben Parker, *Everything About Qat/Khat/Kat* (University of Pennsylvania, African Studies Center, 1995), http://www.sas.upenn.edu/African_Studies/Hornet/qat.html (accessed July, 25 2005). Khat is a commonly used drug in Somalia that is chewed to "produce excitation, banish sleep, and promote communication." The drug was Somalia's largest import and is flown in from Kenya and elsewhere. Chewed by young men, khat is a stimulant which removes the inhibitions of a sober person and enables Somali fighters to wage bloody gang wars.

15. Peterson, "Following Dictator's Removal Somalia Is Torn by Tribal Strife."

16. John L. Hirsch and Robert B. Oakley, *Somalia and Operation Restore Hope: Reflections on Peacemaking and Peacekeeping* (Washington, DC: U.S. Institute of Peace Press, 1995), 14–17.

17. Ibid., 12.

18. Peter Grier, "Dire Straits in Somalia," *Christian Science Monitor,* January 8, 1992.

19. Hirsch and Oakley, *Somalia and Operation Restore Hope,* 16–17.

20. Stevenson, *Losing Mogadishu: Testing U.S. Policy in Somalia,* 37.

21. "In Somali Town, 'Only Six Dead' Is Cause for Hope," *International Herald Tribune,* October 24, 1992.

22. While many aid organizations pulled out of Somalia during the height of the fighting, those who stayed faced a daunting task and lost aid workers to the violence of Somali gangs.

23. Stevenson, *Losing Mogadishu: Testing U.S. Policy in Somalia,* 36.

24. Jonathan Mermin, "Television News and American Intervention in Somalia: The Myth of a Media-Driven Foreign Policy," *Political Science Quarterly* 112, no. 3 (1997).

25. Colin Powell, *My American Journey* (New York: Random House, 1995), 114–15. The Powell Doctrine consists of six basic criteria. (1) Is a vital American interest at stake? (2) Will the United States commit sufficient resources to win? (3) Are objectives clearly defined? (4) Will the United States sustain its commitment? (5) Is there reasonable expectation that Congress and the American people will support the commitment? (6) Have all other options been exhausted?

26. Jon Western, "Sources of Humanitarian Intervention: Beliefs, Information, and Advocacy in the U.S. Decisions on Somalia and Bosnia," *International Security* 26, no. 4 (Spring 2002): 116.

27. See Samuel Makinda, *Seeking Peace from Chaos: Humanitarian Intervention in Somalia* (Boulder, CO: Lynne Reinner, 1993).

28. Grier, "Dire Straits in Somalia."

29. George D. Moffett III, "White House Hints Change in Stance against Putting UN Peacekeepers in Somalia," *Christian Science Monitor,* August 6, 1992.

30. Hirsch and Oakley, *Somalia and Operation Restore Hope,* 19.

31. Ibid.

32. "The U.S. Government's Reaction Time in Aiding Somalia," *Christian Science Monitor,* September 2, 1992. American aid to Somalia began in February 1991 with the United States providing 80,000 tons of food by September 1992.

33. Scott Peterson, "World Shifts Attention to Somalia," *Christian Science Monitor,* September 2, 1992; George D. Moffett III, "Somalia Crisis Prompts Novel Approach to Aid," *Christian Science Monitor,* September 2, 1992; and "Feeding Somalia," *Christian Science Monitor,* September 11, 1992.

34. Stevenson, *Losing Mogadishu: Testing U.S. Policy in Somalia,* 45.

35. "Feeding Somalia."

36. Robert M. Press, "Somalia's Security Crisis Shifts to Remote Villages," *Christian Science Monitor,* October 6, 1992; Stephen Green, "Tough Relief a Must for Future Somalias," *Christian Science Monitor,* October 29, 1992; David D. Newsom, "Somalia: A New Kind of Dilemma," *Christian Science Monitor,* November 10, 1992; "End Somalia's Anguish," *Christian Science Monitor,* November 30, 1992; and Nancy Kassebaum and Paul Simon, "Save Somalia from Itself," *New York Times,* January 2, 1992.

37. Don Oberdorfer, "The Path to Intervention," *Washington Post,* December 6, 1992.

38. Hirsch and Oakley, *Somalia and Operation Restore Hope,* 43.

39. Peter Grier, "Somalia Lawlessness, Despair Behind U.S. Decision to Offer Troops to Protect Food Aid," *Christian Science Monitor,* November 30, 1992.

40. Ron Scherer, "United Nations to Back Bush's Plan on Somalia," *Christian Science Monitor,* December 2, 1992.

41. Hirsch and Oakley, *Somalia and Operation Restore Hope,* 47.

42. George D. Moffett III, "Force in Somalia May Signal More UN Interventions," *Christian Science Monitor,* December 4, 1992.

43. See "CIA Warns Bush on Somalia," *International Herald Tribune,* December 3, 1992; and Fred Barnes, "Last Call," *New Republic,* December 28, 1992.

44. Hirsch and Oakley, *Somalia and Operation Restore Hope.*

45. Moffett, "Force in Somalia May Signal More UN Interventions"; and "The Task in Somalia," *Christian Science Monitor,* December 7, 1992.

46. Peter Grier, "U.S. Relief Startup Goes Well in Somalia," *Christian Science Monitor,* December 11, 1992.

47. Peter Grier, "Logistics Challenges Await Troops in Somalia," *Christian Science Monitor,* December 7, 1992.

48. Robert M. Press, "Relief Troops in Somalia Now Turn to Food," *Christian Science Monitor,* December 11, 1992.

49. Peter Grier, "Focus in Somalia May Shift from Famine to Rebuilding Effort," *Christian Science Monitor,* December 14, 1992.

50. Stanton, *Somalia on $5 a Day,* 101.

51. Ibid., chap. 8.

52. Robert M. Press, "U.S. Marines in Somalia Face Dilemma over Disarmament," *Christian Science Monitor,* December 14, 1992.

53. "Dealing with Somalia's Guns," *Christian Science Monitor*, December 16, 1992.

54. Ibid.

55. Scott Peterson, "UN Seeks Solution to Anarchy in Somalia," *Christian Science Monitor*, December 21, 1992.

56. Hirsch and Oakley, *Somalia and Operation Restore Hope*, 51.

57. Robert M. Press, "U.S. Marines in Somalia Plan to Seize Hidden Arms," *Christian Science Monitor*, December 28, 1992; and Frank Crigler, "A Flaw in the Somalia Game Plan," *Christian Science Monitor*, January 11, 1993.

58. On January 15, 1993, Somali factions signed the Addis Ababa Accords, which promised a cease fire and disarmament of militiamen.

59. "U.S. Crackdown in Somalia," *Christian Science Monitor*, January 7, 1993.

60. Stevenson, *Losing Mogadishu: Testing U.S. Policy in Somalia*, 65.

61. Ibid., 67.

62. Stanton, *Somalia on $5 a Day*, 143–48.

63. Robert M. Press, "U.S. Is Working to Restore Civilian Police in Somalia," *Christian Science Monitor*, January 21, 1993; and Stanton, *Somalia on $5 a Day*, 149.

64. Crigler, "A Flaw in the Somalia Game Plan."

65. Robert M. Press, "First U.S. Troops Exit Somalia, but Full Pullout Still Unclear," *Christian Science Monitor*, January 19, 1993.

66. Along with efforts to reestablish town councils and the national police, UNITAF began publishing a newspaper, *Rajo*, in Mogadishu with useful information about UNITAF and its work. The United Nations and United States also brought Somali intellectuals together in Addis Ababa to work for the restoration of civil society in Somalia.

67. Robert M. Press, "More Doubts Raised About UN Ability to Take Control of Somalia Reconstruction," *Christian Science Monitor*, January 22, 1993.

68. Robert M. Press, "Somalia Tries to Pick up the Postwar Pieces," *Christian Science Monitor*, February 19, 1991; and Robert M. Press and Lucia Mouat, "UN Responds to Critics on Somalia," *Christian Science Monitor*, September 2, 1992.

69. "UN to Take over Somalia Mission on May 1, Chief Says," *Christian Science Monitor*, March 5, 1993. Passed on March 26, 1993, Security Council Resolution 814 called for the establishment of UNOSOM II.

70. Lucia Mouat, "UN to Break New Ground in Plan for Peacekeepers in Somalia," *Christian Science Monitor*, March 16, 1993.

71. Scott Peterson, "Anti-West Mood Imperils Security as Somalia Operation Shifts to UN," *Christian Science Monitor*, March 18, 1993.

72. "Keeping Somalia's Fragile Peace," *Christian Science Monitor*, March 31, 1993; "Changing of the Guard in Somalia," *Christian Science Monitor*, April 30, 1993; and Robert M. Press, "Somalia Faces Tough Rebuilding Task as UN Takes Over," *Christian Science Monitor*, May 5, 1993.

73. David Smock, "Somalia's Next Step: Restoring Economy," *Christian Science Monitor*, March 23, 1993.

74. Scott Peterson, "U.S. Backs Up UN in Somalia, Protecting Its Investment," *Christian Science Monitor,* May 25, 1993.

75. When UNOSOM II took control of Somalia, the German and Indian brigades had not yet arrived, national contingents were without adequate equipment, and essential planning had not been completed.

76. Hirsch and Oakley, *Somalia and Operation Restore Hope,* 116; see also Walter Clarke, "Testing the World's Resolve in Somalia," *Parameters* 23, no. 4 (1993).

77. Hirsch and Oakley, *Somalia and Operation Restore Hope,* 116–20.

78. Peter Grier, "Somalia Crisis Spurs Pentagon to Reorient Training of U.S. Troops," *Christian Science Monitor,* June 16, 1993; and Robert M. Press, "Meeting the Challenges Facing a Troubled Somalia," *Christian Science Monitor,* June 29, 1993. Peter Grier, "Airstrikes in Somalia Show UN Is in for Long Haul," *Christian Science Monitor,* June 14, 1993. The difficulty presented by the urban terrain of Mogadishu led U.S. forces to heavily rely on air power in its attacks against General Aidid's material and forces. Additionally, few of the 10th Mountain soldiers in the QRF were trained in the "door kicking" tactics necessary to kill or capture General Aidid and his associates. Thus, Cobra attack helicopters and C-130 gunships played a major role in strikes.

79. Keith Richburg, "In War on Aideed, UN Battled Itself," *Washington Post,* December 6, 1993.

80. Robert M. Press, "UN Attack in Somalia Seen as Spur to War, Harmful to Aid Effort," *Christian Science Monitor,* July 13, 1993; and "Realism in Somalia," *Christian Science Monitor,* July 15, 1993. Throughout the summer, casualties continued to increase as SNA militiamen attacked UNOSOM II forces in response to strikes against General Aidid.

81. Hirsch and Oakley, *Somalia and Operation Restore Hope,* 124–25.

82. See Ken Menkhaus, "A Second Look at UN's Action in Somalia," *Christian Science Monitor,* July 16, 1993; "Diplomacy Can Help Somalia," *Christian Science Monitor,* July 22, 1993; Lucia Mouat, "UN in Somalia Caught in a Debate over Force Vs. Diplomacy," *Christian Science Monitor,* July 22, 1993; "UN to Strengthen Forces in Somalia after Soldiers Killed," *Christian Science Monitor,* August 10, 1993; and "Staying in Somalia," *Christian Science Monitor,* August 12, 1993.

83. Snow, *Uncivil Wars.*

84. "Staying in Somalia."

85. Hirsch and Oakley, *Somalia and Operation Restore Hope,* 122.

86. Mark Bowden, *Black Hawk Down: A Story of Modern War* (New York: Atlantic Monthly Press, 1999), 29.

87. Ibid., 5.

88. Matt Eversmann and Dan Schilling, *The Battle of Mogadishu: Firsthand Accounts from the Men of Task Force Ranger* (New York: Presidio Press, 2004), xviii.

89. Bowden, *Black Hawk Down,* 20.

90. Ibid., 6–20.

91. Marshall Ecklund, "Analysis of Operation Gothic Serpent: T.F. Ranger in Somalia," *Special Warfare* 17, no. 2 (2004).

92. On the night of September 25 the 101st Airborne Division lost a Black Hawk to an RPG round. During Gothic Serpent, Black Hawks were at their most vulnerable when hovering as Delta assaulters or Rangers fast-roped to the street.

93. Raleigh Cash, "Sua Sponte: Of Their Own Accord," in *The Battle of Mogadishu: First Hand Accounts from the Men of Task Force Ranger,* ed. Matt Eversmann and Dan Schilling (New York: Randon House, 2004).

94. General Aidid saw the single greatest weakness of the Americans to be their unwillingness to die. Thus, in order to force the withdrawal of the United States, the general needed to inflict significant casualties on American forces. Throughout TF Rangers operations, Somali militiamen proved willing to die for little or no gain. The warrior culture of Somalia and a plentiful supply of khat led to aggressive action on the part of the "skinnies," as the Americans called them.

95. Bowden, *Black Hawk Down;* Ecklund, "Analysis of Operation Gothic Serpent: T.F. Ranger in Somalia"; and "U.S. Prepares More Troops for Somalia Operation," *Christian Science Monitor,* October 5, 1993.

96. Scott Peterson, "Somalia Crisis Turns to Quagmire as Clinton Hardens U.S. Resolve," *Christian Science Monitor,* October 6, 1993.

97. The fourth phase of American intervention in Somalia began with the return of American forces in 1995. This period is beyond the scope of this study and offers little additional insight into the broader understanding of asymmetric conflict.

98. Richard Stewart, *The United States Army in Somalia 1992–1994* (Fort McNair, DC: Center for Military History, 1994), 6. While some cynics claim the president sought to appease advocates of intervention while also pleasing an intervention-weary Joint Chiefs of Staff, there is a lack of substantial evidence to support such claims.

99. "Operation Provide Relief," Globalsecurity.org, 1996, http://www.global security.org/military/ops/provide_relief.htm (accessed August 20, 2005).

100. Peter Grier, "As Violence in Somalia Escalates, Senate Steps Up Troop Oversight," *Christian Science Monitor,* September 14, 1993; and "The Somalia Policy," *Christian Science Monitor,* October 6, 1993.

101. Peter Grier, "Clinton Grapples with U.S. Role Abroad after Somalia Attack," *Christian Science Monitor,* October 7, 1993; Linda Feldmann, "GOP's Lugar Urges Vote on Clinton's Somalia Plan," *Christian Science Monitor,* October 12, 1993; and Peter Grier, "U.S. Role in Somalia, Bosnia Raises Concerns at Home," *Christian Science Monitor,* August 12, 1993.

102. Carll Ladd, "U.S. Public and Somalia," *Christian Science Monitor,* October 15, 1993.

103. "Mr. Clinton's Quagmire?" *National Review,* November 1, 1993.

104. Scott Peterson, "U.S. Buildup in Somalia Leaves Many Worried about Further Clashes," *Christian Science Monitor,* October 18, 1993; Mark Sommer, "Leave Somalia to UN," *Christian Science Monitor,* October 19, 1993; and John Hirsch, " U.S. in Somalia: Should the Troops Stay?" *Christian Science Monitor,* October 25, 1993.

105. Bill Clinton, "Somalia: Our Troops Will Leave by March 31, 1994," *Vital Speeches of the Day,* LX, no. 2 (1993).

106. Ibid.

107. Robert M. Press, "Battles Break Out among Rival Clans in Southern Somalia," *Christian Science Monitor,* November 3, 1993; and Robert M. Press, "U.S. Bid for a Political Settlement Faces Tests in Streets of Somalia," *Christian Science Monitor,* November 8, 1993.

108. Robert M. Press, "UN Calls Off Manhunt for Aideed in Somalia," *Christian Science Monitor,* November 18, 1993.

109. Bowden, *Black Hawk Down,* 338.

110. Armed Services Committee, *Somalia,* May 12, 1994; also, from Senate, *United States Rangers in Somalia,* 103rd Cong., November 22, 1993. In this statement by General Garrison, the general explained his view of the Battle of Mogadishu saying, "We accomplished our mission on October 3. We captured 20 of these people that had been killing UN troops, their leadership. We got them out of there, and we tried to defend our men that were trapped in that helicopter. We simply got ourselves in a hell of a fire fight, and we won, too. About 400 Somalis learned that Americans know how to defend themselves, even when they are trapped, pinned down, and you are sniping at them."

111. Stevenson, *Losing Mogadishu: Testing U.S. Policy in Somalia,* 116; and William Go, *The Marine Corps' Combined Action Program and Modern Peace Operations* (Quantico, VA: U.S. Marine Corps, 1997). Go points out that UNITAF functioned in a manner similar to the Marine Corps' Combined Action Program during the Vietnam conflict. Forces worked in specific locations to empower local leaders, arm and train police, eliminate gangs, and build rapport with local populations. This approach may explain the success of UNITAF.

112. Rick Atkinson, "Night of a Thousand Casualties," *Washington Post,* January 31, 1994.

113. Go, "The Marine Corps' Combined Action Program and Modern Peace Operations."

114. Clifford Day, *Critical Analysis on the Defeat of Task Force Ranger* (Montgomery, AL: Air Command and Staff College, 1997). When UNITAF handed over control of Somalia to UNOSOM II on May 4, 1993, not only were the total number of foreign forces in the country significantly lower than during Restore Hope, but also UNOSOM II proved to be a force without a significant advantage in firepower over General Aidid and other faction commanders. If UNOSOM II had not possessed its aviation elements, there is little doubt that the SNA was the better armed military force. Secretary of Defense Aspin's rejection of General Montgomery's request for C-130 gunships, M1 Abrams main battle tanks, and Bradley Fighting Vehicles not only cost American lives during the Battle of Mogadishu, but also dramatically reduced the deterrent effect of UNOSOM II.

115. Stevenson, *Losing Mogadishu: Testing U.S. Policy in Somalia,* 126.

116. Interestingly, the rules of engagement established for UNITAF remained in effect for UNOSOM II. Rather than aggressively engaging and pursuing bandits and factions in breech of disarmament agreements, however, UNOSOM II proved to be a passive force unwilling to act aggressively.

117. Charles A. Stevenson, "The Evolving Clinton Doctrine on the Use of Force," *Armed Forces & Society* 22, no. 4 (1996).

118. Ibid., 2. The failure in Somalia is often credited with playing the primary role in President Clinton's decision not to act when it became apparent that genocide was underway in Rwanda.

119. Hendrickson, *Somalia*, 62.

120. See Harvey Gickman, "Africa in the War on Terrorism," *Journal of Asian & African Studies* 38, no. 2 (2003); Thomas R. Mockaitis, "Reluctant Partners: Civil Military Cooperation in Kosovo," *Small Wars and Insurgencies* 15, no. 2 (2004); and Adekeye Adebajo, "Africa and America in an Age of Terror," *Journal of Asian & African Studies* 38, no. 2 (2003).

CHAPTER 5

1. Stephen Tanner, *Afghanistan: A Military History from Alexander the Great to the Fall of the Taliban* (Cambridge, MA: Da Capo Press, 2002).

2. T. A. Heathcote, *The Afghan Wars, 1839–1919* (Staplehurst, Great Britain: Spellmount, 2003).

3. See Hassan Kakar, *Afghanistan: The Soviet Invasion and the Afghan Response, 1979–1982* (Berkeley and Los Angeles, CA: University of California Press, 1995).

4. Rini Amiri, "Comprehending the Afghan Quagmire," *Sojourner Magazine*, November 1, 2001.

5. *Background Note: Afghanistan* (U.S. State Department, Bureau of South Asian Affairs, 2005), http://www.state.gov/r/pa/ei/bgn/5380.htm (accessed September 10, 2005).

6. Taraki was not killed in the coup but remained a part of the government where he served as president. This position, however, carried no substantial powers with it.

7. *Afghanistan Fact Sheet #2: A Brief History Focusing on 1979–2001* (New York: Center for Economic and Social Rights, 2001); and Marc Morano, "Forged in Soviet Conflict, Taliban Is 'Most Extreme' Islamic Faction," *CNSNews.com,* September 17 2001, http://www.cnsnews.com/ViewForeignBureaus.asp?Page=/For eignBureaus/archive/200109/For20010917a.html (accessed September 14, 2005).

8. *Background Note: Afghanistan.*

9. "The Last Domino—Inevitable End of Afghan President Najibullah's Rule," *National Review,* May 11, 1992.

10. See Larry Goodson, *Afghanistan's Endless War: State Failure, Regional Polities, and the Rise of the Taliban* (Seattle: University of Washington Press, 2002).

11. There is some disagreement as to how and when the Taliban began. The description offered above is accessed by the Taliban and is perhaps as much fable as fact.

12. Tanner, *Afghanistan: A Military History,* 279.

13. "Profile: Gulbuddin Hekmatyar," British Broadcasting Company, January 28 2003, http://news.bbc.co.uk/1/hi/world/middle_east/2701547.stm (accessed September 15, 2005).

14. Davis Anthony, "A Brotherly Vendetta," *Asiaweek*, December 6, 1996.

15. Jason Manning, "Combating Poppy Production," in *Online News Hour,* PBS, USA, 2003.

16. *Afghanistan: Facts and Figures* (The Heritage Foundation, September 17, 2001), http://www.heritage.org/Research/NationalSecurity/WM37.cfm?render forpoint=1. During the rule of the Taliban, Afghanistan's literacy rate stood at 31.5 percent.

17. Heather Nickerson, *Afghanistan, al Qaeda and the Taliban* (Center for Defense Information, August 6 2004), http://www.cdi.org/program/document.cfm? DocumentID=2360&from_page=../index.cfm (accessed September 15, 2005); and from Bob Woodward, "Bin Laden Said to 'Own' the Taliban," *Washington Post,* October 11, 2001. Bin Laden is reported to have given the Taliban over $100 million in aid.

18. Steve Coll, *Ghost Wars: The Secret History of the CIA, Afghanistan, and Bin Laden, from the Soviet Invasion to September 10, 2001* (New York: Penguin Books, 2004), chap. 21.

19. Steve Emerson, *American Jihad: The Terrorists Living among Us* (New York: Free Press, 2003); and Yossef Bodansky, *Bin Laden: The Man Who Declared War on America* (New York: Prima Lifestyles, 2001).

20. Coll, *Ghost Wars,* 371–75.

21. Ibid., 370–79.

22. Ibid., 393; and *The 9/11 Commission Report: Final Report of the National Commission on Terrorist Attacks Upon the United States* (Washington, DC: National Commission on the Terrorist Attacks Upon the United States, 2004), chap. 3.6.

23. "First Bush Memo on al-Qaeda Declassified, Ohmy News International, February 10, 2005, http://english.ohmynews.com/articleview/article_view.asp? at_code=236845&no=210462&rel_no=1 (accessed September 15, 2005); and Coll, *Ghost Wars,* 425–26.

24. After the 1998 bombings of the U.S. Embassies in Dar es Salaam and Nairobi, DCI George Tenet made Osama bin Laden a "Tier 0" target, placing him among the CIA's most sought after persons.

25. Rohan Gunaratna, *Inside al Qaeda: Global Network of Terror* (New York: Berkley Publishing, 2003), 93–101.

26. Edward Girardet, "A More Dangerous Afghanistan," *Christian Science Monitor,* October 18, 2001. There was a strong anti-Taliban sentiment outside the provinces of southern Afghanistan.

27. "Interview with Commander Ahmad Shah Masood," Azadi Afghan Radio, 2000.

28. Paul Wolf, *The Assassination of Ahmad Shah Massoud* (Pincourt, QC: Center for Research on Globalization, 2003).

29. George W. Bush, "President Bush Reaffirms Resolve to War on Terror, Iraq and Afghanistan," The White House, Office of the Press Secretary, March 19, 2004, http://www.whitehouse.gov/news/releases/2004/03/20040319-3.html (accessed December 21, 2004).

30. "List of Attacks Claimed by or Attributed to al-Qaeda," Turkish Press, September 10, 2004, http://archive.turkishpress.com/ (accessed September 15, 2005).

31. Tommy Franks, *American Soldier: General Tommy Franks, Commander in Chief, United States Central Command* (New York: Regan Books, 2004), 243.

32. Ibid., 251. General Franks notes in his memoirs that there was "no stomach" for combat operations in Afghanistan since 1993. Thus, no contingency plan existed prior to 9/11.

33. Ibid., 251–52.

34. Ibid., 243.

35. Michael DeLong, *Inside CentCom: The Unvarnished Truth About the Wars in Afghanistan and Iraq* (Washington, DC: Regnery Press, 2004), 24.

36. Ibid.

37. Paul Richter, "Questions Surface over NATO's Revised Take on the War in Kosovo," *Los Angeles Times,* June 10, 2000.

38. DeLong, *Inside CentCom,* 24.

39. Gary Schroen, *First In: An Insider's Account of How the CIA Spearheaded the War on Terror in Afghanistan* (New York: Presidio, 2005), 51–91.

40. Ibid.

41. Tanner, *Afghanistan: A Military History,* 294–95. The Interservice Intelligence Agency, Pakistan's autonomous intelligence organization, continued limited support of the Taliban even after the beginning of the American offensive on October 7, 2001. It is also believed that ISI continues to support the Taliban and al-Qaeda in the Northwest Frontier Province of Pakistan.

42. Schroen, *How the CIA Spearheaded the War on Terror,* 169. The first Operational Detachment Alpha team, or A-Team, to arrive in Afghanistan landed in the Panjshir Valley one week after air strikes began on Taliban and al-Qaeda targets. These teams joined NA forces where they were responsible for calling in American air strikes against Taliban front lines. They also began conducting special operations such as searching for key al-Qaeda and Taliban leaders. The first of these special operations was a strike against Karnak Farm, al-Qaeda headquarters in Afghanistan, conducted by Army Rangers on October 21.

43. Tanner, *Afghanistan: A Military History,* 303.

44. Air drops were made at night, from high altitude and at high speeds in order to ensure aircraft were not brought down by anti-aircraft missiles. This significantly reduced the accuracy of drops.

45. Peter Popham, "Air Strikes on Afghanistan: Relief: Alarm over Aid Drop in 'World's Biggest Minefield,'" *The Independent,* October 9, 2001.

46. Additional aspects of this effort included gaining the support of Muslim states, limiting destruction of Afghan infrastructure, and winning a broader propaganda campaign.

47. Scott Peterson, "Building a Nation in Afghanistan," *Christian Science Monitor,* October 22, 2001.

48. S. Frederick Starr, "Afghanistan's Biggest Problem—Poverty—Can Be Solved," *Christian Science Monitor,* October 16, 2001.

49. Schroen, *How the CIA Spearheaded the War on Terror,* 326–27.

50. Franks, *American Soldier,* 268–81.

51. Recent communications captured in the first week of October 2005 between al-Qaeda leaders in Pakistan and Abu Musab al-Zarqawi in Iraq suggest that Afghanistan is lost to al-Qaeda.

52. Edward Girardet, "U.S., Beware the Consequences in Afghanistan," *Christian Science Monitor,* October 22, 2001; Edward Girardet, "A Tough Road Ahead in Afghanistan's War," *Christian Science Monitor,* November 6, 2001; and from Franks, *American Soldier,* 326. General Franks notes, "Secretary Rumsfeld and I agreed that we should not flood the country with large formations of conventional troops. 'We don't want to repeat the Soviets' mistakes,' I told the Secretary."

53. DeLong, *Inside CentCom,* 39. General DeLong describes the opening of the American campaign saying, "Operation Enduring Freedom kicked off on October 7, 2001, less than one month after the attacks of September 11. The campaign began with massive air bombardments at targets throughout the country. We hit everything on the target list, including targets in Herat in the east, Kandahar in the south, Kabul and Jalalabad in the west, and Konduz and Mazar-e-Sharif in the north. We dropped one bomb on every known tank; we took out fuel depots; we took out training camps and the tunnels around the camps; we cratered runways so they couldn't get their planes off the ground.... We fired Tomahawk missiles.... And then we did it all again the next night."

54. Philip Smucker, "Taliban Transforms Afghanistan for Total War," *Christian Science Monitor,* October 30, 2001.

55. Girardet, "A Tough Road Ahead in Afghanistan's War"; and see Jack Shafer, "Apple Turnover: *The New York Times'* R.W. Apple Jr. Never Wrote a Piece He Couldn't Contradict," *Slate.com,* April 7, 2003, http://slate.msn.com/id/2081240 (accessed September 15, 2005).

56. Scott Baldauf, "Power Shift in Afghanistan," *Christian Science Monitor,* December 10, 2001.

57. Robin Moore, *The Hunt for Bin Laden: Task Force Dagger on the Ground with the Special Forces in Afghanistan* (New York: Presidio Press, 2003), xix.

58. Tanner, *Afghanistan: A Military History,* 303–5.

59. Franks, *American Soldier,* 350.

60. George W. Bush, "Rebuilding Afghanistan" (The White House, May 19, 2003), http://www.whitehouse.gov/news/releases/2003/05/print/20030519-4.html (accessed September 15, 2004); from Laura Bush, "Radio Address of First Lady Laura Bush to Radio Free Afghanistan" (White House, May 21, 2002), http://www.whitehouse.gov/news/releases/2002/05/20020521-19.html (accessed September 15, 2004): within the first 24 months after hostilities began, $900 million were spent by the United States on the items listed above. George W. Bush, "Remarks by President Bush and President Karzi of the Islamic Government of Afghanistan" (The White House, Office of the Press Secretary, September 12, 2002), http://www.whitehouse.gov/news/releases/2002/09/20020912-6.html (accessed September 15, 2004); and George W. Bush, "Joint Statement on Road Construction in Afghanistan by the President of the United States, the Prime Minister of Japan, and the Foreign Minister of Saudi Arabia" (The White House, Office of the Press Secretary, September 12, 2002), http://www.whitehouse.gov/news/releases/2002/09/20020912-10.html (accessed September 15, 2004).

61. See Rooney, *Guerilla: Insurgents, Patriots and Terrorists from Sun Tzu to Bin Laden.*

62. Howard LaFranchi, "U.S. to Help 'Nation-Build' in Afghanistan," *Christian Science Monitor,* December 18, 2001.

63. George W. Bush, "Fact Sheet: Afghanistan Security and Reconstruction" (The White House, Office of the Press Secretary, May 2, 2002), http://www.whitehouse. gov/news/releases/2002/01/20020128-9.html (accessed September 15, 2004); and from George W. Bush, "President Bush Meets with German Chancellor Schroeder" (The White House, Office of the Press Secretary, January 31, 2002), http://www. whitehouse.gov/news/releases/2002/01/20020131-11.html (accessed September 15, 2004): where Chancellor Gerhard Schroeder proved unwilling to assist the United States in the Iraq War, German assistance in Afghanistan was substantial.

64. Scott Peterson, "UN Action Plan for Afghanistan," *Christian Science Monitor,* November 23, 2001; from Marina Ottaway, "Remaking Afghanistan: Learn from Failures," *Christian Science Monitor,* November 30, 2001: in order to remain relevant, the UN sought a major role in overseeing reconstruction efforts in Afghanistan. Michael J. Jordan, "UN May Be Best Equipped to Rebuild Afghanistan," *Christian Science Monitor,* October 25, 2001; and Michael J. Jordan, "Why You Won't See UN Blue Helmets in Afghanistan," *Christian Science Monitor,* December 18, 2001.

65. Moore, *Hunt for Bin Laden,* chap. 20.

66. DeLong, *Inside CentCom,* 56. British Special Air Service also provided substantial Special Forces support to combat operations at Tora Bora.

67. Scott Baldauf, "Bumpy Rides and Rival Tribes or Afghanistan's Border," *Christian Science Monitor,* December 20, 2001.

68. Moore, *Hunt for Bin Laden,* 313.

69. Scott Baldauf, "Shifting Sands at Afghanistan's Grass Roots," *Christian Science Monitor,* December 26, 2001; Ilene R. Prusher, "Amid Afghanistan's Decay, Hope Rekindles," *Christian Science Monitor,* January 2, 2002; Scott Baldauf, "Help for Survivors of Afghanistan's Land Mines," *Christian Science Monitor,* January 4, 2002; Ilene R. Prusher, "Rich Donors Try to Finesse Flow of $4.5 Billion into Afghanistan," *Christian Science Monitor,* January 23, 2001; and Ilene R. Prusher, "For Woman Minister, Rebuilding Afghanistan Is a Personal Quest," *Christian Science Monitor,* February 7, 2002.

70. Philip Smucker, "Ethnic Split Grows in Afghanistan's Government," *Christian Science Monitor,* February 19, 2002; and "Waging Peace in Afghanistan," *Christian Science Monitor,* February 27, 2002.

71. Among the first Coalition tasks in the aftermath of major combat operations was the establishment of an Afghan National Army, which would integrate factional forces, provide security to the country, and limit intertribal conflict.

72. George W. Bush, "Fact Sheet: Assisting People of Afghanistan" (The White House, Office of the Press Secretary, January 28, 2002), http://www.whitehouse. gov/news/releases/2002/01/20020128-9.html. Aid was among the United States' best weapons against the Taliban and al-Qaeda. By January 2002 the United States and its Coalition partners sent almost $300 million in direct aid, $50 million in credit, and $223 million in unfrozen assets to Hamid Karzai and the people of Afghanistan. In addition to direct aid, Coalition partners provided expertise and equipment for a number of reconstruction projects.

73. Sean Naylor, *Not a Good Day to Die: The Untold Story of Operation Anaconda* (New York: Berkley Books, 2005).

74. Franks, *American Soldier,* 378.

75. General Franks was, however, incorrect in his assessment of enemy casualties, which numbered 800–1,000.

76. Naylor, *Not a Good Day to Die,* 118. Three reconnaissance teams were inserted near the Shah-i-Kot days before Anaconda was set to begin so that they might infiltrate the valley and provide intelligence to mission commanders.

77. William Baker, "The Year in Review 2002: Operation Anaconda," *Naval Aviation News* 50, no. 4: 26–28.

78. "Operation Anaconda Costs 8 U.S. Lives," *CNN.com,* March 4, 2002, http://archives.cnn.com/2002/WORLD/asiapcf/central/03/04/ret.afghan.fighting/index.html (accessed September 15, 2004). During the week-long fight, eight Americans were killed in addition to a small number of Afghan militiamen. More than 40 Americans were also wounded.

79. Moore, *Hunt for Bin Laden,* 370.

80. Patrick Healey and Farah Stockman, "Taliban Flee Kandahar," *Boston Globe,* December 8, 2001.

81. Reports from Afghanistan in fall of 2005 suggest the Taliban is attempting to reconstitute itself in remote regions of western Afghanistan.

82. Scott Baldauf, "Peace Threatened in Afghanistan," *Christian Science Monitor,* September 6, 2002; Scott Baldauf, "A Triangle of Militants Regroups in Afghanistan," *Christian Science Monitor,* April 9, 2003; Owais Tohid, "Southern Afghanistan Suffers as Aid Groups Are Harassed," *Christian Science Monitor,* July 18, 2003; Scott Baldauf, "Aid Groups in Afghanistan Weigh Good Deeds Vs. Safety," *Christian Science Monitor,* October 28, 2003; and "Four Killed in Taliban Attacks in Afghanistan," *Daily Times,* November 21 2003, http://www.dailytimes.com.pk/default.asp?page=story_21-11-2003_pg7_47 (accessed September 15, 2004).

83. "Afghan Attack Leaves 5 Dead, Including NATO Soldier," *Agence France Presse,* November 7, 2006, http://www.metimes.com/; and "Six Killed in Afghanistan Taliban Ambush," *Agence France Presse,* November 3, 2007.

84. Rebecca Grant, "An Air War Like No Other," *Air Force Magazine,* November 1, 2002.

85. George W. Bush, "The Rights and Aspirations of the People of Afghanistan" (The White House, Office of Global Communications, July 9 2003), http://www.whitehouse.gov/news/releases/2003/07/print/20030709-1.html (accessed September 15, 2004); George W. Bush, "Afghanistan: Then and Now" (The White House, 2002), http://www.whitehouse.gov/afac/thenandnow.html (accessed September 15, 2004); and George W. Bush, "President Bush Meets with President Karzai of Afghanistan" (The White House, Office of the Press Secretary, February 27, 2003), http://www.whitehouse.gov/news/releases/2003/02/print/20030227-6.html (accessed September 15, 2004).

86. "U.S. Paratroops Raid Omar Compound near Kandahar," *CNN.com,* October 20 2001, http://edition.cnn.com/2001/WORLD/asiapcf/central/10/20/ret.afghan.attacks/ (accessed September 15, 2004).

87. Kenneth Katzman, *Afghanistan: Post War Governance, Security and U.S. Policy* (Washington, DC: Congressional Research Service, 2004).

88. Moore, *Hunt for Bin Laden.* Moore points out that the combination of American air power, Afghan Mujahideen, and approximately 360 American Special Forces, broken into 6- or 12-man A-Teams, were responsible for the defeat of the Taliban and al-Qaeda, which suffered an estimated 31,000 killed in action.

89. Eric Schmitt, "U.S. May Start Pulling out of Afghanistan Next Spring," *New York Times*, September 14, 2005.

90. Immediately after the end of war in Europe, the number of American soldiers in Germany surpassed one million before declining significantly. In addition to American troops there were British, French, and several million Soviet troops in Germany at war's end. Thus, American troop levels in Afghanistan pale in comparison to the wars of the past.

91. Patrick Healey, "Afghans Want U.S. to Dig Out al Qaeda," *San Francisco Chronicle*, December 27, 2001.

92. Jason Straziuso, "Taliban Support on Rise in Afghanistan," *Los Angelos Times*, November 6, 2006.

93. See Schroen, *How the CIA Spearheaded the War on Terror.*

94. Thomas Johnson, "The Loya Jirga, Ethnic Rivalries and Future Afghan Stability," *Strategic Insights* 1, no. 6 (2002).

95. Ibid; also see PBS, "Filling the Vacuum: The Bonn Conference," WGBH (Boston), 2002, http://www.pbs.org/wgbh/pages/frontline/shows/campaign/withus/cbonn.html (accessed September 15, 2005). In addition to the major ethnic groups in Afghanistan (Pushtun, Hazara, Tajik, and Uzbek), which are predominantly Sunni Muslims, there is a small number of Shiites. They were also included in the Bonn Conference and given several portfolios as well.

96. Jo Johnson, "Afghan Election Worries Monitors," *Financial Times*, October 1, 2005.

97. Stephen Biddle, *Afghanistan and the Future of Warfare: Implications for Army and Defense Policy* (Carlisle, PA: Strategic Studies Institute, U.S. Army War College, 2002), 13.

98. Ibid.

99. Pakistan was also a significant supporter of the Taliban. Through the ISI, Pakistan provided financial support, weapons, and training to the Taliban, which it hoped would unify the country and bring stability to the region.

100. Anthony Davis, "Fateful Victory," *Asia Week,* August 28, 1998. The Northern Alliance, composed of Tajiks, Uzbeks, and Hazaras, refused to join the Taliban government because of long-standing grievances against the Pushtun-dominated Taliban.

101. "Chance: Reports of Taliban Defections," *CNN.com,* October 10, 2001, http://edition.cnn.com/2001/WORLD/asiapcf/central/10/10/ret.chance.otsc/ (accessed September 15, 2004); and Maggie O'Kane, "Alliance Builds New Airstrips and Says Defections Are Aiding Its Advance," *The Guardian* (Manchester), October 8, 2001.

102. Biddle, *Afghanistan and the Future of Warfare,* 13–17.

103. Carl Conetta, *Strange Victory: A Critical Appraisal of Operation Enduring Freedom and the Afghanistan War* (The Project on Defense Alternatives, The Commonwealth Institute, January 30, 2002; http://www.comw.org/pda/0201 strangevic.html.

104. "White House Warns Taliban 'We Will Defeat You,'" *CNN.com,* September 21 2001, http://archives.cnn.com/2001/WORLD/asiapcf/central/09/21/ ret.afghan.taliban/ (accessed September 15, 2004).

105. "In Response to Taliban Offer, Bush Warns 'Time Is Running Out,'" *Houston Chronicle,* October 6, 2001.

106. Julian Borger, "Winter Is Coming and the Taliban Are Strong as Ever. What Now for the War on Terror?" *The Guardian* (Manchester), November 3, 2001; and Barton Gellman, "U.S. Concludes bin Laden Escaped Tora Bora Fight," *Washington Post,* April 17, 2002.

107. Catherine Callaway, "Special Forces Drop into Afghanistan," *CNN.com,* October 20 2001, http://archives.cnn.com/2001/WORLD/asiapcf/central/10/20/ ret.rangers.cnna/ (accessed September 15, 2004).

108. Anthony H. Cordesman, *The Lessons of Afghanistan: Warfighting, Intelligence, Force Transformation, Counterproliferation, and Arms Control* (Washington, DC: Center for Strategic and International Studies, 2002).

109. There is some speculation that Afghan Coalition troops, tasked with sealing off escape routes from Tora Bora, were paid off by al-Qaeda and allowed bin Laden and other al-Qaeda leaders to escape into Pakistan during the December 2001 battle. It is also important to note that the number of American troops engaged in the fighting during these two campaigns was significantly more than one or more A-Teams. The shortage of American troops, however, was a persistent problem in tracking down and cutting off Taliban and al-Qaeda during the ground campaign and its aftermath.

110. Cordesman, *Lessons of Afghanistan.*

111. Ibid. Cordesman sites a number of examples where one faction used American air power to target a rival faction.

112. In the aftermath of the ground campaign in Iraq (2003–2005) insurgents were predominantly secular Sunnis dissatisfied with their loss of power and status within Iraq. It is only recently that foreign fighters are coming to dominate the insurgency.

CONCLUSION

1. Donald Baucom, "Technological War: Reality and the American Myth," *Air University Review* 32, September–October (1981).

2. Spencer Tucker, *The Great War 1914--1918* (Bloomington: University of Indiana Press, 1998).

3. William Allcorn, *The Maginot Line 1928–1945* (London: Osprey Publishing, 2003).

4. D. Clayton James, *Refighting the Last War: Command and Crisis in Korea, 1950–1953* (New York: Free Press, 1993).

5. Jack Pattison, *Something Old, Something New, Something Borrowed, Something Blue: The Marriage of Strategy and Tactics in Vietnam* (Fort

Leavenworth, KS: Command and General Staff College Press, 1989); S.L. Marshall, *Lessons Learned; Vietnam Primer: A Critique of U.S. Army Tactics and Command Practices in the Small Combat Unit Digested from Historical Research of Main States* (Washington, DC: Department of the Army, 1967); and John Nagl, *Counterinsurgency Lessons from Malaya and Vietnam: Learning to Eat Soup with a Knife* (Chicago: University of Chicago Press, 2005).

6. Lind et al., "The Changing Face of War." See earlier chapters for a more detailed discussion of the changing face of warfare.

7. "Remarks to the Senate Armed Services Committee of General Paul X. Kelley."

8. Hammel, *Marines in Beirut.*

9. Hirsch and Oakley, *Somalia and Operation Restore Hope.*

10. UNITAF consisted of more than 35,000 well-armed and trained troops.

11. Stevenson, *Losing Mogadishu: Testing U.S. Policy in Somalia.*

12. Ibid.

13. PBS, "Hunting Bin Laden," in *Frontline*, 120 min., USA, 2005.

14. "Bush: Better Human Intelligence Needed," *CNN.com,* January 18 2005, http://www.cnn.com/2005/ALLPOLITICS/01/18/bush.intelligence/index.html (accessed September 15, 2005).

15. Spiller, "Not War but Like War: The American Intervention in Lebanon."

16. Kelly, *Lebanon: 1982–1984.*

17. Grier, "Logistics Challenges Await Troops in Somalia"; and Hirsch and Oakley, *Somalia and Operation Restore Hope.*

18. Bowden, *Black Hawk Down.*

19. Hendrickson, *Somalia.*

20. Doug Beason, *D.O.D. Science and Technology: Strategy for the Post-Cold War Era* (Washington, DC: National Defense University Press, 2002).

21. Tim McGirk, "A Dearth of Troops," *Time,* December 1, 2003; and Thomas Ricks, "General Reported Shortages in Iraq," *Washington Post,* October 18, 2004.

22. Feldmann, "Beirut: U.S. Marines Take Cover after Ambush." In mid-March 1983 marines moving through Beirut were ambushed, taking a number of casualties.

23. Wright, "Marines in Lebanon Facing Increased Danger." On August 10, 1983, marines returned fire for the first time after a month of small arms fire.

24. Stanton, *Somalia on $5 a Day.*

25. Clarke, "Testing the World's Resolve in Somalia."

26. Jamie McIntyre, "Pentagon: Bin Laden Deputy Complains About Money, Iraq Tactics," *CNN.com,* October 7, 2005, http://www.cnn.com/2005/US/10/07/pentagon.al.qaeda/ (accessed October 25, 2005).

27. "Reconstructing Afghanistan, Freedom in Crisis," Amb. Zalmay Khalilzad testimony (United States Commission on International and Religious Freedom, January 29, 2003), http://uscirf.com/events/hearings/2003/january/01292003_khailzadTestimony.html (accessed September 15, 2005); and Leslie Evans, "Afghan Ambassador Reports on Reconstruction" (Ronald W. Burke Center for International

Relations, UCLA, March 13, 2003) http://www.isop.ucla.edu/bcir/article.asp?parentid=3416 (accessed September 15, 2005).

28. Iraq, on the other hand, has proven to be a much different case with the insurgency continuing to prove effective more than 24 months after it began.

29. Kathleen Bailey, *Understanding "Asymmetric" Threats to the United States* (Washington, DC: National Institute for Public Policy, 2002).

30. From "Lebanon Denies 'Assasination' Story," *BBC News Online,* January 3, 2002, http://news.bbc.co.uk/2/hi/middle_east/1740753.stm (accessed September 5, 2004): in 2002 an attempt was made on the life of pro-Syrian President Emile Lahoud, whose close ties with Syria made the president many enemies. And, from Scott Wilson, "Blast Kills Ex-Premier in Lebanon," *Washington Post,* February 15, 2005: on February 14, 2005, former Lebanese Prime Minister Rafiq Hariri was, allegedly, assassinated by Syrian intelligence agents who continue to operate in Lebanon. A UN report, yet to be released, reportedly blames Syria for the Hariri assassination and continuing violence in Lebanon.

31. "Somalia," World News Network, November 3, 2005, http://worldfactbook.com/country/Somalia/2005 (accessed November 3, 2005).

32. "Blast Kills Three in Western Somalia," *Independent Online,* October 29, 2005, http://www.int.iol.co.za/index.php?click_id=68&art_id=qw1130588821680B254&set_id=#jump (accessed November 1, 2005).

33. Syed Shahzad, "A Chilling Inheritance of Terror," Asia Times Online, October 30 2002, http://www.atimes.com/atimes/South_Asia/DJ30Df01.html (accessed November 1, 2005).

34. John Boyd, *Patterns of Conflict* (Washington, DC: Department of Defense, 1986). Boyd's ideas were never formalized in any report or major written work. Instead, Colonel Boyd gave, to anyone who would listen, a 15-hour presentation, which offered his understanding of conflict and the approach that should be taken toward it. After his retirement from the Air Force, Colonel Boyd worked as a contractor for the Department of Defense where he delivered his presentation more than 400 times to civilian and military personnel.

35. *Joint Doctrine Encyclopedia* (Washington, DC: Department of Defense, 2005), 222.

36. Greg Wilcox and Gary I. Wilson, "Military Response to Fourth Generation Warfare in Afghanistan," d-n-i.net, May 5, 2002, http://d-n-i.net/fcs/wilson_wilcox_military_responses.htm (accessed September 15, 2005).

37. "Is America inside Its Own OODA Loop in Afghanistan and Iraq?" d-n-i.net, October 29, 2003, http://d-n-i.net/fcs/comments/c499.htm (accessed September 15, 2005).

38. Boyd, "Patterns of Conflict," 131.

39. Stephen Walt, "Rigor or Rigor Mortis? Rational Choice and Security Studies," *International Security* 23, no. 4 (1999); and Lisa Martin, "The Contributions of Rational Choice: A Defense of Pluralism," *International Security* 24, no. 2 (1999).

40. Fereydoun Hoveyda, "A Note on Why Islamic Fundamentalists Believe the United States Is a Paper Tiger," *American Foreign Policy Interests* 25 (2003).

41. Bruce Bueno de Mesquita and David Lalman, *War and Reason: Domestic and International Imperatives* (New Haven, CT: Yale University Press, 1994). See the

work of de Mesquita and others for more detailed analysis of formal modeling and game theory.

42. Gabriel Ben-Dor, "The Uniqueness of Islamic Fundamentalism and the Fourth Wave of International Terrorism," *Totalitarian Movements & Political Religions* 4, no. 3 (2003); Martha Crenshaw, "The Causes of Terrorism," *Comparative Politics* 13, no. 4 (1981); and Jean-Pierre Derriennic, "Theory and Ideologies of Violence," *Journal of Peace Research* 9, no. 4 (1972).

Works Cited

ABC News. *Asking for Help,* 2002. http://abcnews.go.com/?lid=ABCCOM Menu&lpos=ABCNews (accessed September 11, 2004).

Abdullah, Ibrahim. *Between Democracy and Terror: The Sierra Leone Civil War.* Dakar: Codesria, 2004.

Adebajo, Adekeye. "Africa and America in an Age of Terror." *Journal of Asian & African Studies* 38, no. 2 (2003): 175–91.

Ahmed, Ali Jimali. *The Invention of Somalia.* Trenton, NJ: Red Sea Press, 1995.

Ali, S. Mahmud. *The Fearful State: Power, People and Internal War in South Asia.* London: Zed Books, 1993.

Allcorn, William. *The Maginot Line 1928–1945.* London: Osprey Publishing, 2003.

Allison, Graham. *Essence of Decision: Explaining the Cuban Missile Crisis.* 2nd ed. New York: Longman, 1999.

———. *Nuclear Terrorism: The Ultimate Preventable Catastrophe.* New York: Times Books, 2004.

Amiri, Rini. "Comprehending the Afghan Quagmire." *Sojourner Magazine,* November 1, 2001.

Anable, David. "On Keeping a Great Nation on Course, Rather Than Tacking between Extremes." *Christian Science Monitor,* November 9, 1983.

Anthony, Davis. "A Brotherly Vendetta." *Asiaweek,* December 6, 1996.

ArabicNews.com, "Bush Warns Syria, Iran from the Consequences of Interfering in Iraq," December 16, 2004. http://www.arabicnews.com/ansub/Daily/Day/ 041216/2004121607.html (accessed September 15, 2005).

Arrian. *The Campaigns of Alexander.* Translated by Aubrey de Selincourt. New York: Penguin Classics, 1958.

Assyrian International News Agency. "Rice Criticizes Alleged Syrian Support for Terrorists in Iraq," May 21, 2005.

Atkinson, James D. "Liddell-Hart and Warfare of the Future." *Military Affairs* 29, no. 4 (1965): 161–63.

Atkinson, Rick. "Night of a Thousand Casualties." *Washington Post,* January 31, 1994.

Azadi Afghan Radio. "Interview with Commander Ahmad Shah Masood." Afghanistan, 2000.

Bailey, Kathleen. *Understanding "Asymmetric" Threats to the United States.* Washington, DC: National Institute for Public Policy, 2002.

Baker, William, and Mark L. Evans. "The Year in Review 2002: Operation Anaconda." *Naval Aviation News* 50, no. 4 (July–August 2003): 24–26.

Baldauf, Scott. "Aid Groups in Afghanistan Weigh Good Deeds Vs. Safety." *Christian Science Monitor,* October 28, 2003.

———. "Bumpy Rides and Rival Tribes or Afghanistan's Border." *Christian Science Monitor,* December 20, 2001.

———. "Help for Survivors of Afghanistan's Land Mines." *Christian Science Monitor,* January 4, 2002.

———. "Peace Threatened in Afghanistan." *Christian Science Monitor,* September 6, 2002.

———. "Power Shift in Afghanistan." *Christian Science Monitor,* December 10, 2001.

———. "Shifting Sands at Afghanistan's Grass Roots." *Christian Science Monitor,* December 26, 2001.

———. "A Triangle of Militants Regroups in Afghanistan." *Christian Science Monitor,* April 9, 2003.

Barnes, Fred. "Last Call." *New Republic,* December 28, 1992, 11–13.

Barnett, Roger W. *Asymmetrical Warfare: Today's Challenge to U.S. Military Power.* Washington, DC: Brassey's, 2003.

Barnett, Thomas P.M. *The Pentagon's New Map: War and Peace in the Twenty-First Century.* New York: G.P. Putnam's Sons, 2004.

Bassford, Christopher. *Clausewitz in English: The Reception of Clausewitz in Britain and America.* New York: Oxford University Press, 1994.

Baucom, Donald. "Technological War: Reality and the American Myth." *Air University Review* 32 (September–October 1981).

BBC News Online, "In Full: Al-Qaeda Statement," October 10, 2001. http://news.bbc.co.uk/1/low/world/middle_east/1590350.stm (accessed September 5, 2004).

———, "Lebanon Denies 'Assassination' Story," January 3, 2002. http://news.bbc.co.uk/2/hi/middle_east/1740753.stm (accessed September 15, 2005 2005).

Beason, Doug. *D.O.D. Science and Technology: Strategy for the Post Cold War Era..* Washington, DC: National Defense University Press, 2002.

Beckett, I.F.W. *The Encyclopedia of Guerilla Warfare.* New York: Facts on File, 2001.

Beliaev, Igor, and John Marks. *Common Ground on Terrorism: Soviet-American Cooperation against the Politics of Terror.* New York: W.W. Norton, 1991.

Belsie, Laurent. "Fallout from Beirut Bombing." *Christian Science Monitor,* April 19, 1983.

————. "Schultz Raises Hope in Lebanon." *Christian Science Monitor,* April 29, 1983.

————. "U.S. Marine Commander Escapes Injury in Lebanon." *Christian Science Monitor,* May 6, 1983.

Ben-Dor, Gabriel. "The Uniqueness of Islamic Fundamentalism and the Fourth Wave of International Terrorism." *Totalitarian Movements & Political Religions* 4, no. 3 (2003): 71–90.

Berkowitz, Bruce. "Fighting the New War." *Hoover Digest,* no. 3 (2002): 1–7.

————. *The New Face of War: How War Will Be Fought in the 21st Century.* New York: Free Press, 2003.

Beyerchen, Alan. "Clausewitz, Nonlinearity, and the Unpredictability of War." *International Security* 17, no. 3 (1992): 59–90.

Biddiscombe, Perry. *The Last Nazis.* Charleston, SC: Tempus Publishing, 2000.

————. *Werwolf! The History of the National Socialist Guerrilla Movement.* Toronto: University of Toronto Press, 1997.

Biddle, Stephen. *Afghanistan and the Future of Warfare: Implications for Army and Defense Policy.* Carlisle, PA: Strategic Studies Institute, U.S. Army War College, 2002.

"Biotechnology and the Future of the Biological and Toxin Weapons Convention." Solna, Sweden: Stockholm International Peace Research Institute, 2001.

Black, Jeremy. *Warfare in the 18th Century.* London: Cassell, 2002.

Blank, Stephen J. "Rethinking Asymmetric Threats." Carlisle, PA: Strategic Studies Institute, Army War College, 2003.

Bodansky, Yossef. *Bin Laden: The Man Who Declared War on America.* New York: Prima Lifestyles, 2001.

Bonaparte, Napoleon. "Correspondence from Napoleon to Eugene," 1805. In *Napoleon on the Art of War,* edited by Jay Luvaas. New York: Free Press, 1999.

————. "Napoleon to the Executive Directory," 1796. In *Napoleon on the Art of War,* edited by Jay Luvaas. New York: Free Press, 1999.

————. "Order of the Army No. 14552," 1808. In *Napoleon on the Art of War,* edited by Jay Luvaas. New York: Free Press, 1999.

Boot, Max. *The Savage Wars of Peace: Small Wars and the Rise of American Power.* New York: Basic Books, 2002.

Borger, Julian. "Winter Is Coming and the Taliban Are Strong as Ever. What Now for the War on Terror?" *The Guardian* (Manchester), November 3, 2001.

Bowden, Mark. *Black Hawk Down: A Story of Modern War.* New York: Atlantic Monthly Press, 1999.

Boyd, John. *Patterns of Conflict.* Washington, DC: Department of Defense, 1986.

Brehmer, Berndt. *The Dynamic O.O.D.A. Loop: Amalgamating Boyd's O.O.D.A. Loop and the Cybernetic Approach to Command and Control.* Stockholm: Swedish National Defense College, 2004.

Breitbart.com, "Hacker Attacks in U. S. Linked to Chinese Military: Researchers," December 13, 2005. http://www.breitbart.com/news/2005/12/12/0512122 24756.jwmkvntb.html (accessed December 13, 2005).

British Broadcasting Company. "France Bolsters Ivory Coast Peace Force,"
2003. http://news.bbc.co.uk/2/hi/africa/2728909.stm (accessed September 3,
2004).

———. "Profile: Gulbuddin Hekmatyar," January 28, 2003. http://news.bbc.co.uk/
1/hi/world/middle_east/2701547.stm (accessed September 15, 2005).

Buchan, Glenn C. *Future Directions in Warfare: Good and Bad Analysis, Dubious
Rhetoric, and the "Fog of Peace."* Santa Monica, CA: Rand, 2003.

Bueno, de Mesquita. *War and Reason: Domestic and International Imperatives.*
New Haven, CT: Yale University Press, 1994.

Bush, George W. "Afghanistan: Then and Now." The White House, 2002. http://
www.whitehouse.gov/afac/thenandnow.html (accessed September 15, 2004).

———. "Fact Sheet: Afghanistan Security and Reconstruction." The White House,
Office of the Press Secretary, May 2, 2002. http://www.whitehouse.gov/news/
releases/2002/05/20020502-18.html (accessed September 15, 2004).

———. "Fact Sheet: Assisting People of Afghanistan." The White House, Office of
the Press Secretary, January 28, 2002. http://www.whitehouse.gov/news/
releases/2002/01/20020128-9.html.

———. "Joint Statement on Road Construction in Afghanistan by the President of
the United States, the Prime Minister of Japan, and the Foreign Minister of Saudi
Arabia." The White House, Office of the Press Secretary, September 12, 2002.
http://www.whitehouse.gov/news/releases/2002/09/20020912-10.html (accessed
September 15, 2004).

———. "President Bush Meets with German Chancellor Schroeder." The White
House, Office of the Press Secretary, January 31, 2002. http://www.whitehouse.
gov/news/releases/2002/01/20020131-11.html (accessed September 15, 2004).

———. "President Bush Meets with President Karzai of Afghanistan." The
White House, Office of the Press Secretary, February 27, 2003. http://www.
whitehouse.gov/news/releases/2003/02/print/20030227-6.html (accessed
September 15, 2004).

———. "President Bush Reaffirms Resolve to War on Terror, Iraq and Afghanistan." The White House, Office of the Press Secretary, March 19, 2004. http://
www.whitehouse.gov/news/releases/2004/03/20040319-3.html (accessed
December 21, 2004).

———. "Rebuilding Afghanistan." The White House, May 19, 2003. http://
www.whitehouse.gov/news/releases/2003/05/20030519-4.html (accessed
September 15, 2004).

———. "Remarks by President Bush and President Karzi of the Islamic Government
of Afghanistan." The White House, Office of the Press Secretary, September 12,
2002. http://www.whitehouse.gov/news/releases/2002/09/20020912-6.html
(accessed September 15, 2004).

———. "Results in Iraq: 100 Days toward Security and Freedom." Washington, DC:
The White House, 2003.

———. "The Rights and Aspirations of the People of Afghanistan." The
White House, Office of Global Communications, July 9, 2003. http://www.
whitehouse.gov/news/releases/2003/07/print/20030709-1.html (accessed
September 15, 2004).

Bush, Laura. "Radio Address of First Lady Laura Bush to 'Radio Free Afghanistan.'" The White House, May 21, 2002. http://www.whitehouse.gov/news/releases/2002/05/20020521-19.html (accessed September 15, 2004).

Caesar. *The Civil Wars*. Translated by A.G. Peskett. Cambridge, MA: Harvard University Press, 1984.

———. *The Conquest of Gaul*. New York: Penguin Books, 1983.

———. *The Gallic Wars*. Translated by H.J. Edwards. Cambridge, MA: Harvard University Press, 2000.

Callaway, Catherine. "Special Forces Drop into Afghanistan." *CNN.com*, October 20, 2001. http://archives.cnn.com/2001/WORLD/asiapcf/central/10/20/ret.rangers.cnna/ (accessed September 15, 2004).

Cameron, Gavin, et al. "The 1999 W.M.D. Terrorism Chronology: Incidents Involving Sub-National Actors and Chemical, Biological, Radiological and Nuclear Materials." *The Nonproliferation Review*, no. 3 (2000): 157–74.

Carey, T. Elaine. "American Marines Meet the P.L.O." *Christian Science Monitor*, August 26, 1982.

Carr, Caleb. *The Lessons of Terror: A History of Warfare against Civilians*. New York: Random House, 2003.

Castelfranco, Sabrina. "Italian PM Announces Phased Withdrawal from Iraq." *Voice of America*, March 16, 2005. http://www.voanews.com/english/archive/2005-03/2005-03-16-voa1.cfm?CFID=6396882&CFTOKEN=13361206 (accessed December 15, 2005).

Cebrowski, Arthur K. "The Small, the Fast and the Many." *Net Defense*, January 15, 2004.

Center for Economic and Social Rights. *Afghanistan Fact Sheet #2: A Brief History Focusing on 1979–2001*. New York, 2001.

Central Intelligence Agency. *The World Factbook*. Washington, DC, 2005. https://www.cia.gov/cia/publications/factbook/index.html (accessed July, 25 2005).

Chace, James. *Acheson: The Secretary of State Who Created the American World*. Cambridge, MA: Harvard University Press, 1999.

Chandler, David G. *The Campaigns of Napoleon*. New York: Schribner, 1973.

Christian Science Monitor, "Changing of the Guard in Somalia," April 30, 1993.

———, "Dealing with Somalia's Guns," December 16, 1992.

———, "Diplomacy Can Help Somalia," July 22, 1993.

———, "End Somalia's Anguish," November 30, 1992.

———, "Feeding Somalia," September 11, 1992.

———, "France Reducing the Size of Its Beirut Contingent," January 3, 1984.

———, "How the Marines Fared in Lebanon," February 22, 1984.

———, "Keeping Somalia's Fragile Peace," March 31, 1993.

———, "Reagan Team Tells Senate Marines Needed in Beirut," January 13, 1984.

———, "Realism in Somalia," July 15, 1993.

———, "Somalia Chronology," July 22, 1991.

———, "Staying in Somalia." August 12, 1993.

———, "The Somalia Policy," October 6, 1993.

———, "The Task in Somalia." December 7, 1992.

———, "The U.S. Government's Reaction Time in Aiding Somalia," September 2, 1992.

———, "UN To Take over Somalia Mission on May 1, Chief Says," March 5, 1993.

———, "UN To Strengthen Forces in Somalia after Soldiers Killed," August 10, 1993.

———, "U.S. and Syria," December 6, 1983.

———, "U.S. Crackdown in Somalia," January 7, 1993.

———, "U.S. Prepares More Troops for Somalia Operation." October 5, 1993.

———, "Waging Peace in Afghanistan," February 27, 2002.

Chuikov, Victor. *The End of the Third Reich*. New York: Imported Publications, 1978.

Clarke, Walter. "Testing the World's Resolve in Somalia." *Parameters* 23, no. 4 (1993).

Clinton, Bill. "A National Security Strategy for a New Century." Washington, DC: The White House, 1999.

———. "Presidential Decision Directive/N.S.C.–63." Washington, DC: The White House, 1998.

———. "Somalia: Our Troops Will Leave by March 31, 1994." *Vital Speeches of the Day* LX, no. 2 (1993): 34–36.

Cloarec, Yann, ed. *How to Make War*. Paris: Ediciones La Calavera, 1998.

CNN.com, "Bush: Better Human Intelligence Needed," January 18, 2005. http://www.cnn.com/2005/ALLPOLITICS/01/18/bush.intelligence/index.html (accessed September 15, 2005).

———, "Chance: Reports of Taliban Defections," October 10, 2001. http://edition.cnn.com/2001/WORLD/asiapcf/central/10/10/ret.chance.otsc/ (accessed September 15, 2004).

———, "Congress to Reconvene Tuesday Despite Continuing Anthrax Tests," October 22, 2001. http://www.cnn.com/2001/HEALTH/conditions/10/22/anthrax/ (accessed September 16, 2004).

———, "Operation Anaconda Costs 8 U.S. Lives," March 4, 2002. http://archives.cnn.com/2002/WORLD/asiapcf/central/03/04/ret.afghan.fighting/index.html (accessed September 15, 2004.

———, "Transcript of President Bush's Address," September 20, 2001. http://archives.cnn.com/2001/US/09/20/gen.bush.transcript/ (accessed September 15, 2005).

———, "U.S. Missiles Pound Targets in Afghanistan, Sudan," August 20, 1998. http://www.cnn.com/US/9808/20/us.strikes.01/ (accessed February 10, 2005).

———, "U.S. Paratroops Raid Omar Compound near Kandahar," October 20, 2001. http://edition.cnn.com/2001/WORLD/asiapcf/central/10/20/ret.afghan.attacks/ (accessed September 15, 2004).

———, "White House Warns Taliban 'We Will Defeat You,'" September 21, 2001. http://archives.cnn.com/2001/WORLD/asiapcf/central/09/21/ret.afghan.taliban/ (accessed September 15, 2004).

———, "Zimbabwe's Mugabe Warns Britain," May 2, 2001. http://www.cnn.com/ 2001/WORLD/africa/05/02/mugabe.threat/ (accessed September 4, 2004).

Cohen, William S. *Annual Report to the President and Congress.* Washington, DC: Department of Defense, 1999.

———. *Report of the Quadrennial Defense Review.* Washington, DC: Department of Defense, 1997.

Coll, Steve. *Ghost Wars: The Secret History of the CIA, Afghanistan, and Bin Laden, from the Soviet Invasion to September 10, 2001.* New York: Penguin Books, 2004.

Collier, Ellen D. "Instances of Use of United States Forces Abroad, 1798–1993." Naval Historical Center, Department of the Navy, 1993.

Collins, Edward M. "Clausewitz and Democracy's Modern Wars." *Military Affairs* 19, no. 1 (1955): 15–20.

Conetta, Carl. *Strange Victory: A Critical Appraisal of Operation Enduring Freedom and the Afghanistan War.* Project on Defense Alternatives, The Commonwealth Institute, January 30, 2002. http://www.comw.org/pda/0201strangevic.html.

Corbett, Julian. *Some Principles of Maritime Strategy.* New York: Longman, Green and Company, 1911.

Cordesman, Anthony H. *The Lessons of Afghanistan: Warfighting, Intelligence, Force Transformation, Counterproliferation, and Arms Control.* Washington, DC: Center for Strategic and International Studies, 2002.

———. *Military Balance in the Middle East XIV: Weapons of Mass Destruction.* Washington, DC: Center for Strategic and International Studies, 1999.

Cragin, Kim, and Sara A. Daly. "The Dynamic Terrorist Threat: An Assessment of Group Motivations and Capabilities in a Changing World." Santa Monica, CA: RAND, 2004.

Crenshaw, Martha. "The Causes of Terrorism." *Comparative Politics* 13, no. 4 (1981): 379–99.

Crigler, Frank. "A Flaw in the Somalia Game Plan." *Christian Science Monitor,* January 11, 1993.

Croddy, Eric. *Chemical and Biological Warfare.* New York: Copernicus Books, 2002.

Cyrulik, Joseph C. "Asymmetric Warfare and the Threat to the American Homeland." *Landpower Essay Series.* (Association of the U.S. Army, The Institute of Land Warfare, 1999).

Daily Times (Pakistan), "Four Killed in Taliban Attacks in Afghanistan," November 21, 2003. http://www.dailytimes.com.pk/default.asp?page=story_21-11-2003_pg7_47 (accessed September 15, 2004).

Davies, Jack. "Reunification of the Somali People." Chevy Chase, MD: Davies Consulting, 2001.

Davis, Anthony. "Fateful Victory." *Asia Week,* August 28, 1998.

Davis, Lynn. *Individual Preparedness and Response to Chemical, Radiological, Nuclear and Biological Terrorist Attacks.* Santa Monica, CA: RAND, 2002.

Day, Clifford. "Critical Analysis on the Defeat of Task Force Ranger." Montgomery, AL: Air Command and Staff College, 1997.

Deeb, Marius. *Syria's Terrorist War on Lebanon and the Peace Process.* New York: Palgrave Macmillan, 2004.

de Jomini, Antoine Henri. *The Art of War.* London: Greenhill Books, 1996.

DeLong, Michael. *Inside CentCom: The Unvarnished Truth About the Wars in Afghanistan and Iraq.* Washington, DC: Regnery Press, 2004.

Derriennic, Jean-Pierre. "Theory and Ideologies of Violence." *Journal of Peace Research* 9, no. 4 (1972): 361–74.

Dick, C.J. "Conflict in a Changing World: Looking Two Decades Forward." Surrey: Conflict Studies Research Center, Royal Military Academy Sandhurst, 2002.

d-n-i.net. "Is America inside Its Own OODA Loop in Afghanistan and Iraq?" October 29, 2003. http://d-n-i.net/fcs/comments/c499.htm (accessed September 15, 2005).

Douhet, Giulio. *Command of the Air.* Washington, DC: Office of Air Force History, 1983.

Drew, Dennis. *Making Strategy: An Introduction to National Security Processes and Problems.* Montgomery, AL: Air University Press, 1988.

Dryburgh, Marjorie. *North China and Japanese Expansion 1933–1937: Regional Power and the National Interest.* London: Curzon Press, 2000.

Ecklund, Marshall. "Analysis of Operation Gothic Serpent: T.F. Ranger in Somalia." *Special Warfare* 17, no. 2 (2004).

Elder, Larry. "The Battle Over Islam." LarryElder.com, September 15, 2004. http://www.larryelder.com/islambattle.html (accessed September 15, 2005).

Ellis, Stephen. *The Mask of Anarchy: The Destruction of Liberia and the Religious Dimension of an African Civil War.* New York: New York University Press, 2001.

Elshtain, Jean Bethke. *Just War against Terror: The Burden of American Power in a Violent World.* New York: Basic Books, 2004.

Elting, John R. "Jomini: Disciple of Napoleon." *Military Affairs* 28, Spring (1964): 17–26.

Emerson, Steve. *American Jihad: The Terrorists Living among Us.* New York: Free Press, 2003.

English, J.A. "Kindergarten Soldier: The Military Thoughts of Lawrence of Arabia." *Military Affairs* 51, no. 1 (1987): 7–11.

Epstein, Rafael. "Iran Accused of Interfering in Iraq." Australian Broadcasting Corporation, April 24, 2003. http://www.abc.net.au/cgi-bin/common/print friendly.pl?http://www.abc.net.au/am/content/2003/s839157.htm (accessed September 15, 2005).

Eula, Michael J. "The Classical Approach: Giulio Douhet and Strategic Air Force Operations: A Study in the Limitations of Theoretical Warfare." *Air University Review* (September–October 1986): 1–5.

Evans, Leslie. "Afghan Ambassador Reports on Reconstruction." Ronald W. Burke Center for International Relations, UCLA, March 13, 2003. http://www.isop.ucla.edu/bcir/article.asp?parentid=3416 (accessed September 15, 2005).

Eversmann, Matt, and Dan Schilling. *The Battle of Mogadishu: Firsthand Accounts from the Men of Task Force Ranger.* New York: Presidio Press, 2004.

Fact-index.com. *Asymmetric Warfare.* http://www.fact-index.com/a/as/asymmetric_warfare.html (accessed May 15, 2004).

Falkenrath, R.A., ed. *America's Achilles Heel: Nuclear, Biological and Chemical Terrorism and Covert Attack.* Cambridge, MA: MIT Press, 1999.

Feldmann, Linda. "Beirut: U.S. Marines Take Cover after Ambush." *Christian Science Monitor,* March 17, 1983.

———. "G.O.P.'s Lugar Urges Vote on Clinton's Somalia Plan." *Christian Science Monitor,* October 12, 1993.

———. "Shultz Accuses Syria of Blocking Cease-Fire." *Christian Science Monitor,* September 22, 1983.

———. "U.S. Officer in Beirut Averts an Israeli Tank Crossing." *Christian Science Monitor,* February 3, 1983.

Ferguson, Charles. *The Four Faces of Nuclear Terrorism.* New York: Routledge, 2005.

Forde, Steven. "Varieties of Realism: Thucydides and Machiavelli." *The Journal of Politics* 54, no. 2 (1992): 372–93.

Fort Lauderdale City Commission. "City Commission Workshop Fire-Rescue Department Planning." Fort Lauderdale, FL, 2002.

Fox News.com, "Anthrax Reaches the Senate," October 15, 2001. http://www.foxnews.com/story/0%2C2933%2C36527%2C00.html (accessed September 16, 2004).

Frank, Benis M. *U.S. Marines in Lebanon, 1982–1984.* Washington, DC: History and Museums Division Headquarters, U.S. Marine Corps, 1987.

Franks, Tommy. *American Soldier: General Tommy Franks, Commander in Chief, United States Central Command.* New York: Regan Books, 2004.

Friedman, Norman. "Russians Offer E.M.P. Counter." *Proceedings* 123 (1997).

Fuller, J.F.C. *Armament and History: The Influence of Armament on History from the Dawn of Classical Warfare to the End of the Second World War.* Cambridge, MA: Da Capo Press, 1998.

———. *Memoirs of an Unconventional Soldier.* London: Nicholson and Watson, 1936.

———. *A Military History of the Western World: From the Earliest Times to the Battle of Lepanto.* Cambridge, MA: Da Capo Press, 1987.

Gellman, Barton. "U.S. Concludes bin Laden Escaped Tora Bora Fight." *Washington Post,* April 17, 2002.

George, Alexander, and Richard Smoke. *Deterrence in American Foreign Policy: Theory and Practice.* New York: Columbia University Press, 1974.

Geraghty, Timothy. "Situational Report No. 25." United States Marine Corps, 1983.

Giap, Vo Nguyen. *How We Won the War.* Philadelphia: Recon, 2001.

———. *People's War People's Army.* New York: Bantam Books, 1962.

Gickman, Harvey. "Africa in the War on Terrorism." *Journal of Asian & African Studies* 38, no. 2 (2003): 162.

Girardet, Edward. "A More Dangerous Afghanistan." *Christian Science Monitor,* October 18, 2001.

————. "A Tough Road Ahead in Afghanistan's War." *Christian Science Monitor,* November 6, 2001.

————. "U.S., Beware the Consequences in Afghanistan." *Christian Science Monitor,* October 22, 2001.

Glenn, Russell W. *Marching under Darkening Skies: The American Military and the Impending Urban Operations Threat.* Santa Monica, CA: RAND, 1998.

GlobalSecurity.org, "Homeland Security Planning Scenarios," June 1, 2005. http://www.globalsecurity.org/security/ops/hsc-scen-1.htm (accessed December 15, 2005).

————, "Operation Provide Relief," 1996. http://www.globalsecurity.org/military/ops/provide_relief.htm (accessed August 20, 2005).

Go, William. "The Marine Corps' Combined Action Program and Modern Peace Operations." Quantico, VA: U.S. Marine Corps, 1997.

Godsell, Geoffrey. "'Send in the Marines': Decisive U.S. Action Tends to Favor P.L.O." *Christian Science Monitor,* July 8, 1982.

Goldstone, Jack. "State Failure Task Force Report: Phase 3 Findings." McLean, VA: Science Applications International Corporation, 2000.

Goodson, Larry. *Afghanistan's Endless War: State Failure, Regional Politics, and the Rise of the Taliban.* Seattle: University of Washington Press, 2002.

Gould, Harold, and Franklin Spinney. "New Generation of War Changes the Paradigm." *The Virginian Pilot,* October 3, 2001.

Goulding, Vincent J., Jr. "Back to the Future with Asymmetric Warfare." *Parameters,* no. 4 (Winter 2000–01): 21–30.

Grange, David L. "Asymmetric Warfare: Old Method, New Concern." *National Strategy Forum Review* (Winter 2000).

Grant, Rebecca. "An Air War Like No Other." *Air Force Magazine,* November 1, 2002, 30–37.

Green, Stephen. "Tough Relief a Must for Future Somalias." *Christian Science Monitor,* October 29, 1992.

Greene, Thomas C. "Security Fears Tip Spanish Election." *The Register,* 2004.

Grier, Peter. "Airstrikes in Somalia Show UN Is in for Long Haul." *Christian Science Monitor,* June 14, 1993.

————. "As Violence in Somalia Escalates, Senate Steps Up Troop Oversight." *Christian Science Monitor,* September 14, 1993.

————. "Clinton Grapples with U.S. Role Abroad after Somalia Attack." *Christian Science Monitor,* October 7, 1993.

————. "Dire Straits in Somalia." *Christian Science Monitor,* January 8, 1992.

————. "Focus in Somalia May Shift from Famine to Rebuilding Effort." *Christian Science Monitor,* December 14, 1992.

————. "Logistics Challenges Await Troops in Somalia." *Christian Science Monitor,* December 7, 1992.

————. "Somalia Crisis Spurs Pentagon to Reorient Training of U.S. Troops." *Christian Science Monitor,* June 16, 1993.

———. "Somalia Lawlessness, Despair Behind U.S. Decision to Offer Troops to Protect Food Aid." *Christian Science Monitor,* November 30, 1992.

———. "U.S. Relief Startup Goes Well in Somalia." *Christian Science Monitor,* December 11, 1992.

———. "U.S. Role in Somalia, Bosnia Raises Concerns at Home." *Christian Science Monitor,* August 12, 1993.

Grossman, Zoltan. "From Wounded Knee to Afghanistan: A Century of U.S. Military Interventions." *Z Magazine* 14, no. 8 (2001): 1–13.

Guevara, Che. *Guerrilla Warfare.* Lincoln: University of Nebraska Press, 1998.

Gunaratna, Rohan. *Inside Al Qaeda: Global Network of Terror.* New York: Berkley Publishing, 2003.

Gurr, Robert Ted. *Why Men Rebel.* Princeton, NJ: Princeton University Press, 1971.

Hadd, H. A. "Who's a Rebel? The Lessons Lebanon Taught." *Marine Corps Gazette* 46, no. 3 (1962).

Hammel, Eric. *The Root: The Marines in Beirut, August 1982–February 1984.* Pacifica, CA: Pacifica Press, 1985.

Handel, Michael. "Corbett, Clausewitz and Sun Tzu." *Naval War College Review* 53, no. 4 (2000).

———. *Masters of War: Sun Tzu, Clausewitz and Jomini.* London: Frank Cass, 1992.

Hanson, Victor Davis. *An Autumn of War: What America Learned from September 11 and the War on Terrorism.* New York: Anchor Books, 2002.

———. *The Soul of Battle: From Ancient Times to the Present Day, How Three Great Liberators Vanquished Tyranny.* New York: Anchor Books, 1999.

Harrison, Lawrence E. *Culture Matters: How Values Shape Human Progress.* New York: Harper Collins, 2001.

Harsch, Joseph C. "The Case of Captain Johnson." *Christian Science Monitor,* February 10, 1983.

Healey, Patrick. "Afghans Want U.S. To Dig Out Al Qaeda." *San Francisco Chronicle,* December 27, 2001.

Healey, Patrick, and Stockman, Farah. "Taliban Flee Kandahar." *Boston Globe,* December 8, 2001.

Heathcote, T. A. *The Afghan Wars, 1839–1919.* Staplehurst, Great Britain: Spellmount Limited, 2003.

Hendrickson, Alan. "Somalia: Strategic Failures and Operational Successes." Marine Corps Command and Staff College, 1995.

The Heritage Foundation. "Afghanistan: Facts and Figures." September 17, 2001. http://www.heritage.org/Research/NationalSecurity/WM37.cfm?renderfor point=1.

Herodotus. *The Histories.* Translated by George Rawlinson. New York: Alfred A. Knopf, 1997.

Hildreth, Steven A. *Cyberwarfare.* Washington, DC: Congressional Research Service, 2001.

Hippolyte, Jacques. *Stratégiques, Classiques De La Stratégie.* Paris: l'Hern, 1977.

Hirsch, John. "U.S. in Somalia: Should the Troops Stay?" *Christian Science Monitor,* October 25, 1993.

Hirsch, John L., and Robert B. Oakley. *Somalia and Operation Restore Hope: Reflections on Peacemaking and Peacekeeping.* Washington, DC: United States Institute of Peace Press, 1995.

Hohenzollern, Frederick. *Frederick the Great on the Art of War.* Translated by Jay Luvaas. Cambridge, MA: Da Capo Press, 1999.

Houston Chronicle, "In Response to Taliban Offer, Bush Warns 'Time Is Running Out,'" October 6, 2001.

Hoveyda, Fereydoun. "A Note on Why Islamic Fundamentalists Believe the United States Is a Paper Tiger." *American Foreign Policy Interests* 25 (2003): 499–503.

Hudson, Walter M. "The Continuing Influence of Clausewitz." *Military Review,* March–April (2004): 60–62.

Hughes, Patrick M. "Future Conditions: The Character and Conduct of War, 2010 and 2020." In *Seminar on Intelligence, Command, and Control.* Cambridge, MA: Center for Information Policy Research, Harvard University, 2003.

Huntington, Samuel P. *The Clash of Civilizations and the Remaking of World Order.* New York: Simon and Schuster, 1998.

Icasualties.org, "Iraq Coalition Casualty Count," 2004. http://icasualties.org/oif/ Stats.aspx (accessed September 15, 2004).

Institute for National Strategic Studies. "Strategic Assessments: Engaging Power for Peace." Washington, DC, 1998.

International Herald Tribune, "CIA Warns Bush on Somalia," December 3, 1992.

———, "In Somali Town, 'Only Six Dead' Is Cause for Hope," October 24, 1992.

IOL. "Blast Kills Three in Western Somalia." *Independent Online,* October 29, 2005. http://www.int.iol.co.za/index.php?click_id=68&art_id=qw113058882 1680B254&set_id=#jump (accessed November 1, 2005).

Jalali, Ali. *Afghan Guerrilla Warfare: In the Words of the Mujahideen Fighters.* St. Paul, MN: MBI Publishing, 2001.

James, D. Clayton. *Refighting the Last War: Command and Crisis in Korea, 1950– 1953.* New York: Free Press, 1993.

Jenkins, Brian M., ed. *Countering the New Terrorism.* Santa Monica, CA: RAND, 1998.

Joes, Anthony James. *Resisting Rebellion: The History and Politics of Counterinsurgency.* Lexington: University of Kentucky Press, 2004.

Johnson, Jo. "Afghan Election Worries Monitors." *Financial Times,* October 1, 2005.

Johnson, Maxwell. "The Arab Bureau and the Arab Revolt: Yanbu to Aqaba." *Military Affairs* 46, no. 4 (1982): 194–201.

Johnson, Thomas. "The Loya Jirga, Ethnic Rivalries and Future Afghan Stability." *Strategic Insights* 1, no. 6 (2002).

Johnston, Alastair. *Cultural Realism: Strategic Culture and Grand Strategy in Chinese History.* Princeton, NJ: Princeton University Press, 1998.

Jones, Archer. *The Art of War in the Western World.* Urbana: University of Illinois, 1987.

Jordan, Michael J. "UN May Be Best Equipped to Rebuild Afghanistan." *Christian Science Monitor,* October 25, 2001.

———. "Why You Won't See UN Blue Helmets in Afghanistan." *Christian Science Monitor,* December 18, 2001.

Josephus, Flavius. *The Jewish War.* Translated by G. A. Williamson. New York: Penguin Classics, 1984.

Kadim, Karim. "Insurgent Attacks Kill 8; Iraqi Official Discourages Protests." *USA Today,* March 28, 2005.

Kakar, Hassan. *Afghanistan: The Soviet Invasion and the Afghan Response, 1979–1982.* Berkeley and Los Angeles: University of California Press, 1995.

Kassebaum, Nancy, and Paul Simon. "Save Somalia from Itself." *New York Times,* January 2, 1992.

Katzman, Kenneth. *Afghanistan: Post War Governance, Security and U.S. Policy.* Washington, DC: Congressional Research Service, 2004.

Kegley, Charles W., Jr. *The New Global Terrorism: Characteristics, Causes, Controls.* New York: Prentice Hall, 2003.

Kelley, General Paul X. *Remarks by the Commandant of the Marine Corps to the Senate Armed Services Committee,* October 31, 1983.

Kelly, John H. *Lebanon: 1982–1984.* Santa Monica, CA: RAND Corporation.

Khan, Ayez Ahmed. "Terrorism and Asymmetrical Warfare International and Regional Implications." *DefenseJournal.com,* 2002. http://www.defencejournal. com/2002/february/terrorism.htm (accessed September 15, 2005).

Kindlebarger, Charles. *The World in Depression 1929–1939.* Berkeley and Los Angeles: University of California Press, 1974.

Klein, Yitzhak. "Long Defensives: Victory without Compellence." *Comparative Strategy* 15 (1996): 233–49.

Knickerbocker, Brad. "Open-Ended Role for U.S. Marines in Beirut Makes Pentagon Brass Edgy." *Christian Science Monitor,* September 30, 1982.

———. "Pentagon Begins Offensive to Support Defense Buildup." *Christian Science Monitor,* September 13, 1983.

———. "U.S. Buildup in Lebanon." *Christian Science Monitor,* September 14, 1983.

———. "U.S. Looks Beyond Beirut to Future of Palestinians." *Christian Science Monitor,* August 24, 1982.

———. "U.S., Syria Flex Muscles in Mideast." *Christian Science Monitor,* November 9, 1983.

———. "Weinberger: U.S. Blames Syria for Attack on Marines." *Christian Science Monitor,* November 23, 1983.

Knott, Stephen F. "Congressional Oversight and the Crippling of the CIA." George Mason University's History News Network, November 4, 2001. http://hnn.us/ articles/380.html (accessed June 27, 2005).

Krauthammer, Charles. "The Unipolar Moment." *Foreign Affairs* 70, no. 1 (1990).

Krepinevich, Andrew. *Meeting the Anti-Access and Area Denial Challenge.* Washington, DC: Center for Strategic and Budgetary Assessment, 2003.

Kuby, Erich. *The Russians and Berlin, 1945.* New York: Hill and Wang, 1968.

Ladd, Carll. "U.S. Public and Somalia." *Christian Science Monitor,* October 15, 1993.

LaFranchi, Howard. "Two U.S. Marines Killed in Beirut." *Christian Science Monitor,* August 30, 1983.

———. "U.S. To Help 'Nation-Build' in Afghanistan." *Christian Science Monitor,* December 18, 2001.

Landes, David S. *The Wealth and Poverty of Nations: Why Some Are So Rich and Some Are So Poor.* New York: W.W. Norton, 1999.

Laqueur, Walter, ed. *Voices of Terror: Manifestos, Writings and Manuals of Al Qaeda, Hamas, and Other Terrorists from around the World and Throughout the Ages.* New York: Reed Press, 2004.

Larsen, R.J., and R.P. Kadlec. *Biological Warfare: A Post Cold War Threat to America's Strategic Mobility Forces.* Pittsburgh, PA: Matthew B. Ridgeway Center for International Security Studies, University of Pittsburgh, 1995.

Larson, Robert H. "B.H. Liddell-Hart: Apostle of Limited War." *Military Affairs* 44, no. 2 (1980): 70–74.

Lawrence, T.E. *The Seven Pillars of Wisdom: A Triumph.* New York: Anchor, 1991.

———. "T.E. Lawrence on Guerrilla Warfare," 2004. http://pegasus.cc.ucf.edu/~eshaw/lawrence.htm (accessed February 15, 2004).

Levitt, Matthew. *Targeting Terror: U.S. Policy toward Middle Eastern State Sponsors and Terrorist Organizations, Post-September 11.* Washington, DC: Washington Institute for Near East Policy, 2003.

Lewis, I.M. *A Modern History of Somalia: Nation and State in the Horn of Africa.* New York: Longman, 1980.

Libicki, Martin. "Illuminating Tomorrow's War." In *McNair Paper 61.* Washington, DC: Institute for National Strategic Studies, 1999.

———. "Rethinking War: The Mouse's New Roar?" *Foreign Policy,* no. 4 (1999).

Liddell-Hart, B.H. *Strategy.* 2nd ed. New York: Meridian, 1991.

Lind, William S., Colonel Keith Nightengale (USA), Captain John F. Schmitt (USMC), Colonel Joseph W. Sutton (USA), and Lieutenant Colonel Gary I. Wilson (USMCR). "The Changing Face of War: Into the Fourth Generation." *Marine Corps Gazette,* October (1989).

Livy, Titus. *The War with Hannibal.* Translated by Aubrey De Selincourt. New York: Penguin Classics, 1972.

Longworth, Philip. *The Art of Victory: The Life and Achievements of Generalissimo Suvorov.* London: Constable and Company, 1965.

Luvaas, Jay, ed. *Napoleon on the Art of War.* New York: Free Press, 1999.

MacAuley, Neill. *The Sandino Affair.* Micanopy, FL: Wacahoota Press, 1998.

Machiavelli, Niccolo. *The Art of War.* Translated by Ellis Farneworth. Cambridge, MA: Da Capo Press, 1965.

Mack, John E. *Prince of Disorder: The Life of T.E. Lawrence.* Cambridge, MA: Harvard University Press, 1998.

MacLachlan, Bruce. *Operational Art in the Counter-Terror War in Afghanistan.* Newport, RI.: Naval War College, 2002.

Mahan, A.T. *Armaments and Arbitration*. New York: Harper, 1912.

———. *The Influence of Sea Power Upon History, 1660–1783*. New York: Little Brown & Co., 1980.

———. *The Influence of Sea Power Upon the French Revolution, 1793–1812*. Boston: Little & Brown, 1892.

Makinda, Samuel. *Seeking Peace from Chaos: Humanitarian Intervention in Somalia*. Boulder, CO: Lynne Reinner, 1993.

Malone, Julia. "Congress Calls for Security for Marines Amid Skepticism." *Christian Science Monitor*, October 25, 1983.

Manning, Jason. "Combating Poppy Production." In *Online News Hour*. USA: PBS, 2003.

Manwaring, Max. "Internal Wars: Rethinking Problem and Response." Carlisle, PA: Strategic Studies Institute, 2001.

Mao, Zedong. *The Situation and Tasks in the Anti-Japanese War after the Fall of Shanghai and Taiyuan*. New York: Foreign Language Press, 1956.

Marshall, S.L. *Lessons Learned; Vietnam Primer: A Critique of U.S. Army Tactics and Command Practices in the Small Combat Unit Digested from Historical Research of Main States*. Washington, DC: Department of the Army, 1967.

Martin, Lisa. "The Contributions of Rational Choice: A Defense of Pluralism." *International Security* 24, no. 2 (1999): 74–83.

McAllister Linn, Brian. *The Philippine War, 1899–1902*. Lawrence: University of Kansas Press, 2002.

———. *The U.S. Army and Counterinsurgency in the Philippine War, 1899–1902*. Chapel Hill: University of North Carolina Press, 2000.

McClintock, Robert. "The American Landing in Lebanon." *United States Naval Institute Proceedings* 88, no. 10 (1962): 65–79.

McCready, Douglas M. "Learning from Sun-Tzu." *Military Review,* May–June (2003): 85–88.

McGirk, Tim. "A Dearth of Troops." *Time,* December 1, 2003.

McIntyre, Jamie. "Pentagon: Bin Laden Deputy Complains about Money, Iraq Tactics." *CNN.com,* October 7, 2005. http://www.cnn.com/2005/US/10/07/pentagon.al.qaeda/ (accessed October 25, 2005).

McKenzie, Kenneth, Jr. "The Revenge of the Melians: Asymmetric Threats and the Q.D.R." In *McNair Paper*. Washington, DC: Institute for National Strategic Studies, National Defense University, 2000.

Meigs, Montgomery C. "Unorthodox Thoughts About Asymmetric Warfare." *Parameters,* no. 3 (2003): 4–18.

Menkhaus, Ken. "A Second Look at UN's Action in Somalia." *Christian Science Monitor,* July 16, 1993.

Menning, Bruce W. "Train Hard, Fight Easy: The Legacy of A.V. Suvorov and His 'Art of Victory.'" *Air University Review,* November–December (1986): 79–88.

Mermin, Jonathan. "Television News and American Intervention in Somalia: The Myth of a Media-Driven Foreign Policy." *Political Science Quarterly* 112, no. 3 (1997): 385–403.

Messmer, Ellen. "U.S. Army Kick-Starts Cyberwar Machine." *CNN.com*, November 22, 2000. http://archives.cnn.com/2000/TECH/computing/11/22/cyberwar.machine.idg/index.html (accessed September 15, 2004).

Meyers, Gene. "Getting to the Fight: Aerospace Forces and Anti-Access Strategies." *Air and Space Power Chronicles*, VII (2001).

Miller, Stuart. *Benevolent Assimilation: The American Conquest of the Philippines, 1899–1902.* New Haven, CT: Yale University Press, 1984.

Mockaitis, Thomas R. "Reluctant Partners: Civil Military Cooperation in Kosovo." *Small Wars and Insurgencies* 15, no. 2 (2004): 38–50.

Moffett, George D., III. "Force in Somalia May Signal More UN Interventions." *Christian Science Monitor*, December 4, 1992.

———. "Somalia Crisis Prompts Novel Approach to Aid." *Christian Science Monitor*, September 2, 1992.

———. "White House Hints Change in Stance against Putting UN Peacekeepers in Somalia." *Christian Science Monitor*, August 6, 1992.

Molloy, Herbert. *The Great Pursuit.* New York: Smithmark Publishers, 1995.

Moody, Peter R. "Clausewitz and the Fading Dialectic of War." *World Politics* 31, no. 3 (1979): 417–33.

Moore, Robin. *The Green Berets.* New York: St. Martin's Press, 2002.

———. *The Hunt for bin Laden: Task Force Dagger on the Ground with the Special Forces in Afghanistan.* New York: Presidio Press, 2003.

Moosa, Matti. *The Maronites in History.* Syracuse, NY: Syracuse University Press, 1986.

Morano, Marc. "Forged in Soviet Conflict, Taliban Is 'Most Extreme' Islamic Faction." *CNSNews.com*, September 17, 2001. http://www.cnsnews.com/View ForeignBureaus.asp?Page=/ForeignBureaus/archive/200109/For20010917a.html (accessed September 14, 2005).

Morgan, John G., and Anthony D. McIvor. "Rethinking the Principles of War." *Proceedings*, October (2003): 34–38.

Mouat, Lucia. "UN in Somalia Caught in a Debate over Force Vs. Diplomacy." *Christian Science Monitor*, July 22, 1993.

———. "UN To Break New Ground in Plan for Peacekeepers in Somalia." *Christian Science Monitor*, March 16, 1993.

Nagl, John. *Learning to Eat Soup with a Knife: Counterinsurgency Lessons from Malaya and Vietnam.* Chicago: University of Chicago Press, 2005.

National Center for Policy Analysis. "The Cost of Terrorism." *Daily Policy Digest*, May 15, 2002. http://www.ncpa.org/iss/ter/2002/pd051502f.html (accessed September 11, 2004).

National Commission on the Terrorist Attacks Upon the United States. *The 9/11 Commission Report: Final Report of the National Commission on Terrorist Attacks Upon the United States.* Washington, DC, 2004.

National Review, "Mr. Clinton's Quagmire?" November 1, 1993.

———, "The Last Domino—Inevitable End of Afghan President Najibullah's Rule," May 11, 1992.

Navy Historical Center. *Quasi-War with France 1798–1801*. Department of the Navy, 1996. http://www.history.navy.mil/faqs/stream/faq45-3.htm (accessed September 2, 2004).

Naylor, Sean. *Not a Good Day to Die: The Untold Story of Operation Anaconda.* New York: Berkley Books, 2005.

NewsMax.com, "China Dragon Bares Its Claws for Cyberwar," November 17, 1999. http://www.newsmax.com/articles/?a=1999/11/17/45206 (accessed September 15, 2005).

Newsom, David D. "Somalia: A New Kind of Dilemma." *Christian Science Monitor,* November 10, 1992.

Nickerson, Heather. *Afghanistan, Al Qaeda and the Taliban.* Center for Defense Information, August 6, 2004. http://www.cdi.org/program/document.cfm?DocumentID=2360&from_page=../index.cfm (accessed September 15, 2005).

Nielson, Keith, and Elizabeth Jane Errington, ed. *Navies and Global Defense: Theories and Strategy.* Westport, CT: Praeger, 1995.

Nunn, Sam. "Nuclear Terrorism: Unite against the Gravest Threat." *International Herald Tribune,* May 28, 2003.

Oberdorfer, Don. "The Path to Intervention." *Washington Post,* December 6, 1992.

O'Hanlon, Michael E. *Defense Policy Choices for the Bush Administration.* Washington, DC: Brookings Institution Press, 2001.

Ohmy News International. "First Bush Memo on Al-Qaeda Declassified," February 10, 2005. http://english.ohmynews.com/articleview/article_view.asp?at_code=236845&no=210462&rel_no=1 (accessed September 15, 2005).

O'Kane, Maggie. "Alliance Builds New Airstrips and Says Defections Are Aiding Its Advance." *The Guardian* (Manchester), October 8, 2001.

Olson, Kyle B. "Aum Shinrikyo: Once and Future Threat?" *Emerging Infectious Diseases* 5, no. 4 (2000): 513–17.

Olson, Mancur. *The Logic of Collective Action.* Cambridge, MA: Harvard University Press, 1965.

Olson, Steven P. *Terrorist Attacks: The Attack on U.S. Marines in Lebanon on October 23, 1983.* New York: Rosen Publishing, 2003.

Ottaway, Marina. "Remaking Afghanistan: Learn from Failures." *Christian Science Monitor,* November 30, 2001.

Paret, Peter, ed. *Makers of Modern Strategy from Machiavelli to the Nuclear Age.* Princeton, NJ: Princeton University Press, 1986.

Parker, Ben. *Everything About Qat/Khat/Kat.* University of Pennsylvania, African Studies Center, 1995. http://www.sas.upenn.edu/African_Studies/Hornet/qat.html (accessed July 25, 2005).

Pattison, Jack. *Something Old, Something New, Something Borrowed, Something Blue: The Marriage of Strategy and Tactics in Vietnam.* Fort Leavenworth, KS: Command and General Staff College Press, 1989.

PBS. "1 Megaton Surface Blast: Pressure Damage." WGBH (Boston), 2004. http://www.pbs.org/wgbh/amex/bomb/sfeature/1mtblast.html (accessed September 14, 2004).

————. "Filling the Vacuum: The Bonn Conference." WGBH (Boston), 2002. http://www.pbs.org/wgbh/pages/frontline/shows/campaign/withus/cbonn.html (accessed September 15, 2005).

————. "Hunting Bin Laden." *Frontline;* 120 min. USA: PBS, 2005.

————. "Target America." *Frontline;* 120 min. USA: PBS, 2001.

Peterson, Scott. "Anti-West Mood Imperils Security as Somalia Operation Shifts to UN" *Christian Science Monitor,* March 18, 1993.

————. "Building a Nation in Afghanistan." *Christian Science Monitor,* October 22, 2001.

————. "Following Dictator's Removal Somalia Is Torn by Tribal Strife." *Christian Science Monitor,* October 22, 1991.

————. "Somalia Crisis Turns to Quagmire as Clinton Hardens U.S. Resolve." *Christian Science Monitor,* October 6, 1993.

————. "UN Action Plan for Afghanistan." *Christian Science Monitor,* November 23, 2001.

————. "UN Seeks Solution to Anarchy in Somalia." *Christian Science Monitor,* December 21, 1992.

————. "U.S. Backs Up UN in Somalia, Protecting Its Investment." *Christian Science Monitor,* May 25, 1993.

————. "U.S. Buildup in Somalia Leaves Many Worried About Further Clashes." *Christian Science Monitor,* October 18, 1993.

————. "World Shifts Attention to Somalia." *Christian Science Monitor,* September 2, 1992.

Pike, John. *Unmanned Aerial Vehicles.* Federation of American Scientists, Intelligence Resource Program, 2004. http://www.fas.org/irp/program/collect/uav.htm (accessed September 21, 2004).

Polybius. *The Rise of the Roman Empire.* Translated by Ian-Scott Kilvert. New York: Penguin Books, 1980.

Popham, Peter. "Air Strikes on Afghanistan: Relief: Alarm over Aid Drop in 'World's Biggest Minefield.'" *The Independent,* October 9, 2001.

Powell, Bill. "The Man Who Sold the Bomb." *Time,* February 14, 2005.

Powell, Colin. *My American Journey.* New York: Random House, 1995.

Press, Daryl G. "Urban Warfare: Options, Problems and the Future." Bedford, MA: MIT Security Studies Programs, 1999.

Press, Robert M. "Battles Break Out among Rival Clans in Southern Somalia." *Christian Science Monitor,* November 3, 1993.

————. "First U.S. Troops Exit Somalia, but Full Pullout Still Unclear." *Christian Science Monitor,* January 19, 1993.

————. "Meeting the Challenges Facing a Troubled Somalia." *Christian Science Monitor,* June 29, 1993.

————. "More Doubts Raised About UN Ability to Take Control of Somalia Reconstruction." *Christian Science Monitor,* January 22, 1993.

————. "Relief Troops in Somalia Now Turn to Food." *Christian Science Monitor,* December 11, 1992.

———. "Somalia Faces Tough Rebuilding Task as UN Takes Over." *Christian Science Monitor,* May 5, 1993.

———. "Somalia Tries to Pick up the Postwar Pieces." *Christian Science Monitor,* February 19, 1991.

———. "Somalia's Security Crisis Shifts to Remote Villages." *Christian Science Monitor,* October 6, 1992.

———. "UN Attack in Somalia Seen as Spur to War, Harmful to Aid Effort." *Christian Science Monitor,* July 13, 1993.

———. "UN Calls Off Manhunt for Aideed in Somalia." *Christian Science Monitor,* November 18, 1993.

———. "U.S. Bid for a Political Settlement Faces Tests in Streets of Somalia." *Christian Science Monitor,* November 8, 1993.

———. "U.S. Is Working to Restore Civilian Police in Somalia." *Christian Science Monitor,* January 21, 1993.

———. "U.S. Marines in Somalia Face Dilemma over Disarmament." *Christian Science Monitor,* December 14, 1992.

———. "U.S. Marines in Somalia Plan to Seize Hidden Arms." *Christian Science Monitor,* December 28, 1992.

Press, Robert M., and Lucia Mouat. "UN Responds to Critics on Somalia." *Christian Science Monitor,* September 2, 1992.

Preston, Diane. *The Boxer Rebellion.* New York: Berkley Publishing, 2001.

Press Trust of India. "Chinese Plans for Cyberwar Pose a Threat to U.S., Says Pentagon." *IndianExpress.com,* November 21, 1999. http://www.indianexpress.com/fe/daily/19991121/fec21059.html (accessed September 15, 2005).

Prusher, Ilene R. "Amid Afghanistan's Decay, Hope Rekindles." *Christian Science Monitor,* January 2, 2002.

———. "For Woman Minister, Rebuilding Afghanistan Is a Personal Quest." *Christian Science Monitor,* February 7, 2002.

———. "Rich Donors Try to Finesse Flow of $4.5 Billion into Afghanistan." *Christian Science Monitor,* January 23, 2001.

Qiao, Liang, and Xiangsui Wang. *Unrestricted Warfare.* Beijing: PLA Literature and Arts Publishing House, 1999.

Reagan, Ronald. "Address to the Nation on Events in Lebanon and Grenada." American Reference Library, October 27, 1983.

———. "Interview with Bruce Drake of the *New York Daily News.*" American Reference Library, December 12, 1983.

———. "Interview with Members of the Editorial Board of the *New York Post* in New York City." American Reference Library, September 16, 1983.

———. "Letter to the Speaker of the House and the President Pro Tempore of the Senate Reporting on United States Participation in the Multinational Force in Lebanon." American Reference Library, September 29, 1982.

———. "Question-and-Answer Session with Reporters on Domestic and Foreign Policy Issues." American Reference Library, December 14, 1983.

———. "Radio Address to the Nation on the Situation in Lebanon." American Reference Library, October 8, 1983.

————. "Remarks and a Question-and-Answer Session with Reporters on the Pentagon Report on the Security of United States Marines in Lebanon." American Reference Library, December 27, 1983.

————. "Remarks to Military Personnel at Cherry Point, North Carolina, on the United States Casualties in Lebanon and Grenada." American Reference Library, November 4, 1983.

————. "Statement by Deputy Press Secretary Speaks on the Death of Two United States Marines in Lebanon." American Reference Library, August 29, 1983.

————. "Statement by Deputy Press Secretary Speaks on the Situation in Lebanon." American Reference Library, September 23, 1982.

Reimer, Dennis J. "Dominant Maneuver and Precision Engagement." *Joint Forces Quarterly*, no. 4 (1996).

Richburg, Keith. "In War on Aideed, UN Battled Itself." *Washington Post*, December 6, 1993.

Richey, Warren. "All Quiet on Beirut Front: Marines in Lebanon Boost U.S. Image." *Christian Science Monitor*, October 21, 1982.

Richter, Paul. "Questions Surface over N.A.T.O.'s Revised Take on the War in Kosovo." *Los Angeles Times*, June 10, 2000.

Ricks, Thomas. "General Reported Shortages in Iraq." *Washington Post*, October 18, 2004.

Ridgeway, James. "Chinese Army Pushes Cyberwar Barbarians at the Gate." GlobalSecurity.org, November 24, 1999. http://www.globalsecurity.org/intell/library/news/1999/11/991124-ridgeway.htm (accessed September 15, 2005).

Ritter, Gerhard. *Frederick the Great: A Historical Profile*. Translated by Peter Paret. Berkeley and Los Angeles: University of California Press, 1968.

Rooney, David. *Guerilla: Insurgents, Patriots and Terrorists from Sun Tzu to bin Laden*. London: Brassey's, 2004.

Rosenblatt, Alan J. "Aggressive Foreign Policy Marketing: Public Response to Reagan's 1983 Address on Lebanon and Grenada." *Political Behavior* 20, no. 3 (1998): 225–40.

Roskill, Stephen W. *The Strategy of Sea Power: Its Development and Application*. London: Collins, 1962.

Rubin, Trudy. "Israel's Bill for War: Less Than Expected." *Christian Science Monitor*, August 26, 1982.

————. "Knesset Debate on War Likely to Echo across Israel." *Christian Science Monitor*, September 9, 1982.

————. "Opening of Airport Gives Beirutis a Psychological Boost." *Christian Science Monitor*, October 1, 1982.

————. "Syria Reacts with Threats to U.S. Navy Salvos as 'Defensive' Role of the Marines Expands." *Christian Science Monitor*, September 19, 1983.

————. "U.S. Marines in Lebanon: A Solution?" *Christian Science Monitor*, July 7, 1982.

Rumsfeld, Donald. *Nuclear Posture Review Report*. Washington, DC: Department of Defense, 2002.

Saikowski, Charlotte, and Daniel Southerland. "Beirut Bombings Lend Urgency to Search for a Settlement in Lebanon." *Christian Science Monitor,* October 24, 1983.

Salibi, Kamal. *A House of Many Mansions: The History of Lebanon Reconsidered.* Berkeley and Los Angeles: University of California Press, 1990.

———. *Modern History of Lebanon.* Los Angeles: Caravan Books, 1996.

Savino, Adam. "Cyber-Terrorism." The University of Dayton School of Law, 2004. http://www.cybercrimes.net/Terrorism/ct.html (accessed September 17, 2004).

Sawyer, Ralph D., trans. *The Seven Military Classics of Ancient China.* Boulder, CO: Westview Press, 1993.

Scarborough, Rowan. "Drug Money Sustains Al Qaeda." *Washington Times,* December 23, 2003.

Scherer, Ron. "United Nations to Back Bush's Plan on Somalia." *Christian Science Monitor,* December 2, 1992.

Schmitt, Eric. "U.S. May Start Pulling Out of Afghanistan Next Spring." *New York Times,* September 14, 2005.

Schnabel, James. "Policy and Direction: The First Year." In *The United States Army in the Korean War.* Washington, DC: Government Printing Office, 1972.

Schom, Alan. *Napoleon Bonaparte: A Life.* New York: Perennial, 1998.

Schroen, Gary. *First In: An Insider's Account of How the CIA Spearheaded the War on Terror in Afghanistan.* New York: Presidio, 2005.

Shafer, Jack. "Apple Turnover: *The New York Times'* R.W. Apple Jr. Never Wrote a Piece He Couldn't Contradict." *Slate.com,* April 7, 2003. http://slate.msn.com/id/ 2081240 (accessed September 15, 2005).

Shahzad, Syed. "A Chilling Inheritance of Terror." *Asia Times Online,* October 30, 2002. http://www.atimes.com/atimes/South_Asia/DJ30Df01.html (accessed November 1, 2005).

Shanahan, Vice Adm. Jack (USN Ret.), Col. Chet Richards (USAF Ret.), and Frank Spinney. "Bury Cold War Mindset: Fourth-Generation Warfare Rewrites Military Strategy." *Defense News,* August 5–11, 2003.

Shaw, Martin. "New Wars of the City: 'Urbicide' and 'Genocide.'" University of Sussex, 2000. http://www.sussex.ac.uk/Users/hafa3/city.htm (accessed May 15, 2004).

Shelton, Henry H. *Joint Vision 2020.* Washington, DC: U.S. Joint Chiefs of Staff, 2000.

Shulimson, Jack. *Marines in Lebanon 1958.* Washington, DC: Department of the Navy, Headquarters U.S. Marine Corps.

Shutt, Anne. "Israeli Planes Hit Lebanon Again." *Christian Science Monitor,* September 14, 1982.

———. "Marines End Beirut Task, Secretary of Defense Says." *Christian Science Monitor,* September 2, 1982.

———. "Marines Return to Lebanon." *Christian Science Monitor,* September 30, 1982.

Smock, David. "Somalia's Next Step: Restoring Economy." *Christian Science Monitor,* March 23, 1993.

Smucker, Philip. "Ethnic Split Grows in Afghanistan's Government." *Christian Science Monitor,* February 19, 2002.

———. "Taliban Transforms Afghanistan for Total War." *Christian Science Monitor,* October 30, 2001.

Snidal, Duncan. "The Limits of Hegemonic Stability Theory." *International Organization* 39, no. 4 (1985): 579–614.

Snow, Donald M. *Distant Thunder: Third World Conflict and the New International Order.* New York: St. Martin's Press, 1993.

———. *From Lexington to Desert Storm and Beyond.* Armonk, NY: M.E. Sharpe, 2000.

———. *Uncivil Wars: International Security and the New Internal Conflicts.* Boulder, CO: Lynne Rienner Publishers, 1996.

———. *When America Fights: The Users of U.S. Military Force.* Washington, DC: CQ Press, 2000.

Sommer, Mark. "Leave Somalia to UN" *Christian Science Monitor,* October 19, 1993.

Southerland, Daniel. "Cost to Eject Syrians from Lebanon Has Israel, U.S. Considering Other Options." *Christian Science Monitor,* December 6, 1983.

———. "Keeping Peace in Beirut: First Step in Lebanon Recovery." *Christian Science Monitor,* September 21, 1982.

———. "Lebanon Urges More U.S. Muscle." *Christian Science Monitor,* September 9, 1983.

———. "U.S. Marines Only One Part of Complex Lebanon Package." *Christian Science Monitor,* July 8, 1982.

———. "Will Lebanon's Peacekeepers Be Domestic or Multinational?" *Christian Science Monitor,* October 26, 1982.

Spacewar.com, "Iraq Withdrawal Heads Agenda for New Spanish Cabinet," April 14, 2004. http://www.spacewar.com/2004/040419164753.rriav7ye.html (accessed December 15, 2005).

Special Oversight Panel on Terrorism. Committee on Armed Services. *Cyberterrorism,* May 23, 2000.

Spiller, Roger J. "Not War but Like War: The American Intervention in Lebanon." In *Leavenworth Papers.* Fort Leavenworth, KS: Combat Studies Institute, U.S. Army Command and General Staff College, 1981.

Stanton, Martin. *Somalia on $5 a Day: A Soldier's Story.* New York: Presidio Press, 2001.

Starr, S. Frederick. "Afghanistan's Biggest Problem—Poverty—Can Be Solved." *Christian Science Monitor,* October 16, 2001.

Staten, Clark L. "Asymmetric Warfare, the Evolution and Devolution of Terrorism: The Coming Challenge for Emergency and National Security Forces." Emergency Response and Research Institute, April 27, 1998. http://www.emergency.com/asymetrc.htm (accessed May 15, 2004).

Stedman, Steven. "International Actors and Internal Conflict." In *Project on World Security.* New York: Rockefeller Brothers Fund, 1999.

Stevenson, Charles A. "The Evolving Clinton Doctrine on the Use of Force." *Armed Forces & Society* 22, no. 4 (1996): 511–36.

Stevenson, Jonathan. *Losing Mogadishu: Testing U.S. Policy in Somalia.* Annapolis, MD: Naval Institute Press, 1995.

Stewart, John. *Russian Government Blames Chechnya, Al Qaeda.* Australian Broadcasting Corporation, 2004. http://www.abc.net.au/lateline/content/2004/s1193459.htm (accessed September 10, 2004).

Stewart, Richard. *The United States Army in Somalia 1992–1994.* Fort McNair, DC: Center for Military History, 1994.

Sumida, Jon. "New Insights from Old Books." *Naval War College Review* 54, no. 3 (2001).

Sun-tzu. *The Art of War.* Translated by Ralph D. Sawyer. New York: Barnes & Noble Books, 1994.

Tacitus. *The Annals of Imperial Rome.* New York: Penguin Classics, 1956.

Tanner, Stephen. *Afghanistan: A Military History from Alexander the Great to the Fall of the Taliban.* Cambridge, MA: Da Capo Press, 2002.

Temko, Ned. "Rising Risks for Reagan in Lebanon." *Christian Science Monitor,* December 19, 1983.

———. "Syria Moves to Speed Exit of Marines." *Christian Science Monitor,* January 4, 1984.

Tenet, George. *Global Trends 2015: A Dialogue About the Future with Nongovernmental Experts.* Washington, DC: National Intelligence Council, 2000.

Thompson, Leroy. *The Counter-Insurgency Manual.* London: Greenhill Books, 2002.

Thucydides. *History of the Peloponnesian War.* Translated by Rex Warner. New York: Penguin Books, 1954.

Tohid, Owais. "Southern Afghanistan Suffers as Aid Groups Are Harassed." *Christian Science Monitor,* July 18, 2003.

Tse-tung, Mao. *On Guerrilla Warfare.* Translated by Samuel B. Griffith II. Urbana Champagne: University of Illinois Press, 1961.

———. *Selected Works of Mao Tse-Tung.* Vol. 1. London: Lawrence and Wishart, 1954.

Tucker, Jonathan B. "Asymmetric Warfare." *FORUM for Applied Research and Public Policy,* no. 2 (1999).

———. *Toxic Terror: Assessing Terrorist Use of Chemical and Biological Weapons.* Cambridge, MA: MIT Press, 2000.

Tucker, Spencer. *The Great War 1914–1918.* Bloomington: University of Indiana Press, 1998.

TurkishPress.com, "List of Attacks Claimed by or Attributed to Al-Qaeda," September 10, 2004. http://www.turkishpress.com/ (accessed September 15, 2005).

U.S. Armed Services Committee. *Somalia.* Washington, DC: May 12, 1994.

USA Today, "Nature, Structure of Al-Qaeda Changing," March 8, 2003.

U.S. Commission on International Religious Freedom. "Reconstructing Afghanistan: Freedom in Crisis": Amb. Zalmay Khalilzad testimony. January 29, 2003. http://uscirf.com/events/hearings/2003/january/01292003_khailzadTestimony.html (accessed September 15, 2005).

U.S. Commission on National Security for the 21st Century. *Road Map for National Security: Imperative for Change.* Washington, DC, 2001.

U.S. Congress. *Act to Authorize the Defense of the Merchant Vessels of the United States against French Depredations,* 5th Cong., June 25, 1798, 572, 50–51.

U.S. Congress. Senate. "United States Rangers in Somalia," 103rd Cong., November 22, 1993.

U.S. Department of Defense. *Joint Doctrine Encyclopedia.* Washington, DC, 2005.

———. *Report of the D.O.D. Commission on Beirut International Airport Terrorist Act, October 23, 1983.* Washington, DC, 1983.

U.S. Department of State. Bureau of Near Eastern Affairs. *Background Note: Libya.* Washington, DC, 2004.

U.S. Joint Chiefs of Staff. *Joint Vision 2010.* Washington, DC, 1996.

U.S. Marine Corps. *Small Wars Manual.* Manhattan, KS: Sunflower University Press, 1940.

U.S. Navy. *Aircraft Carriers—C.V., C.V.N.* U.S. Navy, 2004. http://navysite.de/carriers.htm (accessed September 13 2004).

U.S. State Department. Bureau of South Asian Affairs. *Background Note: Afghanistan.* Washington, DC, 2005. http://www.state.gov/r/pa/ei/bgn/5380.htm (accessed September 10, 2005).

Utgoff, Victor A. *The Challenge of Chemical Weapons.* New York: St. Martin's Press, 1991.

Utley, Robert E., and Wilcomb E. Wasburn. *Indian Wars.* New York: Mariner Books, 2002.

Van Crevald, Martin. *The Art of War: War and Military Thought.* London: Cassell, 2002.

———. *Technology and War: From 2000 B.C. to the Present.* New York: Free Press, 1989.

———. *The Transformation of War: The Most Radical Reinterpretation of Armed Conflict since Clausewitz.* New York: Free Press, 1991.

Vegetius, Flavius Renatus. *The Military Institutions of the Romans.* Translated by John Clark. Westport, CT: Greenwood Press, 1985.

Verton, Dan. *Black Ice: The Invisible Threat of Cyber-Terrorism.* New York: McGraw-Hill, 2004.

von Clausewitz, Carl. *On War.* New York: Alfred A. Knopf, 1993.

Walt, Stephen. "Rigor or Rigor Mortis? Rational Choice and Security Studies." *International Security* 23, no. 4 (1999): 5–48.

Ward, Mark. "Cyber Terrorism Overhyped." BBC News, 2003. http://news vote.bbc.co.uk/ (accessed September 18, 2004).

Washington Post, "Transcript: 9/11 Commission Hearing," April 13, 2004. http://www.washingtonpost.com/wp-dyn/articles/A9088-2004Apr13.html (accessed June 27, 2005).

Webb, R.C., et al. "The Commercial and Military Satellite Survivability Crisis." *Defense Electronics* 24 (1995).

Weiss, Kenneth. *The Soviet Involvement in the Ogaden War.* Washington, DC: Center for Naval Analysis, 1980.

Wesleyan University, *The U.S. Marines in Lebanon*. Wesleyan University Department of Government, August 7, 2001. http://www.wesleyan.edu/gov/ (accessed 2004).

Western, Jon. "Sources of Humanitarian Intervention: Beliefs, Information, and Advocacy in the U.S. Decisions on Somalia and Bosnia." *International Security* 26, no. 4 (Spring 2002): 112–42.

Westwell, Ian. *Warfare in the 18th Century*. Austin, TX: Raintree Steck-Vaughn, 1999.

Wheelan, Joseph. *Jefferson's War: America's First War on Terror*. New York: Carroll and Graf, 2003.

Wheeler, Ed, and Craig Roberts. *Doorway to Hell: Disaster in Somalia*. Tulsa, OK: Consolidated Press International, 2002.

Whiting, Charles. *Hitler's Werewolves*. New York: Playboy Press, 1972.

Whitney, Craig R. "France's 'Cowboy' Judge: A Relentless Tracker of International Terrorists." *International Herald Tribune*, December 5, 1996.

Wieviorka, Michel. "French Politics and Strategy on Terrorism." In *The Politics of Counter-Terrorism: The Ordeal of Democratic States*, edited by Barry Rubin. Washington, DC: School of Advanced International Studies, 1990.

Wilcox, Greg, and Gary I. Wilson. "Military Response to Fourth Generation Warfare in Afghanistan." d-n-i.net, May 5, 2002. http://d-n-i.net/fcs/wilson_wilcox_military_responses.htm (accessed September 15, 2005).

Wilkinson, Paul. "The Strategic Implications of Terrorism." *Terrorism & Political Violence. A Sourcebook*, edited by Prof. M.L. Sondhi. India: Har-anand Publications, 2000. http://biblioteca.upeace.org/masters/documents/Wilkinson%201997.%20The%20media%20and%20terrorism.pdf (accessed May 15, 2004).

Williams, Brian. "The Atlantic Wall." Militaryhistoryonline.com, 2000. http://www.militaryhistoryonline.com/wwii/dday/prelude.aspx (accessed February, 1 2004).

Wilson, G.I., John P. Sullivan, and Hal Kempfer. "4GW: Tactics of the Weak Confound the Strong." Military.com, September 8, 2003. http://d-n-i.net/fcs/comments/c490.htm (accessed May 15, 2004).

Wilson, Scott. "Blast Kills Ex-Premier in Lebanon." *Washington Post*, February 15, 2005.

Wilson, Thomas R. *The Four Thrusts*. Washington, DC: Defense Intelligence Agency, 2001.

Winder, David. "What's Behind the Major Debate About Foreign Troops in Lebanon?" *Christian Science Monitor*, October 31, 1983.

Wolf, Paul. "The Assassination of Ahmad Shah Massoud." Pincourt, QC: Center for Research on Globalization, 2003.

Woodward, Bob. "Bin Laden Said to 'Own' the Taliban." *Washington Post*, October 11, 2001.

World News Network. "Somalia," November 3, 2005. http://worldfactbook.com/country/Somalia/2005 (accessed November 3, 2005).

Wright, Robin. "As Marine Exit Begins, Pressure Increases on Gemayel to Resign." *Christian Science Monitor*, February 19, 1984.

———. "Beirut Deadlock Keeps Marines Issue Alive." *Christian Science Monitor,* January 13, 1984.

———. "Can Beirut Forces Be Safe?" *Christian Science Monitor,* November 2, 1983.

———. "Fighting in Lebanon Escalates Following Israeli Pullback." *Christian Science Monitor,* September 7, 1983.

———. "Lebanese Druze Guns Shoot Holes in U.S. Peace Efforts." *Christian Science Monitor,* September 9, 1983.

———. "Lebanon: The Politics Behind Gunfire and Kidnapping." *Christian Science Monitor,* August 12, 1983.

———. "Marines in Lebanon Facing Increased Danger." *Christian Science Monitor,* August 25, 1983.

———. "Rapid Escalation of U.S. Forces in Lebanon Concerns Allies." *Christian Science Monitor,* September 14, 1983.

———. "U.S. Role in Beirut Goes on Despite Exit of Marines from Peace Force." *Christian Science Monitor,* February 27, 1984.

———. "U.S. Marine–Israeli Relations Tense." *Christian Science Monitor,* January 26, 1983.

Xenophon. *Anabasis.* Translated by Carleton Brownson. Cambridge, MA: Harvard University Press, 1998.

Yemma, John. "Hawks Are Overshadowing Diplomats in Besieged Beirut." *Christian Science Monitor,* July 7, 1982.

———. "Shattered State in the Mideast." *Christian Science Monitor,* February 4, 1983.

Zakaria, Fareed. *The Future of Freedom: Illiberal Democracy at Home and Abroad.* New York: W.W. Norton, 2003.

Zinni, General Anthony. *4 G.W. & Zinni's Question: What Is Nature of Victory?* Arlington, VA: Naval Institute Forum, 2003.

Index

1st Marine Division, 110, 112
10th Mountain Division, 123
160th SOAR, 135

Adolphus, Gustavus, 28
Aeneas the Tactician, 20
Afghan Reconstruction Steering Group (ARSG), 137
Aguinaldo, Emilio, 62, 63
Aidid, Muhammad Farah, 54, 105, 115, 118, 150
al-Qaeda, 11, 56, 66, 74, 129
Amaal, 89, 95, 152
American embassy, 97; Beirut, Lebanon, 88; Dar es Salaam, 74; Nairobi, 131
Anthrax, 66, 71
Aum Shinrikyo, 66, 71

Baghdad, 36, 80
Barre, Siad, 10, 102, 105, 117
Battalion Landing Team (BLT) 2/8, 149
Beirut International Airport (BIA), 11, 84, 97, 98, 123
bin Laden, Osama, 2, 24, 55, 130
Bir, General Cevik, 111, 115, 152
Blair, Prime Minister Tony, 134
Bonaparte, Napoleon, 31, 32

Boutros-Ghali, Secretary General Boutros, 108, 120
Bush, President George H. W., 90, 109, 124
Bush, President George W., 1, 35, 63, 131, 132, 157; Afghanistan, 140, 141

Central Command (CENTCOM), 110, 117
Central Intelligence Agency (CIA), 67, 80, 100, 128, 134
Central Intelligence Agency: Bin Laden Unit, 130; Counterterrorism Unit (CTU), 130; Operations Bureau, 67
China, 2, 15, 24, 57, 73
Cicero, 16
Civil war: Beirut, 83; Somalia, 108
Clinton, President William J., 11, 60, 74, 132; conflicts of asymmetry, 3, 14, 46, 81; Delenda Plan, 131; national security strategy, 54; Somalia, 102, 110, 124
Corbett, Julian, 39, 40

DeLong, Lieutenant General Michael, 133
Druze, 83, 91, 97, 156

Federal Bureau of Investigation: Counter Terrorism Unit, 67
Fourth Generation Warfare (4GW), 2, 77, 146
Franks, General Tommy, 132, 145
Frederick II, the Great, 23, 27, 29
Fuller, J.F.C., 21, 43

Garrison, Brigadier General William, 117, 150
Gemayel, Amin, 87
Gemayel, Bashir, 87
Geneva Conventions on the Laws of War (1949), 55
Geraghty, Lieutenant Colonel Timothy J., 89, 99
Gerlach, Lieutenant Colonel Howard L., 89, 99
Giap, Vo Nguyen, 15, 27, 46, 53
Global War on Terror (GWOT), 2, 7, 68, 150
Guevara, Che, 49, 53

Habr-Gidr, 116, 119
Hamas, 36, 68, 159
Hezbollah, 10, 156, 159
Howe, Admiral Jonathan, 111, 115, 151

Interservice Intelligence Agency (ISI), 128, 131
Iraq War (2003–present), 9, 72
Israel, 10, 57, 73; Beirut, Lebanon, 85
Israeli Defense Force (IDF), 85

Jihad, 134
Johnston, Lieutenant Colonel Robert B.: Beirut, Lebanon, 87; Somalia, 110
Joint Chiefs of Staff (JCS), 107, 110
Jomini, Baron Antoine Henri de, 27, 33–35
Josephus, 17–19
Julius Caesar, 8, 17–21

Kabul, 80, 127–35
Karnak Farm, 130–31
Karzai, Hamid, 138–56

Khobar Towers bombing (1996), 65, 74

Lawrence of Arabia, 41–43
Liddell-Hart, B.H., 41–44
Long Commission, 91, 98, 99–101
Loya Jurga, 137, 154

Machiavelli, Niccolo, 23–24
Mahan, Alfred Thayer, 39–40
Mao Zedong, 44–48
Maronite, 83–87
Massoud, General Ahmed Shah, 129–34
Mazar-i-Sharif, 135–37
Mead, Colonel James M., 86–97
Montgomery, Major General Thomas M., 115–19, 151
Mujahideen, 10, 128–36
Musharraf, President Pervez, 134

Northern Alliance (NA), 2, 129–42

Omar, Mullah Muhammad, 2, 128–45
OODA Loop, 14, 157
Operation Anaconda, 38, 139–40
Operation Enduring Freedom, 76, 132–42
Operation Restore Hope, 10, 111–17

Pakistan, 70, 128, 138, 151
Palestinian Liberation Army (PLA), 85
Palestinian Liberation Organization (PLO), 151
People's Army of Vietnam (PAVN or NVA), 47
People's Democratic Party of Afghanistan (PDPA), 127
Phalange, 85–97
Powell Doctrine, 107, 124
Pushtun, 130–42, 156

Rabbani, Burhanuddin, 10, 144
Reagan, President Ronald, 85–100, 121, 151
Revolution in Military Affairs (RMA), 2, 77

Rules of Engagement (ROE), 87–99, 109–13, 152

Sandino, Augusto, 6, 81
September 11, 2001, 1, 6, 11, 24, 56, 149, 159
Shah-i-Kot Valley, 139–45
Somali National Alliance (SNA), 105–22, 153
Soviet-Afghan War (1979–1989), 128, 135
Soviet Union, 2, 6–7, 59, 63–65; Afghanistan, 127–28; biological weapons program, 70
Special Forces, 12–13, 67–68, 80; Afghanistan, 134–35; Somalia, 117
Sun-tzu, 15, 24–27
Syria, 41–42, 85–91

Taef Agreement (1989), 156
Taliban, 2, 10–12, 127–42
Tarnak Farm, 131
Task Force 11, 138
Task Force 64 (TF 64), 140
Task Force Dagger (TF Dagger), 138

Task Force K-Bar (TF K-Bar), 139
Task Force Rakkasan, 139
Task Force Ranger (TF Ranger), 117
Thucydides, 16
Tora Bora, 137–39

UNOSOM I, 108, 113
UNOSOM II, 111–16
United Nations, 10; Afghanistan, 137–41; Somalia, 103–09, 111–16
United Nations Security Council, 108–9
United Somali Congress (USC), 105–6
United States Congress, 74, 95; Beirut, 96–100; Somalia, 103–9
United Task Force (UNITAF), 110–24
USS Cole, 1, 40, 130

Vegetius, 17–20
von Clausewitz, Carl, 36–39

Weapons of Mass Destruction (WMD), 54, 65–67, 71, 81
World Trade Center, 6, 131–32

About the Author

ADAM B. LOWTHER is Assistant Professor of Political Science at Arkansas Tech University. He received his Ph.D. from the University of Alabama at Tuscaloosa. He is the author of articles in *Military Review, Journal of Chinese Political Science, Proceedings,* and *An Army at War.*